TOP
MAN

Also by Stewart Lansley and Andy Forrester:

Stewart Lansley

Poverty and Progress in Britain
Housing and Public Policy
Poor Britain (with Joanna Mack)
Beyond Our Ken (with Andy Forrester and Robin Pauley)
Councils in Conflict (with Sue Goss and Christian Wolmar)
After the Gold Rush
Rich Britain (forthcoming)

Andy Forrester

Britain from Waterloo to the Great Exhibition (with Michael Moss)
Beyond Our Ken (with Stewart Lansley and Robin Pauley)
Sid's Heroes (with Syd Joynson)
The Man Who Saw the Future: A Biography of William Paterson,
  Founder of the Bank of England

TOP
MAN

HOW PHILIP GREEN BUILT HIS HIGH STREET EMPIRE

Stewart Lansley & Andy Forrester

First published 2005 by
Aurum Press Limited
25 Bedford Avenue
London WC1B 3AT
www.aurumpress.co.uk

A catalogue record for this book is available from the British Library.

ISBN 1 84513 100 2

10 9 8 7 6 5 4 3
2009 2008 2007 2006

Text design by Geoff Green

Typeset by SX Composing DTP, Rayleigh, Essex

Printed and bound in Great Britain by Creative Print & Design (Wales) Ltd, Ebbw Vale

CONTENTS

PREFACE

P hilip Green is one of the most controversial and colourful businessmen in Britain. A little over a decade ago he was a rag-trader, a mere millionaire and barely known. Today he is worth over £4.5 billion and is estimated to be Britain's fifth richest person. In his climb up the wealth ladder, he has overtaken the likes of Richard Branson, the Reuben brothers and the Sainsbury family, and made his first billion in record time, faster than anyone else in British history. He then went on to quadruple his wealth in a handful of years.

Green commands a sprawling retail empire of 2,500 shops from Bhs and Burton to Miss Selfridge and Topshop. His influence is pervasive – there can hardly be a chief executive in retail from Sainsbury's to Woolworth's that has not felt his breath at some stage in their careers. Many still glance over their shoulder in case they are next in his plans. In the summer of 2004, he burst upon the consciousness of the wider British public when he tried for a second time to seize control of Marks & Spencer – the crown jewels of British retailing – with an audacious takeover bid that would have cost more than £11 billion. It was one of the bloodiest takeover battles in British history, a clash of high drama marred by controversy, ill-feeling and bitter personal rivalry.

The rise of this chain-smoking and irascible entrepreneur is all the more remarkable when you consider who he is – a brash outsider who has brushed with the establishment, the City and some of the biggest retailers in Britain. This is the story of how Green has moved from obscurity to fame; of how, in less than a decade, he has emerged from the shadows to become one of Britain's most formidable retail take-over tycoons; of what accounts for his breathless rise to the top.

Green left school early without a qualification to his name and set out, at the age of sixteen, to make his fortune in business, only to come to grief in a number of ill-starred ventures. He then came under criticism for the way he attempted to run a public company, Amber Day, as a private fiefdom. It was only in the mid-1990s, when the memory of his controversial past was fading, that he began to display the one quality that the City values above all: the ability to make money.

The book not only explains how Green has made his money, and examines the roots of his extraordinary drive and determination; it also asks the questions that Green would prefer to be ignored. What is he really worth? How much of a transformation has he achieved at Bhs and Arcadia? Should he be let loose on M&S? Does he have a magic retail touch that sets him apart from other pioneering and contemporary retail entrepreneurs?

Despite his undoubted success, Green remains a figure who provokes strong views. There is his decision to live in Monaco with his family, an arrangement that brings huge tax benefits. There is his unpredictable behaviour and fiery temperament. He may be one of Britain's most successful entrepreneurs, but he continues to divide opinion amongst bankers, retailers and the public – between those who see his abrasiveness, vulgarity and expletive-strewn language as a sign of weakness, and those who consider him a man of unique talent, an iconoclast who has done more than most to lift the stuffy image of the British high street.

Many of his contemporaries and colleagues are certainly wary of him; just how wary we discovered during the research for this book. We have approached scores of people – friends, former colleagues and competitors alike. Many wanted Philip's permission. Yet almost from the word go, he has refused to cooperate with this project. Despite repeated requests, he eventually decided not to be interviewed.

As business journalists, we have set out to write as accurate and fair an account of Green's rise and of his record as an entrepreneur as is possible without his co-operation. We have been greatly helped by the company records filed by Green at Companies House over the years, sketchy though some of them are. Some of those we approached have refused to talk at all. Typical of the comments made were: 'it's too sensitive'; 'it's more than my job's worth'; 'but I may end up working for him one day'. Others have been happy to help, even some of his friends and associates. Most have preferred to do so on the understanding that we would not reveal the source. A large number, though not all, of the accounts therefore remain anonymous.

Philip Green's shadow has certainly hung over the writing of this book. It seems to have been present even during some of the interviews we have conducted. During one conversation with a leading figure in the retail industry who spoke glowingly of Green's strengths, he let it slip that he also had weaknesses. When he was asked what those were, he looked thoughtful and, with a smile, replied, 'I think I'll pass on that.' Another interviewee was happy to give us his reminiscences of Green during a long career in the fashion business, but on one strict condition: 'I do not want my name to be mentioned in this book under any circumstances.' One who agreed to speak warned us: 'I don't intend to fall out with Philip Green. Retail is a small world.'

On the basis of Wordsworth's adage that the child is the father of the man, we have looked at Green's years as a schoolboy at Carmel College in Oxfordshire with the help of a number of his contemporaries, both pupils and teachers, who remember him well. We are indebted to Gerald and Vera Weisfeld for their reminiscences of the early years of Green's business career in the rough-and-ready rag-trade. A number of his associates from his middle and later years as a businessman have freely spoken to us, both on and off the record. We are also grateful to the retail analysts, experts and journalists who have been willing to share their expertise on his skill and performance as a retailer.

We are particularly grateful to Robert Clark for providing figures on sales per square foot used in chapter fourteen. We would also like to thank Louise Foster for making available the full transcript of interviews she conducted with both Philip Green and Stuart Rose in November 2004 for *Drapers* magazine. At the London College of Fashion Rosalie Dobson was enormously helpful in guiding us to the many articles written about Philip Green over the last twenty-five years. Chris Garston read several draft chapters and gave invaluable advice on financial interpretation.

Working with Aurum Press has been a delight. We would like to thank Piers Burnett for taking on this project and for the encouragement and support he has given to us at all times.

For any errors that remain we must take full responsibility.

Stewart Lansley and Andy Forrester
August 2005

Chapter 1

THIS IS YOUR LIFE

I t was planned with the precision of a military operation. In January 2002, invitations arrived at the homes of around 200 very select guests. Those lucky enough to be on the list were told to prepare themselves for a long weekend abroad in March. Little else was given away. The venue was, intriguingly, to remain an absolute mystery.

There were some clues, but not many. The guests were to come prepared for formal evening events and for warm sunny days by the sea. Curiously, the dress code extended to one specific and highly unusual requirement. Each person should bring flesh-coloured (or failing that plain white) underwear for a fancy-dress occasion on the Saturday evening. There was no need to pack costumes. They would be supplied by the organisers.[1] All the guests needed to do was rendezvous early on 14 March 2002 at Luton airport.

There was one other critical piece of information. They were going to celebrate the fiftieth birthday of one of Britain's richest men, the retail entrepreneur Philip Green.

The morning of 14 March was distinctly chilly and blustery. At the airport terminal a procession of upmarket cars, many with personalised number plates and darkened windows, disgorged their cargoes of party-goers and trim designer suitcases. There was an undoubted sense of drama about the occasion, as the well-dressed and well-heeled occupants slipped into the terminal building, many sheltering their identities behind dark glasses.

There was glamour, too. One person recognised by curious onlookers was Jilly Johnson, a former 'page 3 girl'. According to a report in the *Daily Mail* the following day: 'You didn't have to be blonde, glamorous and clad in designer casuals yesterday to win a place on Philip Green's birthday jet. But it certainly helped . . . Dozens of ladies answering that description descended on Luton airport to prove that making a great deal of money can buy you the most attractive "close friends" going.'[2]

None of those gathering in the VIP area that morning, exchanging greetings and effecting introductions, had any idea of what lay ahead of them, but all the appearances were that it was not to be a modest affair. Outside on the airport apron sat a large white jet aeroplane, an Airbus 300. On its tail fin, in two-metre-high letters, had been painted the logo 'PG50'. It was testimony to the trust placed in the Greens that nobody had objected to flying off to an unknown destination, carrying flesh-coloured underwear in their bags. Only one invitee – the film-director turned insurance salesman Michael Winner – is known to have declined the invitation. He stated that it was simply because he hated being a guest.[3]

Although the build-up had all the hallmarks of a Philip-style event, it was in fact being masterminded not by him but by his wife, Tina, who had herself passed her half-century a couple of years before. Philip had been kept very much in the dark about the details. The concept of a lavish and expensive party held in an exotic foreign location had already had a dry run. In 2001, Tom Hunter, the richest man in Scotland, and a close friend of Philip's, had celebrated his fortieth birthday in the French Riviera resort of Saint Jean Cap Ferrat, east of Nice. Tom's wife Marion had hired a London-based events firm called Banana Split to organise the party – a lavish fancy-dress ball built around the theme of Hollywood movies. Two giant 'Oscar' statuettes had been shipped in to frame a stage fully wired for lighting and sound. Tom himself, who was prematurely balding, had dressed up as Yul Brynner in *The King and I*, while Sir Richard Branson had come along as Darth Vader.

Entertainment had been provided by two of Tom's favourite musical acts, the American funk group Kool and the Gang, followed even more spectacularly by Tom's great hero, the blind American superstar and Motown legend Stevie Wonder. The stars – and the large entourage that supports them – had been shipped over from the States especially for the occasion. All of this had, as intended, taken Tom completely by surprise. As Hunter mingled with the party-goers, and received their congratulations, he bumped into his family bank manager. He found himself asking just how much this had all cost. The banker replied with a good-natured grin: 'You don't want to know.' The bill for the party in fact came in at around £750,000.[4]

The Greens were among the guests, and were much taken by the idea. It seems that the decision to celebrate Philip's half-century in a similar but even more spectacular way was taken shortly afterwards. Certainly Tina had engaged the same Banana Split team to plan the whole event and to come up with ideas on how to surprise both the birthday boy and the guests. Banana Split, already known for the scale and ambition of its parties, had pulled out all the stops and come up with a scheme that meant the transport of sets and set-designers, caterers and catering equipment, lighting men and sound riggers, and a mass of paraphernalia, thousands of miles across land and sea.

That the Greens could afford to splash out was not open to question. Philip Green had recently made it into the billionaire camp. Over the previous year his wealth had jumped sixfold from some £200 million to a staggering £1.2 billion, due to his acquisition of British Home Stores and his remarkable success in turning the business around. The contract Tina had signed with Banana Split was the biggest of its kind the company had ever won, with a budget reported to be some £5 million.[5]

Some of the cost was swallowed up in security. Because of the risk of terrorist attacks following 9/11, nothing could be left to chance. So the blanket of secrecy normally imposed on these big celebrity occasions was even thicker than usual. The venue had to be able to maintain tight security at all times, but it also had to be in a sunny and warm place, and large enough to accommodate the 200 guests and the same again in entertainers, technicians and security men. Tina and Banana Split eventually settled on a luxury hotel in an isolated and beautiful setting, not in Spain or Morocco or the Canaries, but in the rather more downmarket holiday destination of Cyprus. The Anassa, standing on the northern side of the Akamas Peninsula at the very western tip of Cyprus, seemed to meet most of their needs.

It was the island's only really de luxe hotel, with 184 spacious rooms, all with private balconies and panoramic views, and its own substantial 35-acre grounds, securely fenced. It was modern but stylish, a tasteful adaptation of ancient Byzantine architecture style with cool marble corridors, white walls and mosaics. There was a private beach, and several outdoor swimming pools. Within the landscaped gardens, dotted with bougainvillea and cypress trees, were clusters of superbly appointed villas.

Finding a place for the evening celebrations presented the only real headache. But Banana Split had the perfect solution. They would erect a huge marquee over the hotel's tennis courts and convert it into an atmospheric nightclub that could be themed on each successive night by a quick change in the decor and lighting. A special PG50 logo was prominently worked into the design. Wining and dining had to be of the highest quality. A top-class champagne, Kristal 95, retailing at £125 a bottle, had been flown out to Cyprus, and a French chef drafted in.

Aboard the plane the party mood had set in long before the guests reached Cyprus. The cabin crew had joined in the spirit of the occasion. As the high, snow-topped mountains of Cyprus appeared through the port windows, the plane's public address system was switched on. A voice announced that the plane was about to land. Passengers should please note that only Louis Vuitton suitcases – or luggage of similar quality – would be off-loaded on arrival. It was a rather feeble in-joke, but appreciated for all that.

On the ground at Paphos International Airport word had spread that a party of VIPs was flying in from London. But no other details had leaked out. Even when the plane taxied up to the terminal building and a red carpet was rolled out to meet it – in the best Hollywood tradition – to reveal the PG50 logo woven into it in large gold letters, it meant nothing to a local journalist sniffing around the terminal building. The first report to the outside world, carried by a French news agency, simply reported that 'a rich British couple' had come to Cyprus to stage a party.[6]

It was only when the guests had reached the Anassa and settled in that they received the first hint of what lay in store for them. The great marquee had been kitted out sumptuously, with twenty flower-decked tables arranged along two sides with a large bow-fronted stage dominating the far end. Above it hung a canopy from which gleamed a thousand spots of light.[7]

After dinner, the party's first big attraction was introduced – George Benson, the iconic black American entertainer who had taken soul and married it to jazz. He was booked for seventy-five minutes, but played for two hours. It was a good start.

The next day more guests arrived. In the world of the super-rich, owning a private jet is only one step up from owning a Bentley or a Rolls, and the airport had welcomed a small squadron of them. Speculation on what exactly was going on at the Anassa had begun to grow.

Outside the gates to the hotel, curious locals and a rash of stringers employed by the big news agencies had by this time gathered, desperately seeking any intelligence on just who the big names were. Perhaps the staff at the gate enjoyed winding them up. The name of Michael Jackson was bandied about. Others thought to be coming included Kevin Costner, Diana Ross, Eric Clapton and Kate Moss. All these names duly featured in some of the first newspaper reports.[8]

One guest was correctly identified. This was the then heir to the Monaco throne, the forty-three-year-old Prince Albert, whom Philip Green counted as a friend. The two men had met through the work of Tina on the Monaco charity circuit and played tennis together.

But Albert, for all his celebrity, was really a peripheral figure in the world of Philip Green. It was the other guests, the friends of Philip, or FOPs, who had featured more prominently in his remarkable story. They could be divided roughly into relatives and friends, bankers and business associates.

The first group was headed by Alma Green, Philip's still formidable mother, now in her eighties. Then there was his older sister, Elizabeth, and Tina's sister Susie, married to Sir Stirling Moss. There was a large contingent of Jewish friends, people that Green had met through his career and his social life – which included a love for Tottenham Hotspur and an even greater liking for the gaming table. The close-knit Jewish community of north London was the bedrock of what is popularly known as the rag-trade. Green owed them not a little. But he also had a great many friends outside the rag-trade. One of the guests was Anita Land, sister of the present chairman of the BBC, Michael Grade. Another was Jeremy Beadle.[9]

Also invited was a remarkably powerful group of investment bankers. One of them was Peter Cummings, head of corporate finance at the Bank of Scotland. Cummings had worked himself up from a lowly position within the bank to become one of Britain's most successful deal-makers. He had made his reputation by backing Tom Hunter and Philip Green in some of their earliest business deals. Over the years he had come to admire Green's business acumen, willing to bet his shirt on the entrepreneur's capacity to cut profitable deals. He had never been proved wrong.

A second banker at the party – a striking and vivacious figure – was Robin Saunders, the thirty-nine-year-old dashing American woman who handled the deal-making in London for the German bank

WestLB. At the time of the party she was best known as the woman who had made Bernie Ecclestone a billionaire by organising the flotation of what had become famous as 'Bernie Bonds'. But she also raised the vital funds that helped Green take over BHS in 2000. Saunders was at the height of her fame in March 2002 and had not yet fallen under a cloud at WestLB.

Also present were a number of Green's close business associates, a roll-call of people who had been involved, one way or another, in his ever-lengthening list of takeover bids. One was Tom Hunter, who had been given a crucial hand-up by Green in 1996 when he had helped him to expand his Sports Division empire. Then there was Elaine Gray, a Glaswegian who had risen to become managing director of Mark One, a high-profile discount chain part-owned by Green. She had cut her business teeth with Green ten years previously when they had worked together at the time of the great Amber Day controversy, a business venture that had badly scarred Green. Terry Green, no relation, the retailer Green had recruited as chief executive of Bhs, was another guest.

Richard Caring, one of Green's biggest suppliers and closest friends was also there. He was reputed to be worth around £200 million at the time of the party and now owns the world-famous Wentworth Golf Course and celebrity-studded restaurants The Ivy and Le Caprice. In 2002, he was (and he still is) owner and chairman of International Clothing Designs, a London-based fashion supplier with a strong presence in the Far East.

Also among the business associates was one of Green's newest friends, the dapper figure of Stuart Rose, at that time boss of the fashion empire Arcadia, which owned Burton, Topshop, Dorothy Perkins and Miss Selfridge, among others. Rose was in many ways the antithesis to Green. While Green was brash, Rose was urbane; while Green was effusive and out-going, Rose was a rather reserved figure; while Green had the persona of the barrow boy, Rose had that of the respectable City gent. Of all those present at Philip's party Rose was perhaps the man who, in the future, would most grow to regret that he had ever accepted the invitation, although he always denied it was anything but a real pleasure.

One last guest deserves a mention. Jeff Randall was not a business-man but a financial journalist who had worked for the *Sunday Times* and *Sunday Business*. He was now business editor at the BBC.

For a journalist, Randall has had an unusual role in Green's story, as we will see.

Friday, 15 March was Green's actual birthday. In the morning, some of the guests went to explore the sights. Just a few miles along the coast lay the caves and coves that shelter the ancient Baths of Aphrodite, and Paphos was a mere taxi-ride away. Others lounged on the sun terraces or sampled the health spa until it was time for the poolside buffet lunch. The morning was not without excitement. A white fishing boat had come chugging along the coast, heading for Latsi further east. The hotel boasted that its supplies of fish came in daily. But who could be sure that it really was just a fishing boat? The security men, who had kept a low profile so far, decided to take no chances. A motorised rubber dinghy was hurriedly launched, two men carrying sub-machine guns jumped aboard and raced to meet the boat, which was indeed just a fishing vessel.[10]

The alarm over, the rubber boat returned sedately to the hotel beach, the men in black jumping into the shallow water and dragging it up the beach. For the onlookers, it had been like watching a James Bond film.

For the rest of the day, one surprise followed fast upon the heels of another. At one point Richard Caring presented Philip with a brand-new red Ferrari Spider, freshly brought over from Italy and driven to the hotel. It was worth in excess of £100,000. Someone else gifted him a gleaming Harley Davidson, though Green is not known to be a great motorbike enthusiast. For the man who had everything – except at this point his own private jet – the big challenge was to find a birthday present he could still find a use for. Tina had her own answer. Knowing that her husband enjoyed playing real-life Monopoly on the high street, she gave him a solid gold Monopoly board made by the famous London jeweller Asprey. On the board his own properties had been substituted for the more familiar names. The dots in the dice were sparkling diamonds.[11]

Tina, by all accounts an emotional woman, spent much of the time in tears, quite overwhelmed by the whole event. Her husband, according to his brother-in-law, Stirling Moss, was finding it very hard to relax at his own party. A notorious chain-smoker, of short stature and rather overweight, Philip Green had been hospitalised about six years previously in a heart attack scare, but had carried on with his hectic lifestyle with few concessions to either his wife's or his doctor's advice. Sprawling in a lounger by a poolside without his mobile phone at his side seemed almost beyond him.[12]

He would have guessed that Tina had planned a special big surprise for his birthday. He was not to be disappointed. As he and Tina sat on the sun terrace, a mysterious, grey-haired man came up behind him, carrying a crocodile-skinned book. He tapped him on the shoulder, looked him in the eye and said in that distinctively smooth voice: 'Philip Green. This is your life.'

It was Michael Aspel, the presenter of the long-running television programme. Green, not normally one meekly to follow instructions from anyone, rose and, with Tina, followed Aspel to a hotel function room that had been transformed into a TV studio. The guests followed, taking seats in the makeshift auditorium, facing a stage and a large TV monitor.

Aspel first called Alma Green up on to the platform, before beginning a forty-five-minute resumé of Green's life and business achievements. Altogether nine people made their contribution from the platform, but there were also tributes via the medium of the giant TV screen.[13]

One message came from Australia where Gerald and Vera Weisfeld, who had featured in Philip's early career, were on holiday. Gerald had been more than just a business partner; twelve years before, he had acted as best man at Philip and Tina's wedding. Vera, a fun-loving Glaswegian, had once coaxed Philip into doing a Highland dance in front of hundreds of employees, an experience Green was unlikely to forget.[14]

Other messages came from closer to home. On the screen Tina and Philip's children, Chloë and Brandon, sent their love from the Greens' home in Monte Carlo. More greetings came from the crew of their ocean-going motor yacht, *Lionheart*, anchored in Monaco harbour.[15]

There was also glamour from Britney Spears, who sent her best wishes. Nobody suspected that Philip Green could count her as a friend. Sylvester Stallone, who certainly was, sent his best regards. Then came the biggest name of all, Hollywood superstar Bruce Willis. Filmed on an airfield, where a gleaming private jet was waiting to take him and his friends off for the weekend, the star shook up a bottle of champagne, Formula-One-style.

The accolades were wrapped up by Green's own speech, which included a tribute to Tina. One friend remembered it as being like a report to shareholders: 'He was warm and thanked everyone, then he launched into his plan for the next few years for his business. It reminded me of a general addressing his troops.'[16]

Green's television life story was followed that evening by a special birthday dinner in the great marquee. Billed as the 'black and white' evening, the guests were welcomed into the art deco ballroom by a twenty-three-piece band, flown in from Paris and playing Glenn Miller's 'In the Mood', while dancing girls in black bras and white hotpants strutted their stuff.

A team of waiters, also in black and white – with PG logos on their backs – then manoeuvred twenty seashell-shaped silver containers into place on each of the tables. At the heart of each dazzling ice-filled shell – like a pearl inside an oyster – was a dish of the best caviar money could buy, again specially flown in, this time from Russia, at a cost of around £35,000. Washed down with lashings of the Kristal 95 champagne served in Jasper Conran flutes, it was an *hors d'oeuvre* fit for an emperor.

Green had always loved Frank Sinatra, and Tina had hired a Sinatra impersonator, the English singer Frederick Gardner, to sing through-out the feast. Meanwhile, the top-of-the-bill artists were being quietly smuggled into the hotel past a gathering press scrum and shown into the 'green rooms' immediately behind the stage to prepare for the show.

As the last of the plates were cleared away, the spotlight fell on the curtain. Suddenly the master of the swivel hip and the vocal swerve burst upon them, Tom Jones himself. The Welshman launched into a medley of his hits, culminating in 'It's Not Unusual' and his signature number, 'The Green Green Grass of Home'.[17]

It was a hard act to follow but the next group was more than up to the challenge. The lights dimmed and a hush fell over the tables. Then the music came beating out and the curtain rose to reveal the legendary American soul band Earth, Wind and Fire, a band that had produced its first great hit when Green had been a struggling young garment trader. The performance of the nine-man ensemble was for many the highlight of the entire weekend. While some, including Stirling Moss, slipped away to bed, many got down to the serious business of dancing the night away.[18]

The next morning there was much hammering and rebuilding within the marquee. Banana Split were putting together one of their more ambitious sets, a wooden version of a Roman arena. By early evening the guests had duly put on the regulation underwear, though not all had managed flesh. The party organisers, dressed as sturdy centurions in full military uniform, handed out the costumes – white toga-like garments with gold trimmings, ankle-high gold-strapped sandals and laurel wreaths dipped in golden paint.

There was some degree of choice. Jeff Randall observed in a newspaper article that Stuart Rose had chosen an elaborate creation that made him 'as camp as knickers, in an outfit that had enough glitter to cover a Christmas tree'.[19] Led by Philip Green and Tina, the guests processed along an olive-lined avenue on a carpet of rosemary and lavender, their way illuminated by flaming torches until they entered the newly finished amphitheatre.

To some at the party, there were few sights more ridiculous than a bunch of middle-aged men displaying their knobbly knees in such costumes. This certainly was the view of Jeff Randall. He confessed to feeling uncomfortable in 'an ill-fitting toga that felt more like a set of Bhs curtains . . . My embarrassment at appearing like an extra from a *Carry On* movie was tempered only by the fact that two of Britain's most highly regarded retailers [Green and Rose] looked even more bizarre than I did.'[20]

Randall was not alone in feeling ill at ease in his costume. At least one other guest confided to his friends that he had never felt so embarrassed in his life.[21] Philip himself had assumed the role of a Roman emperor – 'a physically challenged Nero' as Jeff Randall chose to put it – while Tina played his empress. Whether he thought of himself as Nero is unclear, since he is reported to have referred to himself merely as 'king'. But when reported in the press, Nero it decidedly was. This was, of course, the emperor who fiddled while Rome burned. To add to the occasion, a quartet of male strippers, the Dream Boys, carried the gigantic square birthday cake, all 150 kilograms of it, into the arena. They were dressed as slaves.[22]

That evening the veteran Greek singer Demis Roussos was joined by a troupe of Greek dancers in a let's-not-forget-we-are-in-Cyprus gesture, and the three-day party was wound up by Rod Stewart, who brought the proceedings to a fittingly costly close; he was reportedly paid £750,000 for a performance that lasted forty-five minutes.

The Greens had gone to some lengths to keep the party secret – the staff and artists had been asked to sign a confidentiality agreement –

but details of the weekend, and especially the toga event, inevitably leaked out. Most guests were flattering about the occasion and Green's generosity. As one of his oldest friends described it: 'The party was like going to heaven.'[23] Unsurprisingly, some of the press chose to turn the event into an attack on Green, holding it up as a monument to bad taste. The *Mail on Sunday* described it as an 'orgy of excess' and 'an astonishing display of tasteless ostentation'.[24]

By the time the guests reached Paphos airport the next day a party of journalists had gathered. Green found himself pressed on the stories of excess as he arrived to board his plane home. He told one reporter, 'It wasn't gaudy or horrible or ugly . . . The party was beautifully done and a fabulous success. It was a lot of fun. I am just feeling a little bit tired and my guests are recuperating . . . Most people say it's the best weekend of their lives.'[25]

A COCKY LITTLE BOY

hilip Green was born on 15 March 1952, the only son of Simon and Alma Green. His parents lived in Croydon, a somewhat ordinary district of south London, which had lost any romance it ever had when its airport, the first London airport, had closed down in 1938. Heavily bomb damaged during the war, Croydon had been rebuilt in a dreary post-war style. It was the sort of place that aspiring people would want to leave behind.

Some who know Philip Green, an outgoing man with tremendous energy and the swagger of a Cockney barrow boy, imagine that he must have sprung from an ordinary London family, perhaps of street trader stock. Where else could he have got his blokeish humour and extensive use of expletives? But in fact he was the product of a respectable and enterprising, well-to-do, middle-class Jewish family.

Green once described his father as having been in electrical retailing.[1] The records show he ran a couple of small companies that specialised in servicing radios and renting out TV sets, an idea that may seem passé now but was in fact ahead of its time. Philip's mother, Alma, was also involved in business and seems to have been equally enterprising. In the late 1950s she saw that most women dreamed of having their own automatic washing machines but that few could afford to buy their own. She ran the first American-style coin-operated launderette in Croydon. She also noticed that the traditional petrol station, where motorists queued until an attendant became free to top up their tanks, would soon become obsolete when customers were free to serve themselves. She duly opened her own self-service station, where the young Philip would help out at weekends.[2]

Both parents, in Green's own words, were 'business obsessed'.[3] As well as their retail activities they owned a small property company called Langley Road Investments, which had two properties in South London.[4] They made some money from rent and watched the value of their assets grow, but they were far from being property magnates. Owning property had one great advantage for a small businessman: it could be used as collateral for raising business finance. Interestingly enough, in later life, Philip Green was to prove a master at putting property assets to good business use. Mrs Green has continued to keep an interest in property – even today, aged eighty-six, she manages her own portfolio of property companies.[5]

Simon and Alma Green may not have made it into the top business class, but they did well enough to move to East Finchley, close to the fashionable Hampstead Garden suburb – a favourite haunt of up-and-coming Jewish families – when Philip and his older sister Elizabeth were still children. And they were also able to send him to an expensive Jewish boarding school, Carmel College, when he was nine years of age.

Being sent to boarding school at the age of nine can be a traumatic experience for any child. And this seems to have been the case with Philip Green. Asked about it in 2004 he replied defensively: 'I didn't mind going. It made me independent.' But he shrugged his shoulders as he said it.[6] The body language suggested that he had not relished the experience. Indeed it seems that the years he spent at the school were amongst the unhappiest of his life.

When his parents chose to send Philip to Carmel they no doubt thought it would be in his best interests. In fact, it turned out not to appeal to someone of young Philip's disposition and interests. As his mother told a reporter in June 2002, her son 'always wanted to earn money . . . that was his ambition ever since he helped me out with the business in the summer holidays.'[7] Yet the school was fiercely academic, designed to produce boys who would move into the professions, rather than business. Indeed the college aspired to be the 'Jewish Eton'.[8]

It had been founded in 1948 by Rabbi Kopul Rosen, a distinguished Jewish theologian, with the aim of giving bright Jewish boys an avenue for entry into Oxford and Cambridge universities. It opened modestly on a site on Greenham Common in Berkshire with a roll of just twenty boys. But by 1961 it had moved into a great Victorian country house on the banks of the River Thames at Mongewell, just outside Wallingford near Oxford and had around 300 pupils. The beautiful old house formed the central block and contained the library and dormitories as well as the flat of Kopul Rosen who, as principal of the college, had the privilege – if privilege it was – of living above the school shop. It was a spacious site with lawns running down to the riverbank and new, well-equipped classroom blocks grouped around the old building. The school had its own playing fields and cricket pitch. On the river, the school's oarsmen bent their backs and learnt the art of working as a team.

Compared with many of the older public schools of the time it offered comparative luxury. There was no Spartan regime of cold showers, no plunging into cold outdoor swimming pools as the school had an indoor heated pool. To keep such an establishment going, and to maintain small class sizes, the fees had to be substantial, although there were bursaries available for the brightest boys. Kopul Rosen was descended from Jewish immigrants from Eastern Europe and the ethos of the school was a strange mixture of English public school and Lithuanian *yeshivah* – a school dedicated to the study of Hebrew religious texts. This meant that students had to cope with a fiercely pressurised regime: they were expected to follow the full English academic curriculum but at the same time had to devote much time to religious duties. There were at least two daily Jewish services plus a morning session of religious instruction and regular classes in Hebrew.

The services were held in the new synagogue built during Philip Green's time at the school. It was a spectacularly beautiful building, a statement of the central role played by religion in the life of the school. Designed by a local architect, it took the shape of a giant wedge – with glass walls on three sides and a fourth wall in fashionable concrete. It was good enough to become a listed building.

This was the world that Philip Green entered in the autumn of 1961. It was a school where some of the richest boys were brought down at the start of term by chauffeured limousine. Regardless of their social origin, all Carmelis (a title most pupils were proud to bear) had to wear school uniform, a pretty standard issue of blazer flannels, pullover, shirt, socks and school tie – all available for purchase at Harrods. The school cap featured an extra-long peak in a catching shade of violet. Each pupil brought with them a trunk, packed with a specified range of required articles including underwear, toiletries and sports gear.

Life at Carmel was very much like that at any traditional boys' public boarding school, except for the heavy emphasis on Judaism and the lack of a fagging system. There were strict rules surrounding almost everything from behaviour at communal mealtimes to a strict enforcement of silence after lights out. Boys breaking the rules could be physically punished and there was a liberal use of the slipper on the bottom and the broad ruler on the palm of the hand. Caning, the ultimate sanction, was the preserve of the principal.

From the evidence provided by a number of boys who attended Carmel at the same time as Philip Green, he at first seemed to fit in as well as most boys uprooted from their homes and families and sent off to boarding school. In the school photograph of 1963 he appears in the back row as a good-looking eleven-year-old, distinguished by his thick mop of hair. He looks no less or more at ease with himself than any other boy.

Toni Rauch, an exact contemporary of the young Green during his Carmel years, recalls him as being very much one of the gang, a pretty ordinary lad: 'We were all in it together at boarding school. Philip Green was not particularly a live wire but he wasn't particularly shy. He was quite popular with the group I belonged to.'[9]

But Rauch lost touch with his friend in his later years at the school, years that apparently saw the emergence of a quite different Philip Green. In 1964, when the young Green was only eleven years old, on the very threshold of adolescence, Simon Green suffered a fatal heart attack. His son was later to claim that he and his father had never been close, but at the time he seemed to have been badly affected by the loss. Rauch remembers the young Philip being very upset: 'In a school community as big as Carmel there were bound to be occasions when someone lost a parent. It was quite traumatic when Philip's dad died. He became depressed for a while but I would say no more than anyone else in the same situation.'[10]

But, from the evidence given by other former pupils who knew Philip at school, his father's unexpected death altered both his personality and his behaviour. One told us: 'The death of his father seemed to change him. He became something of a misfit at school, aggressive at times, and unpopular with the other boys. In the classroom he had a disruptive influence, chucking objects around the room when the teacher's back was turned.'[11] Another remembers that in his teens Philip Green had no one he could call a close friend: 'Some boys make friends. Philip Green didn't. I think it was because he could lose his temper at the drop of a hat and could be quite abrasive.'[12]

Another classmate simply remarked that he hoped he might never meet Philip Green again.[13] Even then, it would seem, he had developed an unusual talent for treading on other people's toes.

But there could be a far more straightforward explanation for the aggression he displayed at Carmel College. In a school dedicated to academic high-flyers, boys who would go on to gain entry to the top universities, Philip Green was simply not the sort of person to blossom and feel at ease. It is not that the teaching was necessarily bad – many of the teachers were well-qualified and dedicated to the school – but that the school was bound by a curriculum that gave little scope for making learning exciting or in any way fun. English was a core subject, but much of the time was spent learning the rules of grammar, under-standing the concept of figures of speech or writing notes on great authors. Latin – a compulsory subject – had its own dreary routine of taking ancient Roman texts and translating them into English with each pupil required to translate a passage in front of the whole class. Most boys loathed the subject. Hebrew was not much more popular.[14]

Philip Green was bright enough – like the others boys he had passed the demanding Carmel entrance examination to win admis-sion – but the formal education dished out at the school seems to have completely failed to engage his interest. As he admitted in later life, he was easily bored. As for the religious side of his education, he would not have been unusual if he found it a tedious grind. Most pupils were not particularly religious and found that the whole religious ethos of the school imposed a daunting burden. They would rather have used the time to improve their performance in the mainstream subjects.

But there was one place where the young Green could show his paces – on the playing field. Sport never had the same place at Carmel as it had at Eton, whose playing fields were famously judged by the Duke of Wellington to have won the Battle of Waterloo. The Jewish college possessed no rugby pitches, although an enthusiastic teacher, a Mr Bunney, had attempted to introduce rugby and one game was actually played at the school. Parental protest immediately put a stop to the idea. But there was no such parental prejudice against soccer and the school regularly fielded several elevens and played in local leagues. Football was even then one of Philip Green's great passions. Some of his fellow pupils remember him as a good man to have in the team. His other sport was cricket. Green has sometimes let it be suggested that he shone at the sport. There have even been reports that Green played cricket at county level. But the teacher who ran the cricket team in Green's day does not remember him as being particularly gifted. Anthony Barr-Taylor remembers Philip as a 'cocky little boy' and says he was OK at cricket, but 'nothing special'.[15]

But there is absolutely no dispute about Philip Green's failure to excel in ordinary lessons. By the time he reached the fifth form – at the age of fifteen – he found himself relegated to the bottom class. It had the advantage of being a very small class, with only five or six boys. But it also had the disadvantage of going nowhere. It was generally under-stood that boys in the 'C' stream would not be entered for A levels and would have no chance of gaining entrance to university.[16] Weeding out doubtful candidates in this way may have had the result of boost-ing the school performance in the unofficial A level league.

Although he shared the bottom class with others who were to do well in later life, such as the successful hotelier and entrepreneur Jonathan Wix, we can imagine that those unfairly thought of as dunces by the academic high-flyers may have felt a degree of resentment.

Even among the strugglers of Form 5C, it seems that Philip Green made little progress. He left school without a single O level.[17] It had not helped that he had missed a whole term through being suspended from school, a most unusual distinction to be earned by any Carmeli.[18] In failing to do well at school his experience was very like that of many other successful entrepreneurs. Richard Branson, Greg Dyke, Alan Sugar and Tom Hunter had similarly uninspiring encounters with their schools.

Philip Green was in almost every way a fish out of water at Carmel. Although he came from a relatively affluent background compared with most of the population at the time, many of the boys at school came from Jewish families who had climbed rather higher in social class terms than the Greens had, either in terms of wealth or educa-tional attainment. He was not merely an underdog academically but in class terms as well. Since the Jewish boys at Carmel appear to have been just as sensitive to the nuances of class and hierarchy as any traditional English public schoolboy, Green's failure to make friends may have, at least in part, been down to snobbery. Even his tendency to use coarse language, a habit that his maths teacher, Mrs Evans, recalls as making him unpopular with the boys, may have been a reaction to a sense of being patronised by some of the posher boys he had encountered at school.[19]

That sense of being the underdog at school must have made an abiding impression on him. It is likely to have been one of the key influences on his determination to prove himself at the highest business level. It also helps to explain his subsequent distaste for the 'elitists' who ran the City, and the war of attrition that came to mark his relationships with the business establishment throughout his career.

It was unusual for boys to go home at weekends since celebration of the Sabbath was an important part of school life. But, according to his own account, Philip Green often went home to help his widowed mother run her petrol station. In an in-depth interview with Sally Vincent of the *Guardian* in 2004, he related that he'd 'work in the forecourt on weekends and school holidays. Wipe windscreens, change oil, that sort of thing. The punters would tip him sixpence, two bob, half a crown.' On Saturdays he could knock up as much as five pounds.[20]

All the signs were there. Here was a boy who could scarcely wait to leave school and go into business. There were some role models associated with Carmel. One was Sir Isaac Wolfson, founder of Great Universal Stores or GUS, and king of the mail order catalogue trade. The science block at Carmel was named Wolfson House in honour of the donation he had made to fund it. Another block had been paid for by a generous donation from Marks & Spencer. Even closer to home, the medical centre at the college had been funded by the Wix family, who had made their money in the manufacture of cigarettes. Jonathan, one of the five or six who sat with Philip Green in the class for under-achievers, was a member of the family.

Green certainly does not appear to have looked back with nostalgic pleasure to those schooldays spent on the banks of the Thames at Wallingford. When Carmel College ran into financial difficulties in 1997 and faced closure, Philip Green, by then a multi-millionaire, was approached by a group of former pupils trying to raise money to save it. He simply did not want to know.[21]

For Alma Green, her son's lack of success at his boarding school may not have been a huge blow. Green was close to his mother, a common feature of Jewish family life, and held a deep respect for her opinions and judgement, as he still does. Those who know Philip well maintain that his mother was very much the driving force behind his decision to go into business. Certainly she transmitted to him, through her genes or her influence, a passion for the world of trade. Rather than persuade him to go on to FE College to get some O levels, it appears she used her business and family connections to secure him an apprenticeship in the wholesale shoe trade. It was the first step on a long road that was to end with him becoming one of the richest men in Britain.

In 1968, when Green left school, the British fashion industry was on the brink of a revolution. In a fashion sense the 'swinging sixties', driven by the huge success of British pop bands and artists, had only just begun. Under the influence of rock bands like the Beatles and the Rolling Stones, young people had turned their backs on formal suits for men and skirts and cardigans for women. In London, Carnaby Street and King's Road in Chelsea were setting the trend while a young designer called Barbara Hulanicki was about to open up her trend-setting Biba emporium in Kensington High Street. The fashion business was never to be the same again.

But it wasn't just the switch in fashion that changed the nature of the business. In the 1960s most of the clothes and footwear sold in Britain were made there. But now there was a downward pressure on fashion prices as the youth market blossomed. A suit bought in the new Kensington Market sold for about a fifth of the price of a good traditional suit. Bargain-hunting was the trend of the day and whole-salers began to look overseas to source their products.

The footwear trade was one of the first to make a move. In 1968 the market was dominated by the giant British Shoe Corporation, a creation of the famous takeover king Charles Clore. But new technology was making it possible for foreign suppliers to muscle their way into the UK. Hong Kong, still a British colony and given almost free access to the British market, was in the vanguard. Perhaps by chance, the footwear wholesaler that had employed Philip Green did business with Hong Kong. It gave Green an early insight into the potential of that part of the world to supply the British market, something that made a deep impression on him.

At first he worked in the warehouse, learning how shoes could be stored and retrieved when the orders came in. He was also used as an errand boy, and was sent around London with samples to show retail buyers. The shoes were bottom of the market, sold in some cases for less than £2 a pair. It was his first experience of dealing, the art of striking a profitable deal yet leaving the other side happy. For some-one who liked doing things, rather than sitting at a desk, it was a revelation. He must also have learnt that the rounded vowels taught at Carmel distanced him from down-to-earth customers and his boss. What one of Green's teachers had referred to as 'a certain coarseness' in his speech was the lingua franca at this end of the business. It may be that his distinctive delivery, liberally dispersed with expletives, emerged from this period of apprenticeship.

After four years of learning the ropes Green was allowed to try his hand at selling at a wholesale shoe fair held in the Mount Royal Hotel at Marble Arch. The twenty-year-old apprentice was determined to impress his boss and make his first big sale. When a buyer came to visit the stand and picked up a wooden sandal with a leather strap – a good imitation of a Dr Scholl's – Green told him they would cost him £2 a pair. He was caught on the hop when the buyer asked how much he would charge for 40,000 pairs. He didn't have an answer and had to race over and ask the boss. But when he pointed out the buyer his boss looked sniffy: 'He's got long hair, he can't be serious.'[22]

Green refused to be deterred. He knew the man represented a big retail group. His boss bet him a fiver that he couldn't seal the deal. More than thirty years after the event, Green could still recall the excitement of the challenge: 'So off I went. They wanted them wrapped in a special way, special box, special this, special that, what didn't they want. I said, yes, yes, I'd see to all that.'[23]

He pulled off the deal, and when the order for 40,000 pairs dropped on his desk, he could barely wait to claim his prize from his boss: 'I ran all the way up the five flights, up to the top of our building, slapped it down, said, "There's your order." And he got this old-fashioned leather wallet out of his back pocket, and every note was like it had been ironed. Got the note out, feeling it to make sure it was just the one, and handed me the five quid. That was my first order.'[24]

But he also learned a hard lesson: some customers cannot be trusted. A few weeks later the buyer cancelled the order. Green had to pay the money back.

In 1973, Green celebrated his twenty-first birthday by joining the board of the family property company, Langley Road Investments. But his involvement was never more than a sideline to the business that was now to occupy most of his waking hours – carving a reputation for himself as wheeler and dealer in the London fashion industry, the 'rag-trade'.

Shortly after his birthday, he turned up for a first date with a girl about the same age as himself in a white E-type Jaguar. (One contemporary recalls him first acquiring an E-type when he was as young as eighteen, and adding a personalised number plate once owned by his father, beginning with the letters SG. It was the ultimate status symbol for a young man at the time.) The ostentation didn't impress his date, however. The young woman concerned remembers him as being very full of himself, giving the impression he was in a financial league far above her. Unsurprisingly the relationship did not last beyond the first date.

In any case, his main interest then seems to have been business. In the five years since he first started work the fashion revolution had quickened, especially with the arrival of the age of denim. Jeans were unisex, cheap, hard-wearing and classless. Shops selling them were springing up all over London and in every major city in Britain. They needed supplying. The biggest selling brands were Levis and Lee Jeans but they were relatively expensive. Philip Green was among the first in Britain to see the potential of importing cheap jeans, the classic badge of American youth, from a new and then unlikely source, new textile factories in Hong Kong.

The wholesale side of the London rag-trade was increasingly to be found in an area immediately north of Oxford Street, to the east of Oxford Circus. Green was to spend much of the next twelve years as a trader at the lower end of the market, buying and selling imported clothing, always ready for a deal, always trying to keep one step ahead of his rivals. In the mid-1970s, with the country first on a three-day week, and then suffering a serious bout of stagflation as a result of the 1973 Yom Kippur War and the hike in oil prices, it was a tough time to make a go of business.

Britain had been short of entrepreneurs for as long as anyone could remember. As Anthony Sampson put it: 'To many foreigners in the 1950s and 1960s, the British, from dons to dustmen, seemed stubbornly united in their lack of interest in money.'[25] Indeed, in the 1960s, a worried government had even set up a special inquiry to find out what had happened to the once famed spirit of British enterprise. The committee found few answers, suggesting only that banks had been too tough on those who wanted to run their own companies. Certainly finding money to start the business has always been one of the great challenges facing any would-be entrepreneur, although money of itself can't guarantee success.[26]

Green has never quite fitted the mould of the self-made man that some journalists have liked to portray. When Simon Green died in 1964 he left an estate valued at some £14,000, equivalent to £180,000 at today's prices.[27] In addition his mother had run her own businesses for many years, opening doors for him that would have remained closed to someone with no business background in the family. At the age of twenty-one he was given a business loan of £20,000 by the family bank, a sum equivalent to some £150,000 in today's money.[28] Even so, without the help of friends and businessmen he met, he might have found those early years in business even tougher than they proved to be.

In his early twenties Philip Green first met a man, ten years his senior, who was to have a profound influence on him. Gerald Weisfeld, a Londoner and also Jewish, had built a hugely successful business around his ability to trade at the bottom end of the market, and ran a cash-and-carry clothing business in Great Titchfield Street, near Oxford Circus with the catchy name of Fash 'n' Carry. Weisfeld appears to have treated Green almost as a son, and the two men struck up a long and lasting friendship as fellow wholesale traders.

Gerald also had a growing business in Scotland which had started as What Every Woman Wants in 1971. He had recruited an energetic second-in-command, a Glasgow woman called Vera MacDonald, a business partnership that was soon to blossom into marriage. One day, when Vera was in charge at the Glasgow head office, she received a telephone call from Gerald's secretary in Great Titchfield Street to say: 'There is an arrogant, confident young guy here and he says he wants a desk.'[29]

'Ruby,' said Vera, 'show him the door.' Shortly afterwards Gerald phoned to tell her that the young man was Philip Green and that he had promised him a desk at Fash 'n' Carry from which he could run his business.

According to Gerald Weisfeld, Green was at this time a supplier to his business, a man who offered him clothes at very competitive prices. The pair would go off together to London's docklands to cavernous warehouses, where, as Weisfeld remembers, they would sometimes 'climb over mountains of stock to find the goods we wanted'.[30]

Green was a born negotiator, spending much of his time talking people into doing deals. He often dealt in cash and drove around London in a flashy car. Vera Weisfeld tells of the time he arrived at Great Titchfield Street in a Mercedes sports car carrying a briefcase full of money. She remembers him at that time as 'a very dashing young man, I would say a handsome young man'.[31] She recalls one occasion when she was squeezed into the back seat of the Mercedes, listening to Green describing some of his recent deals. Finally she tapped him on the shoulder and said: 'Excuse me, Philip, how old are you?' He replied that he was twenty-four. 'Oh,' she said, 'the way you were talking, all these deals you have been doing, I thought you must be at least a hundred.'[32]

It was a gentle putdown, but the story captures the somewhat flash character that had already emerged. Green also possessed a quality possessed by most successful entrepreneurs: he never knew when to give up. Vera Weisfeld admired him for it: 'He's always been involved in business and has had periods when he was wealthy and periods when he was down. But my impression of Philip is that when he is down he will find ways to get back up. That is what I respect him for. He is not a loser – nothing will hold him back.'[33]

On one occasion, he and Gerald Weisfeld made a trip to Hong Kong together. Green found the energy there invigorating, as he later commented: 'It's very fast moving, Hong Kong. Very fast. Very quick. Nobody goes to sleep. They work seventeen hours a day and nobody's tired. Hong Kong. Very built up. You wouldn't imagine it. Every inch built up, crammed full of people. All working.'[34]

He was in some ways a prophet of the benefits of globalisation before the word was invented. According to the Weisfelds, he and Gerald returned from their trip to the Far East with so many pairs of jeans that they had enough to supply the whole of Britain. But there were hard lessons to be learned in turning that sort of coup into a profitable and sustainable business.

In November 1976, Green set up his first import and export business. It was called Tarbrook Ltd, an off-the-shelf name that he did not feel the need to change. But its articles of association certainly indicated no lack of ambition. One of its stated aims was 'to carry on business in any part of the world as wholesalers, manufacturers, factors, agents, retailer of textiles, and materials of any description'.[35]

For a company with such ambitious aims the start-up capital of just £9,500 – money raised by means of a short-term bank loan – seems hardly adequate, but the ambitious young Green, already a persuasive salesman with good contacts in the Far East, may have hoped to fund the business largely through cashflow.

His mother was appointed co-director, although she seems to have had no experience of the sort of business her son planned to build. It was the first of several similar partnerships she was to form with Philip. In the company records he signed all the official returns as director and salesman, while Alma Green's occupation was described as 'property owner'.[36] It seemed that Philip would run the day-to-day business while his mother took more of a behind-the-scenes role, providing encouragement, inspiration and advice in matters such as dealing with the accounts and the VAT inspector.

The now familiar Philip Green signature with its great looping capitals appears on the company registration papers and has changed little over the years. In 2003, it was analysed by a handwriting expert who did not know the author's identity. She detected 'a sharp intellect', a person who was 'a realistic and practical thinker who mistrusts woolly thoughts, vague concepts, or subjective thinking', who believed in 'calling a spade a spade' and was 'admired and reviled in equal measure for doing so'. Allied to this was 'an enormous potential for rebelliousness with perceived authority'.[37]

For the first eighteen months of its existence Tarbrook had a turnover of nearly £175,000 and made a profit of just over £10,505, hardly a strong performance, but not a failure either. This was the only set of accounts ever filed.

Amongst those he did business with were the Weisfelds. He may have been a young man with a flash car and a touch of arrogance but Vera Weisfeld remembers his role as 'a trader buying parcels of goods. Very often we would have had deals brought our way through Philip.'[38] It seems his main activity was acting as a go-between between suppliers and wholesalers, striking bargains that left both sides satisfied.

It was only in 1981 that he came to public notice for the first time with an eye-catching scheme to launch the first British celebrity-branded jeans. In the United States Gloria Vanderbilt had already lent her name to a brand of jeans with great commercial success. Vanderbilt, a rich American heiress, had made a name for herself both as an actress and a designer, creating her own range of sunglasses and perfumes. In 1979 (at the age of fifty-four) she allowed herself to be used to promote a new style of very tight jeans with her name emblazoned on the back pocket. They had sold like hot cakes.

Philip Green soon spotted the potential in Britain. He looked around to find a UK equivalent for Gloria Vanderbilt and came up with the idea of Joan Collins. The actress was then forty-eight years old and had recently put new life into her faltering career by starring in the sex-thrillers *The Stud* and *The Bitch*, both based on the raunchy novels of her sister Jackie. She was soon to depart to the United States to star in a television series called *Dynasty*, a move that transformed her status as a celebrity. When Green approached her agents to ask whether she would agree to become Britain's answer to Gloria Vanderbilt, she signed up to the deal, turning up at the launch and being featured in the advertising campaign. She would receive royalties on every pair of jeans sold.

In 1981, Eric Musgrave was a news reporter on the weekly trade magazine *Drapers Record*. In April of that year he went to an office in Conduit Street to cover this breaking news story. There he met Philip Green, then twenty-nine years old, for the first time: 'I found him to be a rather typical chippy Jewish rag-trader guy. He was working in a small untidy office, with phones ringing all the time. But at least he was in the upmarket Conduit Street, close to New Bond Street, rather than north of Oxford Street in the wholesale rag-trade district around Great Portland Street.'[39] The reporter was certainly impressed by the energy of the man and by his enthusiasm for his new product. Green assured him that the early signs were so encouraging he was having to rush the goods to market: 'We were planning to deliver the merchandise in August,' he said, 'but because of the response we are hoping to get the supplies through by next month.'[40] The ambitious Green planned a whole range of casual clothes bearing the Joan Collins label. He publicly staked his reputation on their success, and told Musgrave, 'I believe British girls have an affinity with Joan Collins.'[41]

Today Green likes to give the impression that he has his finger on the pulse of fashion. But in the case of Joan Collins Jeans he badly misjudged the tastes of young British women, the target market.

American youth might be keen to wear the same clothes as the ageing but still glamorous Gloria Vanderbilt: their British equivalents probably regarded Joan Collins as a B-movie actress who had seen better days.[42] They resolutely refused to open their purses and pay up the £16.95, which, in 1981, was a high price for a pair of rather ordinary jeans. Instead of launching Philip Green's career as a fashion trendsetter, much of the stock had to be sold off at heavily discounted prices.

The failure of Joan Collins Jeans was Green's first great setback as the fortunes of the company closely followed those of the jeans. The following year, on the petition of a supplier whose bills had not been settled, the company suffered the indignity of being compulsorily wound up.[43]

Typically, Green had several other business projects on the go. In 1980, he had somehow found time to launch another company called Cupcraft Ltd with a new partner called Peter Solemani, a fellow north Londoner. Although Green and Solemani each held 50 per cent of the shares, Green was clearly the man in charge, since he grandly listed himself as 'chairman'. Like Tarbrook, Cupcraft had an ambitious prospectus, but survived only a year before the partners decided to call it a day. It was put into liquidation only a month after the final bringing down of the curtain on Joan Collins Jeans. The company records, filed with Companies House, do not contain detailed accounts, but it was piling up debts that could not realistically be paid off.[44]

If Green had any hopes that Tarbrook might sort out its financial difficulties, they were to be dashed. As 1983 drew to a close the two directors – Philip and Alma Green – called a special meeting (of themselves) and resolved: 'That it has been proved to the satisfaction of this meeting that the company by reasons of its liabilities cannot continue its business, and that it is advisable to wind up the same, and accordingly that the company be wound up voluntarily.'[46] When the sums were totted up the company was found to owe its creditors a hefty £239, 348. It had assets of just £436.

Now thirty-one years of age, Philip Green had spent fifteen years of his life in pursuit of an elusive fortune in the wholesale fashion trade. Almost without exception, everything he had touched had turned to lead. With the Thatcher government determinedly tightening the screws to squeeze inflation out of the British economy, nobody would have blamed him if he had simply given up and taken a regular job as a buyer or property manager with some big retail group. But Green was no quitter, and the recession was throwing up new business opportunities. He had already begun to take them.

THE DEL BOY YEARS

P hilip Green had yet to make his mark in the business that was to ultimately make him famous and rich – fashion retail. He had been first tempted to try his hand in the extraordinary market conditions of 1979, before his energies had been diverted into Joan Collins Jeans. In that year, Mrs Thatcher's chancellor, Sir Geoffrey Howe, had tried to tackle rising inflation by hiking British interest rates. Coming after a decade of great stress – the four-day week, galloping inflation and increasing industrial unrest – it was the last straw for many of Britain's smaller retailers. It was especially difficult for those on leases, which, extraordinarily, did not provide for rent reductions even in hard times. In the circumstances of 1979 this inflexibility quickly became a recipe for the closing down of shops in all the high streets of Britain.

In London the streets that commanded the highest rents were hardest hit – prestigious places such as Oxford Street and New Bond Street. Many smaller fashion retailers, hit by a triple whammy of falling sales, rising interest rates and a sharply rising rate of VAT, made the only decision they felt they could, which was to sell up and pull out. Under the terms of the standard shop lease they had to return the premises to the landlord free of stock. It was a glorious opportunity for a sharp young dealer like Philip Green to pick up supplies at knock-down prices. In the late autumn of 1979 a number of 'designer label' outlets were shutting up shop in London's West End. Haute couture had been replaced by a new mass-market form. Top designers were now selling ready-to-wear garments using quality materials and carrying the endorsement of that all-important label. One of the designer label shops that announced its closure was Originelle, a one-off store run by a brother and sister partnership in Berners Street. Green hurried over to find the premises crammed with trendy but slightly care-worn Bruce Oldfield and Jacques Azagury clothes, highly regarded British designer names that were not quite Yves St Laurent but sold well all the same. The retail value of the unsold stock was reckoned to be £35,000, but since Originelle was desperate to clear the shop Green was able to buy the stock for much less. It might have sold well, heavily discounted, on the capital's many street markets. His plan was at first to sell it on. But when he had time to examine the job lot more closely he realised he could dress it up a bit and sell it at a premium: 'It didn't look all that bad to me . . . so I sent it all to the dry cleaners, got it put on nice satin hangers and polythened it up so it looked brand new.'[1] Philip Green waited a quarter of a century before he revealed this detail to a journalist as an illustration of his inventiveness, without perhaps realising how such tales helped to confirm the prejudice of some that he was something of a Del Boy character.

But the decision not to sell the stock on to any of his usual retailers, or indeed to any third party, also had logic. He took a look around, saw the large number of empty shops coming on the market and decided to take his first plunge into retailing. He knew that Sammy Stewart, a clothing retailer who ran his own shop at 41 Conduit Street, just around the corner from fashionable New Bond Street, was getting out. He struck a deal and took over in his place. In September 1979, he had opened his first shop. His Bruce Oldfield and Jacques Azagury stock was soon flying off the racks. He was still there two years later when he was using the shop as the base from which to launch the Joan Collins Jeans range and Eric Musgrave first came across him, phones ringing, clutter everywhere.

Green had caught the retail bug. In 1981, the British high street was still stretched out on the rack of recession with closing down sales and empty shops a common enough sight. Green appears to have been on the prowl for new shops to lay the foundations of an embryonic clothing discount chain. In the trade press he had noticed a shop lease for sale in New Bond Street, one of the capital's most exclusive shopping streets and just round the corner from Conduit Street. It asked for offers. One Friday afternoon he went round to inspect the shop and, according to his own account, reached an agreement in what seems to have been a matter of minutes that he would pay £75,000 for the lease and £75,000 for the stock and move in right away.[2]

The stock consisted of fashionable Italian designer wear, much of it in leather. According to Green he sold the whole lot in just a week and then went out to Italy to find more of the same. It proved an exhilarating experience as he recounted it to the *Guardian*:

> Some of these designers, they've got stock for years. Warehouses big as old aeroplane hangars, full of it . . . I bought the lot . . . We filled this shop, floor to ceiling, put up these great big posters and had them queueing all down Bond Street. Wasn't popular with the rest of the street, but what could they do?[3]

This was something of an understatement. The street prided itself on its exclusivity: it housed Asprey the royal jewellers, and some of London's top fashion boutiques. The new style of retailing that Philip Green brought into the street was out of keeping with the image they wanted to project, and his decision to name his shop Bond Street Bandit hardly helped. One insider in the trade at the time describes him as the first fashion importer to bring designer label clothes to Britain using the grey or unofficial markets that could be found in the great European fashion centres. 'When he brought in top fashion brands and started to sell them at discount prices through Bond Street Bandit, he rocked quite a few boats. At that time nobody did that sort of thing – take very high class merchandise and sell it cheaply; it was just not playing the game.'[4]

But the real battle was still to come. The boutiques selling the top designer labels – names such as Giorgio Armani, Chloe, Christian Dior and Yves St Laurent – initially ignored Green. Under an arrangement that was meant to guarantee the right sales ambience for upmarket shoppers, the fashion houses had granted selected boutiques the exclusive right to sell their labels, and had backed it up with an elaborate set of legal guarantees.

Green was the first to challenge this cosy relationship. Over the summer of 1981 he had taken on as buyer the strikingly named Andrea Von Tiefenbach, a woman who had previously worked in the designer fashion trade at Browns Boutique in Mayfair's South Molton Street, the 'exclusive stockist' of Giorgio Armani's elegant Italian womenswear. With her help he was able to find an unofficial source in Europe willing to supply the top designer labels at huge discounts, on the basis that they were last year's designs. In October he unveiled his coup, offering Yves St Laurent silk dresses, Armani trouser suits and Christian Dior creations all at less than half the usual prices.[5]

For the first time in his career Green found himself making

headlines in the popular press, putting himself forward as the champion of designer fashions for the masses. Browns was amongst the first to raise objections, a protest that brought a team of Armani representatives beating a path to Green's door in Conduit Street. They negotiated to buy the Armani stock back from Green at the full retail price, bringing Green a healthy profit.[6]

There were more fireworks to come. In New Bond Street was the 'Rive Gauche' boutique which held the licence to sell the Yves St Laurent fashion label – YSL. It was run by a London socialite and fashion guru called Claire, Lady Rendlesham. She had an aristocratic demeanour and, at fifty-four, was notoriously dismissive of lesser mortals. In her day she had been the fashion editor of *Vogue* Magazine. The famous German fashion photographer Helmut Newton tells in his autobiography how Lady Rendlesham treated him 'like a vulgar peasant who had just come out of his hole'. In another memorable phrase he describes her as 'thin as a nail and as hard as a rock'.[7]

When news reached her that Green was selling YSL fashions at bargain basement prices Rendlesham could hardly contain her anger. Interviewed by a London *Evening Standard* reporter, who described her as the Dragon Lady, she loudly asserted that the matter was now in her lawyer's hands: 'St Laurent clothes are exclusive to me in the UK. We have a very strict contract with Paris. This has never happened to me before.'[8]

She swore that she would track down the illicit supplier. But Green showed no sign of backing off. He told the *Standard* reporter: 'If Lady Rendlesham wants to sue, we'll certainly fight her. If the worse comes to the worst, we'll have to cut the labels out.'[9]

It was the beginning of a long and gruelling struggle that was to run its course over the next three years. The designers and the exclusive boutiques tried to stamp down on the developing 'grey market' for designer clothes, threatening offending suppliers with the loss of their licence to sell the products. Green continued to comb Europe for cut-price supplies. Although the designers considered they had the law on their side there was little public support for their position. To the ordinary shopper it seemed just a way of keeping prices artificially high.

Perhaps because it became increasingly difficult to find grey market suppliers and extra time and effort had to be put in to locate those willing to take a chance, Forty One Conduit Street (as it was now called) and Bond Street Bandit never produced the great profits that Green hoped for. Companies House records show that Philip Green and his mother set up a new company, called Wearstyle Ltd, to run the operation and sold over £400,000 worth of designer stock in the first year and a half. But, the running expenses were high, with over £94,000 being paid out in rent and other charges in the same period.

The profits for the period from the first twenty months of Wearstyle's trading came to only £3740. The company auditors added an interesting rider to the accounts: 'In common with many businesses of similar size and organization, the company's system of control is dependent upon the close involvement of the directors. In these circumstances we have had to rely upon representations from the directors where alternative confirmation of transactions was not available.'[10] Like many budding entrepreneurs, it seems, Philip Green and his mother had found it difficult to keep up with the paperwork.

Eventually the cut-price designer label shops were to close down. Green still held the lease on the premises at 74 New Bond Street in 1985 but the Bond Street Bandit name had gone. Still it was in many ways the making of Green. It had showed him to be an entrepreneur who had not been afraid to rattle a few cages. Others took notice. One of them was a veteran clothing wholesaler based in Taunton in Somerset called George Maldé.

Maldé was going through a particularly difficult time, a victim of the recession and an over-generous bank deal. Maldé, a Kenyan Asian, had come to Britain as a young man in the late 1960s and, in 1971, had set up a wholesale business in imported blue jeans. In 1980 he launched a new brand called Bonanza Jeans, importing the garments from the Far East and distributing them from his warehouse in Taunton. It was a business that required a lot of working capital, a problem that grew more acute as the recession of the early 1980s tightened its grip. Retailers would order large batches of jeans, take delivery, then be slow to pay up. Maldé turned to his bank to help take the strain.

Along with many other businessmen in the industry, Maldé had become a client of the Johnson Matthey Bank, or JMB. The bank – a subsidiary of the respected gold bullion trader Johnson Matthey – was intent on building up business in the rag-trade, and had become a little reckless in its drive to recruit new customers. One of the London jean traders of the time still feels a shiver down his spine when he thinks of how close he came to accepting an enticing offer of JMB credit: 'They had this very pushy young representative who would call round on companies and make them some very seductive offers. Thank God our company did not sign up for the deal.'[11]

In 1984, JMB found it had over-extended itself and spectacularly crashed. It put itself into administrative receivership. A team from the Bristol branch of Price Waterhouse took over the running of the bank and set out to recover bad debts and to look for ways to rescue the bank from bankruptcy. Maldé's company, Blue Jean Sales, had borrowed around £5 million from the bank and was now asked to pay back this vast sum. Maldé found himself in a tight corner, as he recalls: 'Eventually Price Waterhouse wrote to us and said that, if we could not pay our debt to the bank, they would petition for us to be placed into receivership. As far as our company was concerned, it looked very much like the end.'[12]

On 1 July 1985, Maldé put a notice in the trade paper *Menswear*, apologising to his customers for the sudden closure of the firm. He was due to meet Price Waterhouse later in the week and desperately needed an advocate if the business were to be saved. Because of the huge controversy over Bond Street Bandit he had heard of Philip Green. One of his business friends, an energetic entrepreneur called Kenny Tibber, suggested that he might just be the man to help out. Green, Tibber might have added, had plenty of experience dealing with companies faced with liquidation. At that point, there were no fewer than three Green companies in the hands of the receivers.

Tibber arranged for Maldé to meet Philip Green at the Grosvenor House Hotel in London's Park Lane that evening. Green listened to Maldé's tale of misfortune, assured him that something could be done to save Bonanza Jeans, and asked Maldé to give him a week to see what he could do.[13]

The next day Green chartered a helicopter and flew to Bristol with his accountant and his lawyer to hold an urgent meeting with the Price Waterhouse team. Green knew that putting Maldé's company, which traded as Blue Jean Sales, into receivership would be messy. It was a bit like unpeeling an onion. Behind the bottom-line debt were layers of further debt, money owed to them by the retailers who had taken bulk delivery of Bonanza Jeans but had not yet paid for them. So any move to force Maldé into the hands of the receivers might trigger further receiverships.

Green's proposition was clear and simple. He offered Price Waterhouse 20p for each pound owed by Blue Jean Sales. The payment would be immediate (he had apparently already arranged the finance) and without strings. The old company would then be placed into receivership, with any assets it had – such its Taunton warehouse and its unsold stock of 400,000 pairs of jeans – transferred to a new company immediately. He and his team, and not the receivers, would then undertake the arduous task of recovering the debts owed to the old company.

Long hours were spent haggling over details but by 4 a.m. the deal had been struck and largely on Philip Green's terms. His offer of £1.2 million was accepted and the remaining £3.8 million owed to the Johnson Matthey Bank written off. Simultaneously, Blue Jean Sales assigned all its assets to a new off-the-shelf company called Lucasport and went into receivership. Green had agreed with Maldé as part of the rescue plan that he and Kenny Tibber would take two-thirds of Lucasport while Maldé and his wife would jointly own a third.

Since the Maldés would have been bankrupt if Price Waterhouse had pursued its intended policy, Green's plan to give them a 33 per cent share in the business may have seemed generous. But he did not have the time to travel down to Taunton to micro-manage the new firm. By being generous to George and his wife, he tied in their expertise in the business of importing and marketing jeans, although he would be in charge of the purse strings.

But first he had to get back to London. It was now early morning and the costly helicopter was grounded under noise control regulations. Green gave a hilarious account of the return journey in which he, the banker and the lawyer were 'in the middle of nowhere, pitchblack. Police car comes by, gives us a lift to the train station. Quick kip on a bench, caught the milk train back to London. Monday morning we're up and running.'[14] The image of these three men stretched out on a bench in Bristol Temple Meads station in the early hours of a Saturday morning while they waited for the early morning train to London sums up Green's buccaneering approach to business deals.

In mid-July, *Menswear*, which had carried the original small notice announcing that Bonanza Jeans had been forced to close, could now report the last-minute rescue. It also carried an advertisement that ran:

BONANZA BOUNCES BACK

Business is back to normal at Bonanza. We thank all our customers for their solid support while new finance has been secured. Lucasport Ltd now has secured the Bonanza Jeans label and with their substantial backing Bonanza Jeans can only go from strength to strength. The future's looking good.[15]

Chris Astridge, the editor of *MAB News*, a small trade paper, took the view that the practice of firms closing their door one week, only to reappear phoenix-like the next under the control of a new holding company, was often a way of leaving creditors high and dry. The following week a jeans trade fair was due to open at Earls Court. To make the point, Astridge thought it would be fun to carry a spoof ad in the special edition to be issued for the fair, mimicking the 'Bonanza Bounces Back' notice. So they put a strip ad across the bottom of two pages announcing the rescue of Pond-è-Rosa Jeans (a take-off of the long-running television series of the time called *Bonanza*, which was set on the Ponderosa ranch) carrying a similar cowboy logo to that used by Bonanza with a slogan that implied such rescues were dodgy affairs.'[16]

One person was not amused. Green had of course acquired Bonanza fairly and squarely from the receivers. Astridge was manning the *MAB* stall at the show when a smallish man with billowing black hair and a face like thunder came stomping up, a copy of the offending magazine rolled up in his hand. It was Philip Green. 'Did you write this shit?' he thundered, banging the paper down on the counter with a resounding whack. 'I hope you've got a fucking good lawyer.' Even then, Green was not one to enjoy a joke at his own expense.

Sure enough a lawyer's letter did land on the editor's desk the following week demanding an apology for the spoof and substantial damages. One of the journalists working on the paper said: 'We were a pretty small organisation with no resources to fight a legal battle. We spent a very uncomfortable few weeks before the whole matter was quietly settled out of court.'[17] The magazine and its editor had been saved, largely because Green soon had bigger fish to fry.

To finance the Bonanza deal and see through the shake-up he now had in mind, Green had been forced to borrow money. It helped that he had the support of the family company, Langley Road Investments, which made the process less painful than it might otherwise have been. The company accounts show that it raised mortgages on the two properties it owned in Thornton Heath and Beckenham and a sum of £60,000 was put at the disposal of the new company set up to run Bonanza. Added to this was a further mortgage raised on the assets of the Bonanza business in Taunton. The lender in both cases was Bank Leumi, an Israeli bank in London. The deals showed that Green had already developed a shrewd understanding of how to raise large sums of money quickly when it was needed.[18]

But recovering money owed to Bonanza was just as important. In August, he and George Maldé descended on Slough in pursuit of their biggest debtor, a retail jean company called Jean Jeanie, which owed Bonanza Jeans £250,000. With sixty shops, it was one of the country's biggest denim-wear retailers. It was also a legendary player in the story of British jeans. It owned a famous brand name – FU's Jeans. The owner, something of a legend on the British denim fashion scene, was a Liverpudlian called Grant Casey. It was a no-nonsense meeting, held in the unlikely setting of one of Slough's best Chinese restaurants.

A brusque Green laid it on straight: pay up or we'll close you down. But he then threw Casey a lifeline. He and George would accept payment in the form of ten post-dated cheques for £25,000. Casey was hardly in a position to reject the offer and duly handed over the cheques. As they got up to leave he said with a sense of weariness: 'I don't suppose you would like to buy my business, would you?'[19] For Green it was a beguiling prospect. If he could buy Jean Jeanie – owned by Grant Seward Ltd, a company controlled by the Casey family – he could see himself fast becoming the jeans king of Britain, controlling a large chain of stores and two major jeans brands – Bonanza and FU's.

But what, if anything, was Jean Jeanie worth? And could it be turned into an efficient money-making machine? The next week, having checked out that Casey was serious, Philip Green returned to Slough, this time with his accountant, to look at the books. Green could see there were headaches enough to try a lesser man, but there was also potential to turn it into a real money-spinner. For instance, Bonanza and FU's both had their jeans made in China, but by separate suppliers. There was scope here for economies of scale or at least to play one side off against the other.

A week later, Philip Green struck an unusual bargain. He phoned Grant Casey and said: 'There's good news and there's bad news. The good news is I'll buy it. The bad news is you're broke.'[20]

It may have been a typical heavy-handed Green way to open negotiations, but he had come up with an ingenious formula that offered something for both sides. Green claimed that the company was losing £22,000 a week and that Grant Casey's opening price of some £4 million for the company was quite out of the question. However, Green was prepared to offer £65,000 and a further £435,000 in instalments if the company could be turned around. Casey, a man who had been struggling to keep the company steady through the recession, chose to accept the lifeline. They shook on the deal.[21]

Green's immediate headache was that Jean Jeanie had an overdraft of over £3 million. But, convinced he could turn the company around quickly, he went to see the company bankers in Curzon Street, in London's Mayfair. He negotiated a freeze on all interest payments and promised to repay the debt less than six months later – by the end of February 1986.[22]

On completion of the deal, Green then decided to bring his businesses – the two main companies and some smaller subsidiaries – into a single retail/wholesale group under the umbrella of a new company called Lunabond Ltd. He kept all his original partners on board. George Maldé was made head of Bonanza Jeans and eventually took over the wholesale side of Jean Jeanie. Kenny Tibber remained on the board but not in an executive capacity. Green himself was chief executive in charge of overall strategy and the undoubted driving force behind a frantic push towards profitability.

Maldé, who was at this stage his right-hand man, stresses that the first priority was to sort out the suppliers. Bonanza Jeans had already cut out the middleman by having a good Chinese manufacturer supply the company direct, whereas Grant Casey had relied on secondary warehouses in Britain to supply his Chinese-made garments. Within weeks of the Jean Jeanie deal going through Philip Green, Grant Casey and George Maldé set off on a grand tour, reaching China by way of the USA, Japan and Korea, all potential sources of supply.

Although Philip Green had been to Hong Kong, Maldé believes that this was his first trip to China proper. He revelled in it, striking deals with Chinese factories that, according to George Maldé, saved the company a staggering 75 per cent on the price they had previously paid for exactly the same goods.

Back in Britain, Green now applied the squeeze to the few UK suppliers that were still in the chain. One of these was Pepe Jeans, which had a factory in Wembley. Pepe was a popular brand and sold well in Jean Jeanie shops. Nitin Shah, another East African Asian, who ran Pepe Jeans at this time, was one of the suppliers pressurised by Green to cut his prices. But he will have nothing said against him: 'When he was running Jean Jeanie Philip always paid his bills on time and paid a fair price. Of course he liked doing a few large deals, rather than many small ones. But that made business sense. He was a man of total honesty, a man of integrity whose word was his bond.'[23] Despite his willingness to strike bargains where necessary to keep suppliers like Nitin Shah sweet, Green was able to negotiate substantial discounts across the board.

George Maldé maintains that, within a matter of weeks of Green taking over ultimate control, they also managed to recover over £2 million owed to them by the shops that stocked Bonanza Jeans. This, and the huge reduction in costs effected by renegotiating suppliers' contracts, turned round the Lunabond finances very quickly. Now Green could afford to pump money into the refurbishments of the shops most in need of it.

Four months later, by the New Year of 1986, the tide seemed to have turned. With new sales systems installed in the Jean Jeanie shops, staff morale on the rise and Green's obsessive eye poring over weekly sales figures and takings, he pronounced the reconstructed empire of Bonanza and Jean Jeanie to be back in profit.[24]

Word of the turnaround soon reached the ears of the trade press, especially since Philip Green would not have been beyond spreading the good news himself. It was generally well received. A dazzled young reporter on *Menswear* relayed uncritically the Green formula for success: 'Good management, getting people to think commercially, creating a good experienced team, and proper retail systems . . . Jean Jeanie . . . was in a mess when I took it over, with no proper retail systems and low morale among the staff.'[25]

The Del Boy character of Bond Street Bandit days now seemed far in the past. In his place stood a man who had finally proved himself as a deal-maker and problem-solver. Before the decade was out, the trade press had even begun to talk about Jean Jeanie under Philip Green as 'the success story of the 1980s'.[26]

In February 1986, quite out of the blue, Green received a phone call from the best known British jean manufacturer and wholesaler, Lee

Cooper Jeans, based close to the Jean Jeanie head office in Slough. They were developing a new corporate strategy and wondered if Mr Green might like to consider a very interesting proposition they wanted to put to him. With only a few days before the £3 million overdraft needed to be repaid, this opportunity seemed heaven-sent. The two parties arranged to meet.

Lee Cooper was in fact a very old British company (founded by a Lithuanian South African) that had been making jeans long before the craze for blue denim had begun. When the big American jean companies – Nike, Lee and Wrangler – came along in the 1970s, Lee Cooper found its brand name seemed reassuringly American. It had been particularly successful in France where it outsold its American rivals, and had made a healthy profit in 1985. But the top management hankered after high street glory. They were convinced that the Lee Cooper name could be the foundation of a successful nationwide casualwear chain. The big problem was that nobody at Lee Cooper had any retail expertise. Just down the road, on the other hand, was Jean Jeanie, where Philip Green seemed to have won the right to wear his retailing spurs.

So in February the top Lee Cooper management met Green and started negotiations for the takeover of the Lunabond group to transform it into Lee Cooper Retail – the new base for future Lee Cooper expansion in Britain. The Bonanza and FU's range of Jeans would be added to the original Lee Cooper Jeans, broadening the appeal to a younger age range. Their first objective was to persuade Green to join as managing director of the new division. He wanted to bring George Maldé with him. They readily agreed. All that remained was to settle on a price for the business and on a salary package. Green argued Lunabond was turning in a decent profit. He suggested £10 million as the price. This was negotiated down to £7 million, half to be made on the amalgamation and the rest to be paid as a performance bonus, over the next two years. As for salary, they agreed to pay a substantial sum on a rolling contract, and the usual range of management perks. They shook on the deal. Green had owned Jean Jeanie all of six months.

Eighteen years later, in 2004, Green could still recall the excitement when he gave this account of what happened next: 'Went down to the bank in Curzon Street, said, "What do I owe you?" They said, "Dunno, er, three million four hundred and thirty thousand pounds." I said,

"Right, there's your cheque." Slapped it down. Done . . . Can be done is my motto!'[27]

In just three years Green had switched from a struggling small-time trader with a Del Boy image to the man with the golden cheque-book. The man who had taken the decision to wind up operations at Tarbrook, with creditors owed close on a quarter of a million pounds, had now settled into a top job in a public company. It was quite a change.

Now the big challenge was to make a go of Lee Cooper Retail. This was a wholly different world. Could he prove that the Del Boy in him had been sufficiently tamed? Lee Cooper was a publicly quoted company, answerable to shareholders, and an old one at that. It had ways of doing things. Would the volatile Green fit in? Even people like George Maldé who admired him enormously weren't quite sure. Green did not like a culture of meetings; he wanted to get on with the job. He was also notoriously foul-mouthed and could lose his temper at the drop of a hat. Maldé – who went with Green and the Lee Cooper management on a tour of Asia and was in a position to observe the dynamics – was astonished when Green and the head man at Lee Cooper, an urbane but rather arrogant Frenchmen called Pierre Pouillot, had a stand-up row in a hotel in China. He also observed a lack of respect displayed by Green towards people he outranked: 'Sometimes he would greet a salesman or a buyer calling in to see him with a bellow: "Fucking get out!" But then, that is Philip.'[28]

With his shock of bushy hair and the air of a man who knew exactly where he was going, Green at the age of thirty-five exuded an aura of power and wealth, an attraction for many women. He admits to being a bit of a playboy at this time. One acquaintance from these years related that 'his weakness was for slow horses and fast women'.[29] George Maldé remembers him with a different woman on his arm five nights a week.

One girlfriend in the early 1980s was Juliette Owide, daughter of the Soho club owner Oscar Owide. At one stage the attractive Miss Owide seems to have been on the point of being appointed company secretary at Wearstyle Ltd, the company set up in September 1982 to run Bond Street Bandit. In the company records her name was filled in as secretary and then scored out to be replaced by Alma Green, the principal shareholder. Another girlfriend, 'a stunning brunette' as the tabloids would have it, was the film starlet Viviane Ventura.

As to where he might go with such charming company the choice seems to have been between dining out in style, going to the cinema (Philip Green once confessed that his favourite movie was *The Long Good Friday*, a film that made its debut in 1979) or trying his luck at the gaming tables of Mayfair. He was frequently to be seen in the Ritz casino. Horseracing was something of a passion, too. George Maldé had ambitions to own a racehorse that would win the Grand National and thought he had found just the animal in 1985. He persuaded Green to come in on the project and for a year Green could claim to own half a promising racehorse, appropriately called Bonanza Boy, a novice hurdler. Later, when Green had sold his share of the horse back to Maldé, it was to prove a great success, winning the Welsh Grand National in 1989 and coming fourth at Aintree in 1991. While Green's interest in horseracing lasted, he could be seen at such fashionable meets as Cheltenham and Royal Ascot.

But his playboy years were winding down. In 1985, he met the woman who was to become his business partner and his wife. Her name was Christina Palos. She had been born in London to wine merchant parents and brought up in the Far East. In the mid-1980s, she had set up her own fashion boutique, Harabels, in Sloane Street, Knightsbridge. She was already married to a businessman called Robert Palos, had two children – Brett, then thirteen, and Stasha, then ten – and was three years older than Green.

Tina (as everyone called her) was a very attractive and outgoing petite blonde. Introduced to Green through mutual friends, she remembers him as 'awful' at their first meeting. Years later she told the *Daily Mail*, 'I thought he was dreadful actually. I remember him asking me who I was. I said I ran a boutique called Harabels and he said, rather dismissively, "Well, I've never heard of it." . . . I thought, what an arrogant pig.'[30] The next evening the two met again at a party. 'His bow-tie was crooked and without thinking I went right up to him and straightened it. And that was it. It was the oddest thing. I thought, I'm in trouble here. I just fell in love with him at that moment.' Meeting him was to turn her life upside down. Although the relationship took a while to develop, she eventually left Robert and moved in with Green.

Green's other distraction from business at the time was White Hart Lane, the home of Tottenham Hotspur Football Club. Spurs was going through something of a golden period and had won the European Cup

Winners' Cup in 1983. The club had also shown its business acumen off the pitch by becoming the first English football club to float on the Stock Exchange. Perhaps because it was a very business-minded club, it attracted many north London businessmen, a large number of them members of the Jewish community. Green counted many of them as his friends.

In January 1987, Green happened to meet the chairman of Spurs – Jewish property developer, Irving Scholar – in the business class of a jumbo jet bound for Hong Kong. It was a long flight and Green was happy to spend some of the time talking to Scholar about Spurs, a club facing difficulties in trying to upgrade its stadium and facilities in the face of some local opposition. He suggested that a mate of his called Tony Berry would be an asset on the Tottenham Hotspur board because of his business experience. Berry, who had once dreamt of playing for Spurs and had actually been given a trial for the club, had become one of the most successful of a new breed of young entrepreneurs that had prospered in the new era of Thatcherism. His chain of employment agencies, Blue Arrow, had quickly grown to become the largest of its kind in Britain, but he had ambitions to go further.

Thanks to Philip Green's airborne initiative, Scholar met up with Berry, who accepted an offer to join the Spurs board early in 1987.[31] The news went down well with the stock market and the value of shares tripled within a matter of months. Then came the great share crash of October 1987. The Spurs share price slumped along with all the others. But if the Berry magic had faded, he remained a very rich man, happily involved in the football club at the highest level. He had Philip Green to thank for that and he never forgot it. When the time came he was ready to return the favour.

Then there was the larger than life figure of Edward James Ball, some five years older than Green, who was known to his friends as Ted Ball, and to his enemies as 'Caveman' Ball. In 1985, he had teamed up with a City bank called Guinness Mahon to found Landhurst Leasing. Leasing was fast becoming all the rage for cash-strapped firms, and not just for immovable property such as shops and office buildings. Ball was prepared to pay for the ownership of such things as office fixture and fittings and lease them back to the company concerned, at a rate of interest well above what he was paying to the banks who financed his leasing deals. Despite the fact that he lived in East Sussex,

Ball was also a familiar face at White Hart Lane, and close to Green and his circle.

All these men were pleased to be counted as FOPs, 'Friends of Philip'. But the man he seems to have trusted most was a young Londoner called Stephen Kay, a self-made man of the time. He had begun selling used cars and had risen to become king of the cut-price video shop through his company, Intervision. All three men – Berry, Ball and Kay – were to play a crucial role in the next, somewhat chequered, stage of the Green business career.

Chapter 4

NOT A MAN OF HALF MEASURES

I n 1986, Britain was on the edge of a boom. Unemployment was falling and share prices were soaring on the London Stock Exchange. Green should have been enjoying his share of the boom as managing director of Lunabond, the new retail arm of Lee Cooper. He had a three-year contract, money in the bank, a striking company car (with the number plate FU5) and a chance to show that his rescue of Jean Jeanie was no fluke. His negotiation of the right of Lunabond to be the sole agent for Bonanza Jeans in Europe, Canada and the USA suggests he may even have had global ambitions. And yet the time spent at Lee Cooper proved to be among the unhappiest periods of his entire business career. Until now, Green had always been in the driving seat, even if the redoubtable Alma had been looking over his shoulder. Like many thrusting entrepreneurs he was averse to working for other people and expected to be given a free hand to run Lee Cooper Retail. Lunabond continued to exist, albeit now as a subsidiary company within the Lee Cooper Group and he had trusted lieutenants to help him run the business, one of them being his erstwhile partner in *Bonanza Jeans*, George Maldé. Lunabond held board meetings, but they were short and formal affairs called more to conform to company law than to determine policy.[1]

Yet, for all that, Green found working there cramped his style. On the board he was outnumbered three to one by Lee Cooper appointees. One of them was Pierre Pouillot, who spent much of his time in Paris and Germany attending to business and – as a keep fit enthusiast – working out in the gym. It is not hard to imagine that the cultivated Frenchman, who spoke excellent formal English, may have found the plain-spoken and at times hot-tempered Green not to his liking.[2] Equally Green was not a man who enjoyed kowtowing to anyone.

The two men were soon barely on speaking terms. Relations became so bad that Green chose to resign as managing director in

September 1987, barely halfway into his three-year contract and at considerable cost to himself in lost bonuses. It was a traumatic experience from which he took some time to recover. Later he confessed that his irrepressible optimism had taken a knock, so much so that for many months afterwards he spent his days in uncharacteristic idleness. He told a journalist from *Menswear* magazine: 'There were mornings when I woke up and wondered whether I would ever do another deal . . . But there comes a time when you have to pick yourself up, dust yourself off.'[3]

This uncharacteristic lethargy seems to have lasted several months. Then, in the summer of 1988, a new opportunity arose, the prospect of a bid to rescue a publicly quoted company called Amber Day. It was in an altogether higher league, one that would put him in the driving seat at the head of a PLC. The chance came largely as a result of Green's connections to the 'Kosher Nostra' – the close network of north London Jewish entrepreneurs. Helped along by such connections, two of Green's friends in that business group had by 1987 become business leaders in their own right.

The first was Roger Levitt, who had moved rapidly up the financial league after founding his own investment company, the Levitt Group, in 1985. He had already attracted a celebrity clientele, which included film director Michael Winner, novelist Frederick Forsyth and Adam Faith, the pop singer turned actor. The fast-talking Levitt, known as the 'man with the golden grin' and distinguished by his Groucho Marx moustache and bow-tie, had moved into a plush mansion in fashionable Highgate. To advertise the fact that he had made it big, Levitt was conducted to his office in Portland Street each morning in a chauffeur-driven Bentley. He had bought himself a villa at Marbella on the Costa del Sol and was now enjoying the high life, both there and in London.

Even more successful in business terms had been Green's close friend and fellow Spurs supporter, Tony Berry, chairman and chief executive of Blue Arrow. Berry had been the first of the circle to secure one of the exclusive executive boxes at the club's White Hart Lane ground for the entertainment of important clients and close friends. As a keen Spurs fan, Green must have been a regular guest.

By the time Green secured his job as MD at Lee Cooper Retail, Blue Arrow had grown to become the largest business of its kind in Europe, and the energetic Berry started to look across the Atlantic where private employment agencies were booming. He was helped by the stock market surge that had followed that year's 'Big Bang' in the City of London and the introduction of competition that had swept away many of the staid old City stockbroking firms. Berry was able to raise £30 million virtually overnight through selling new Blue Arrow shares to its shareholders, a device known as a 'rights issue'. He used the money to buy a relatively small American company in the same field as Blue Arrow. Some months later, he raised a further £850 million through the largest rights issue ever raised in Britain and bought the American giant Manpower Inc, which was six times larger than Blue Arrow and had offices in thirty-two countries. As a result, in August 1987, his company entered the elite FTSE 100. For a football-crazy youngster brought up in modest circumstances in north London it was no mean achievement.

When Green emerged from his cocoon of inactivity in 1988, Berry was on hand to provide both moral and financial support. Green had already done Berry the considerable favour of giving him a leg-up onto the board of Spurs, so when Green approached him in the summer of 1988 to ask for assistance with his new project, Berry was only too happy to reciprocate.

Amber Day was a struggling fashion business that had lost its way in the economic turbulence of the 1980s. It had been founded by a London Jewish entrepreneur in 1947 as the Dennis Day Dress Company, making womenswear. It expanded in 1971, taking over the Stockport-based Amber Fashions (hence the Amber Day name) to become a force in both the retail and wholesale sides of the business. By 1982 it owned, wholly or in part, some thirty-eight subsidiary companies, including a share in Barbara Hulanicki's Biba in Kensington High Street. But it was now heading for the rocks. Hit by debts and sharp rises in interest charges, Amber Day had been forced to sell most of its assets and seemed to be on the road to nowhere.

In 1987, an attempt had been made by a group headed by another flamboyant Jewish entrepreneur called Irvine Sellar to save Amber Day by transforming it into an upmarket fashion retailer. But the London stock market suddenly went into freefall on 2 October 1987, a day that has gone down in history as 'Black Monday'. In the course of three days, prices on the London Stock Exchange tumbled by almost a third. It would be catastrophic for both Levitt and Berry in the end, but nobody suspected this at the time. One apparent casualty of the slump was the Sellar plan to pump £5.5 million into Amber Day in return for a 29 per cent stake in the company. This was Green's opportunity. With the approval of Sellar, he stepped into the breach and took over the scheme.[4]

But where was Green to find the sum needed to buy out the Sellar interest? He had some personal savings, a product of the success of Jean Jeanie and Bonanza Jeans, but far from the £5.5 million he needed. He turned to his friends. Around £2 million was made available by Tony Berry. Some £300,000 of this was in the form of an unsecured personal loan to Green, the rest in the form of an investment by Blue Arrow in its own block of Amber Day shares.[5] Another friend, the video supremo Stephen Kay, obliged by making a large personal investment in Amber Day. But it appears Green still needed to find some £2.5 million to make up the balance. He claims to have put substantial amounts of his own money into the purchase, but some of this may also have been borrowed from wealthier friends. In any case, on 12 August 1988, now in effective control of 29 per cent of the struggling company, and with a personal 17 per cent holding, Philip Green was duly installed as chairman and chief executive of the first PLC he had ever run.

He began a whirlwind review of the company's operations and decided where the axe should fall. Ever since his first visit to Hong Kong, Green had been convinced that the future of clothes manufacture lay in the low-cost producers of the Far East. Amber Day's manufacturing operations in the UK, though still in narrow profit, were quickly wound up and the sites disposed of.

This left two major activities. The first was the long-established business of importing and distributing clothing. As an experienced and gifted buyer, given to trips overseas, Green might have been expected to make a difference here. And indeed this is what happened. But the main business of Amber Day, from now on, was to be in retail. The group had recently acquired a chain of upmarket menswear shops operating under the name of Review. Philip Green had to show he could make a success of this new operation. At Lee Cooper, and at Jean Jeanie before that, Green had been involved in the fast turnover youth market: jeans and sweatshirts, denim jackets and cowboy boots. At Amber Day he found himself running a business that catered for affluent men aged twenty-five to thirty-five, who were willing to pay a premium for well-designed and well-cut clothes.

Review shops reflected their clientele. They were large and airy with polished wooden floors, high ceilings and a layout designed to maximise sales. A customer who shopped at Review was steered in the direction of buying whole outfits in complementary colours and fabrics in one visit. Their new store in Oxford Street, directly facing Bond Street tube station, was a temple to consumerism. It alone had takings of over £3 million in the first year under Green's stewardship. In the context of a renewed high street mini-boom in 1988 and 1989, Green was probably right to think that more money could be made in this sector than in the over-crowded casualwear market.

Of course, some of the success of Review was down to Michael Barrie, the man who had conceived the idea, sold his chain to Amber Day and now sat with Philip Green on the board. But Green's role was also important. His obsessive attention to detail and his skill in buying in stock that would sell at a good profit improved the bottom line, lowering the break-even point and boosting margins.

The approach paid off. In its first year under Green's command Review made a profit of over £1 million on a turnover of just £8.5 million. Profits before tax for the whole business rose from £503,000 to £2.058 million, a fourfold increase. It was a good start. But, as far as Green was concerned, it was only a beginning.

His vision in the summer of 1989 was to expand and extend the menswear business until it became a force in the British high street to rival a chain such as Burton. Review possessed only ten stores, but many were in prime sites in London – two in Oxford Street, one in King's Road, and one in Kensington High Street. In the early summer of 1989 he bought a second chain of menswear shops, the Woodhouse group. These specialised in the sale of the new designer label clothes produced by Hugo Boss and Giorgio Armani. Green, scourge of the posh shops in the early 1980s, had now well and truly joined their ranks. For this chain of some ten stores Amber Day paid just over £1 million, mainly financed by issuing new Amber Day shares. It seemed a snip.[6]

At the company AGM later that year Green unveiled his plan to put a Woodhouse store in every city in the United Kingdom. He also announced that Amber Day was in the market for many more chains of the right type. Philip Green was beginning to seep into the consciousness of the City.

It did him no harm at all when he defined his business policy in the trade magazines in simple and nakedly honest terms: 'Make no mistake; I am in this business for money.' He also stressed that his fortunes and the fortunes of Amber Day were now inextricably intertwined: 'I am the biggest shareholder with about 17 per cent of the equity and with more than £3 million of my own money invested in the company. I am in this business to make something of it like anyone else and if there are no dividends there is nothing in it for me.'[7] In fact, he had negotiated himself a salary of £250,000 a year and performance bonuses that could raise this to £400,000 a year.[8]

To match his new standing as chairman and chief executive of a PLC, he moved from his flat in Harley Road near Swiss Cottage to a large detached house in Avenue Road, St John's Wood, within easy reach of the Poland Street headquarters of Amber Day. His lifestyle also changed in other ways. He spent £60,000 fitting a new kitchen, and enjoyed staging lavish parties for his friends, business associates and carefully selected journalists. He was now more regularly seen at the exclusive gaming tables of Mayfair and St James's. Some further status symbols were duly acquired, including a holiday villa in Marbella and a £160,000 Cougar Sportcat power boat.[9]

To many financial journalists and City men, Green's sudden emergence as a prowling predator, ready to snap up retail businesses, was an exciting phenomenon. He was a larger-than-life character at a time when much of the retail sector seemed to be in the hands of grey-suited technocrats distinctly short of charisma. He also courted publicity. Soon after taking over at Amber Day, he began a personal telephone offensive, phoning up investors and trusted journalists in a campaign of self-promotion. Fast-talking and unnervingly foul-mouthed when he chose to be, he dispensed his business wisdom in pithy little quotes. Amber Day, a tiny company in stock market terms, started to get press attention way beyond its significance. Detailed and fawning coverage was given to profits forecasts, special in-store promotions and other developments.

Not everyone was pleased. Laing and Cruikshank, Amber Day's official stockbrokers, felt he was encroaching on their territory by ringing clients and advising them to buy Amber Day shares. They quit. But the Green personal offensive paid off. One of his financial advisers confessed to a journalist: 'I have never known a company of Amber Day's size get so much written about it.'[10]

It was not all talk. Since he combined the role of chairman and chief executive and had, in Michael Barrie and David Atkins (the latter representing Blue Arrow), a pair of fellow directors willing to trust his judgement, he was given almost a completely free hand to run the company in the way that he wanted to. Board meetings were held informally and infrequently. He maintained that success in business was not about holding meetings but in making things happen.

One priority was to identify what the next acquisition should be. In 1989 he started wooing one of the nation's most famous high-street institutions, Moss Bros. Here was a name to conjure with, renowned as the provider of formal men's clothing, supplier to the nobility and gentry (famously the Duke of Norfolk had worn a Moss Bros outfit at the coronation of Queen Elizabeth II in 1953) but also to the British man of almost any class requiring a dinner jacket, morning suit or highland dress for a special occasion.

He twice made overtures to Moss Bros in 1989 and was twice rebuffed. Fifty-two per cent of the shares were held by just two big shareholding groups, the Moss family and the Gee family. They viewed Green as jumped-up and brash, and were united in wanting to keep him at bay, the more so because there were rumours he had been briefing the press against them.

His ambition undiminished, Green continued to stalk the high street. Rumours spread that he was interested in acquiring Next, the chain built up so successfully by another fashion entrepreneur, George Davies. Davies had fallen out with his board and had left the company in 1988, one reason it might be considered ripe for a take-over bid. Another name in the frame was Richards, an independent chain catering for women over thirty-five. Then Green was rumoured to be preparing a bid for the mighty Sears Group. That this new kid on the block could have his name seriously linked with the giant shoes-to-fashion empire – an empire that included Selfridge's great emporium in Oxford Street – was a measure of how far Green's star had risen in the course of just eighteen months. Of course, some of these rumours may have come from Green himself. They certainly seem to have provided a convenient smoke-screen for the funda-mental shift in the Amber Day strategy that he was to spring upon a surprised City in May 1990.

The Lawson boom had lasted a couple of years, but had paused in the autumn of 1987 only to pick up again and go into overdrive through 1988 and the first part of 1989. Then the mood changed. Lawson was forced to increase interest rates to cool the economy. Consumer spending began to flag. Soon the high street was facing meltdown.

The profits being made in the Review and Woodhouse chains began to evaporate. Green needed to find another, more profitable line of business. Early in 1990, just such a business unexpectedly came on the market. It had a long record of being 'recession proof' and Green could expect a much warmer reception than he had had from Moss Bros.

The most successful entrepreneurs exude an aura of certainty that disguises the fact that, like everyone else, they are never in control of events. What they do have is an ability to turn the course of events to their advantage. In the case of Philip Green the event in question took place on a DC-10 jetliner in February 1990.

On board were Gerald and Vera Weisfeld, who were taking time off from running their highly successful Scottish-based retail group What Everyone Wants (WEW). Without any warning, one of the jet's three engines exploded and caught fire. The plane went into a steep dive. It was a terrifying experience for all aboard. Both the Weisfelds thought their last moments had come. But, miraculously, the pilot regained control and extinguished the fire. The plane limped into Rio de Janeiro airport.

For Gerald and Vera Weisfeld it was a life-changing experience. They had spent years working hard to build up their business to the exclusion of almost everything else. They decided it was time to pull out and devote themselves to charitable work. Arriving back in Scotland, they immediately put the business up for sale and were delighted to find that their old friend Philip Green was interested. Ever since they had helped kick-start his career by offering him a desk in their Great Titchfield Street warehouse, they had kept in touch and admired his never-say-die attitude. If anybody could take their company and make it a household name all over Britain, Green was the man to do it.

The Weisfelds had built up the business from a single store to a chain of thirty-seven shops over nineteen years, had increased turnover every year they had been in business, and had demonstrated a talent for thriving even through recession. Indeed, Gerald Weisfeld looked on recessions as a time of opportunity when assets could be acquired cheaply and sales increased as bargain-hunting became a national pastime.

What Everyone Wants was a far cry from Review and Woodhouse. The Weisfelds' success had been built on their ability to sell fashionable clothes at a third of the prices charged in the mainstream stores, a quite extraordinary achievement. The secret had been to exploit the anarchic and wasteful nature of the fashion trade. In the 1970s and 1980s manufacturers were in the habit of producing large batches of garments to be sold on to wholesalers, who in turn would attempt to sell them on to the retail shops. Without the modern sophistication of information technology, supply and demand were often badly matched. As the buying season neared its end, there was inevitably an overhang of stock.

Like Green, Weisfeld had learnt a few tricks about the supply business. He would visit the warehouses towards the end of the buying season (the trade still adhered to the convention of a spring/summer and an autumn/winter range, sold months before the seasons began) and drive a hard bargain, arguing that he was doing wholesalers a favour by clearing warehouse space for the incoming stock. He also had an uncanny eye for the fashionable garments that other dealers had missed: 'You would see one special garment in the corner. But you pretended you were not interested in it and beat down the price. You then had a fashionable garment you could sell big time at a low cost.'[11]

As well as bargaining down prices for clothes with fashion appeal, Gerald Weisfeld had also assembled a chain of shops that were close to the big shopping centres without being actually in them. As a result, the running costs of such stores were much lower, since the sites could be bought or leased at a fraction of what the big stores paid for their sites. The company boasted they had never ever paid more than 'peanuts' in rent.[12]

In 1990, WEW was so popular that the police was regularly called in to control the crowds that besieged the new shops on opening day. And it was not just a downmarket phenomenon. According to Weisfeld, even the well-to-do women who normally shopped in Marks & Spencer were unable to resist the lure of the store. He told journalists, half in earnest, that they packed the bargains bought in WEW stores into their Marks & Spencer plastic bags to carry them home.

Both Gerald and Vera Weisfeld were reluctant to make a complete break with WEW and were offered a contract to act as consultants, with Gerald taking a seat on the board. As for the price, it was finally settled at just below £47 million, a sum to be paid in shares, cash and loan notes. The Weisfeld family emerged holding 17 per cent of the Amber Day stock.

On 21 May 1990, Green called a press conference in London to announce Amber Day's sudden change in direction through its acquisition of WEW. In the light of its long history of steady and spectacular growth, the agreed price seemed a bargain. Philip Green's stature as a deal-maker grew overnight. WEW dwarfed Amber Day's other operations, representing 78 per cent of the company's turnover in its first year after the merger.

The takeover of WEW went down well in the City when it quickly showed results. In November it was announced that Amber Day profits had spurted by 47 per cent for the year ending July 1990, a period that included a contribution of only two and a half months' profit from WEW. The headline figure neatly diverted attention from the faltering profits at Review and Woodhouse, badly hit by the deepening recession. The switch in emphasis from menswear to discount trading could not have been better timed.

Green's personal life was also changing. Tina had divorced her husband in 1989 and moved in with Philip in his house on Avenue Road. They were not yet married. As Tina recalls: 'In the end I got so frustrated I had to propose to him. Philip liked it the way it was and I think he was afraid of any commitment.' In August 1990, Philip was photographed outside the couple's home and the next morning's papers carried a photograph of Tina waving him off in her dressing gown with the caption 'Tycoon's gal waved him off'. The feisty Tina thought, I'm nobody's 'gal'. So she told him that it was make-up-your-mind time and took off to Marbella. The shock tactics worked. Within days, he had followed her and proposed. A month later, the couple were married at Westminster Registry Office and held an intimate reception in the garden of their home. 'We barely had an engagement really,' Tina said. 'The thing with Philip is that once he's made up his mind . . . that was it. It's like the way he is in business. He's not a man of half-measures.'[13] Their first child, Chloë, was born the following year.

At first, relations between the Weisfelds and Green seemed to go well enough. Indeed it was Gerald who had been invited to act as best man at the wedding. But the friendship turned sour. Weisfeld believed he had a deal that WEW would remain an autonomous company within Amber Day.[14] He also thought he was to play a key role in buying policy. But Philip Green was determined to be his own master. There was no question of whose will would prevail.

The embarrassing rupture between the two friends came in February 1991. The issue concerned Green's plan to raise prices at WEW. Weisfeld recalls that Green told him he wanted 'to make the business sweat'. Green planned to drive up prices by more than inflation, although keeping prices far below those offered in the main shopping chains or department stores. This offended the Weisfeld principle that WEW prices should remain at a third of those charged in the mainstream shops.[15] The decision of the Weisfelds to sell their shares and break off relations with their twenty-year-old creation received much publicity in Scotland. In London, however, it created scarcely a ripple. In that respect at least, Green was lucky.

Among the Weisfelds' greatest achievements at WEW had been their success in forming a real family atmosphere within the company. The business had a strong culture of loyalty, which paid off in a warm and friendly reception for customers. Vera Weisfeld was a product of a working-class family from Coatbridge, an old steel town badly hit by the decline of heavy industry. She had never lost her down-to-earth friendliness and had built a particularly good relationship with her staff, calling them all by their first names. Her practice of giving away new cars as a reward for success was one later adopted by Green.[16]

For Philip Green, an outsider and a Londoner, she was a hard act to follow. Yet some of those who worked with him seem to have found him an inspiring presence. In 1992, he was followed on a tour of his flagship store in Scotland by a London journalist: 'Watching Mr Green going into his main store in Glasgow's Argyle Street is to see a man in his element. He knows the supervisors by name and immediately starts quizzing them about which lines are moving and criticising the display of some items.'[17]

He liked to be known as 'the governor' (a phrase that in Glasgow is more associated with the city's Barlinnie Prison than with business) and appears to have won respect amongst the people who worked most closely with him, the managers who belonged to the 'executive board'. One of these was Jim McCann, an 'exec' in charge of 'security and audit', a vital job concerned with reducing the quantity of goods lost by 'shrinkage' – in other words, staff pilfering. Soon after Green took over at WEW he spotted that the rate of 'shrinkage' was higher than average and was determined to reduce it. He and McCann worked together on this.

Green commuted by air from London to the Glasgow headquarters of WEW – a pattern of work that he was later to adopt as a lifestyle – bustling into the company's East End office in the shadow of Celtic Park. Green occupied an office in the executive suite and preferred not to use the telephone in communicating with his 'execs', resorting instead to shouting down the corridor. McCann liked his hands-on style. Occasionally an exec would be dragged before the boss for a dressing-down, with both the famous Green temper and his ability to deliver withering criticism already in evidence. Some people were scared of him, says McCann, but his bark was much worse than his bite. At the end of a year battling against 'shrinkage' McCann received a bonus. It was delivered to him by the governor, who signed the cheque personally and handed it to him.[18] Although McCann shared Gerald Weisfeld's view that it was a misjudgement to raise prices in the way that he did, he believes that Philip Green did a good job at WEW.

Another testimony to Green's leadership and business acumen in running WEW comes from the loyalty he inspired in the most senior of his management team. One of these was a thirty-year-old retail manager working for a trendy retail fashion chain called River Island. Ian Grabiner was based in London and Vera Weisfeld had interviewed him as a possible manager over lunch at Claridges. She was so impressed by his talents and personality that she invited him to join her in Glasgow as her successor as managing director.

The second of the bright young management stars at WEW was the buying director Elaine Gray. She was just twenty-eight when Philip Green took over. Like Green, she had left school at sixteen and moved straight to WEW where Vera Weisfeld soon promoted her to a management position. An outgoing young woman, she was to become a star attraction at many of the company's social gatherings for managers, an accomplished song-and-dance act as well as a sharp-minded exec. Like Grabiner, her career since 1990 has been closely interwoven with that of Green himself. Many of Green's legendary buying skills may owe more than he would admit to her ability as a buyer, skills that she in turn acquired with the help of Gerald Weisfeld.

After the Weisfelds sundered their links with WEW in 1991, Green, Grabiner and Gray set about strengthening the company. One outcome was the introduction of new technology to keep a track on sales and stocks through bar-coded labels and a central computer system. This information became a central weapon for increasing profitability by reducing the need for clearance sales – 'markdowns' in trade jargon – and for aligning buying policy with what was actually selling. Another Green priority, and now a central plank of his business philosophy, was to pressure suppliers to lower their prices. His pricing policy was driven by what consumers were willing to pay, not how much it cost producers to produce. At WEW it inevitably led to more dependence on cheap Far Eastern suppliers, a market that Green knew particularly well.

Grabiner and Gray were eventually promoted to sit alongside Philip Green on the board. It seemed a winning formula. In June 1991, Green announced that the recession was being beaten. He forecast that profits would rise threefold from £3 million to a staggering £9.75 million when the results to August 1991 came to hand. Expansion was the order of the day with eight new stores already opened and more to come. All were to be financed by the cash flowing into the company's tills, rather than having to borrow. And the future of the company was to be made even more secure by a rights issue, one new share for every three held. This would raise over £24 million and be used to wipe out any remaining company debt.[19]

The acquisition of WEW seemed to have changed Green. The old Green, always on the prowl for companies in trouble to add to his tally of trophies, was at least temporarily on hold. His letter to shareholders spelt it out loud and clear: 'WEW forms the core of the Amber Day Group's business and the Board intends that it should be the central focus for future growth. The Board's policy is to expand WEW by a process of organic development rather than by acquisition.'[20]

By now, Amber Day was getting noticed. Jeff Randall, the City editor of the *Sunday Times*, was the first to tip the company as a share with potential to go far. Randall would deny that his friendship with Philip Green influenced his judgement, and indeed there were sound reasons for recommending the share. Amber Day was making good profits, despite the recession, and had every prospect of doing better as the tight controls introduced by Green and his team on margins, markdowns and shrinkage took effect.

Not everyone shared Randall's enthusiasm. Some in the City worried that Green was an entrepreneur with a short attention span. As early as April 1991, one City journalist on the *Independent* commented: 'He now appears bored with Review and Woodhouse . . . although both have been owned for less than three years. He owned his previous success, the Jean Jeanie chain, for just six months . . . the group needs decent management who can carry on if his attention is caught elsewhere.'[21] Concerned that Amber Day had all the hallmarks of 'an entrepreneurial one-man band', the paper called on Mr Green to appoint a finance director and an independent director with some experience of running a PLC, something he had promised months before but had so far not delivered.

The prickly Green did not take kindly to criticism of this sort. A few weeks later a short article in the *Independent on Sunday* about Amber Day which he saw as badly informed had led to a volatile response that included a two-page letter and several telephone calls, one of them short and to the point. In a style he went on to make his own he told the startled journalist: 'I just thought you should know I tore your fucking article out and put it under the cat's arse where it belongs!'[22]

For the moment it seemed the shareholders were giving Green the benefit of any doubt. The rights issue of June 1991 was a resounding success with 97 per cent of the shareholders taking up their allocated shares. And respectable City institutions were buying up Amber Day shares as a sound long-term investment. The first had come on board in February 1991 when the Weisfeld shareholding had been snapped up by esteemed City investment groups, chiefly John Govett & Co and Midland Montagu Asset Management, and were later joined by the Prudential Corporation, the TSB Group and Equitable Life Assurance.

Green took the first step to reassure these big investors that Amber Day was not after all a one-man show. In July he recruited Graham Coles, a former finance director at British Home Stores, as group finance director. At the same time Leslie Warman, a former director of Lloyds Merchant Bank, was appointed as non-executive director, a watchdog for City interests.

The share price continued on its upward path, reaching 129p in November 1991 before falling back to 108p by the end of the year. That still meant it had risen by almost 70 per cent in the course of 1991, making it the best performing quoted share of the year. Green was the toast of the City.

Relaxing with his family over the New Year break, Green could have had no inkling of the storms that lay ahead. Times were tough on the high street but WEW continued to show its capacity to run against the tide.

But on Monday, 13 January the share price fell off a cliff. In a single day the value of the shares fell 14 per cent from 107p to 92p, and it went on to fall even further, being worth just 71p by the end of the month.

Green was taken by surprise. He had just flown off on a two-week trip to Sri Lanka and the Far East to negotiate new deals with suppliers. In his absence, Amber Day financial advisers hurriedly issued a state-ment putting the fall down to an organised campaign against the company by anti-Green forces in the City, involving, as reported in one newspaper, 'malicious calls from men in phone booths whisper-ing through handkerchiefs'.[23]

Amber Day had become the victim of what is known in the trade as a 'bear raid'. Broadly speaking, this meant that some City brokers had taken out contracts to deliver Amber Day shares for an agreed price at the end of the traditional Stock Exchange two-week accounting period. They did this without actually having the shares to deliver. They gambled that the share price would fall back, allowing them to buy them at the end of the accounting period for a sum far below the price at which they had agreed to deliver them. The difference between the promised price and the price they had to pay was almost entirely profit.

In the eyes of the stock market, there was nothing wrong with this practice provided it was fairly done. But there was nothing to stop unscrupulous operators spreading false rumours about a company to help the process along. Bear raiders who go about talking down shares in this way are acting against Stock Exchange rules and can be fined and disqualified if they are ever caught. Few ever own up.

There is independent evidence that such practices were going on at the time of the Amber Day stock crash. The *Mail on Sunday* reported on 9 February that 'one person rang up our office a few days ago impersonating a respectable [dealer] and claiming that Philip Green was in a share dealing ring with two brokers that the Stock Exchange had banned from dealing.'[24] The paper established that the caller was bogus and the information untrue.

One of the men accused of organising the January and February bear raid was Simon Cawkwell, an ex-Rugby public schoolboy. Cawkwell has always denied doing anything underhand. He had heard that someone at Amber Day had apparently been predicting that the share price would go up to 300p a share. This had led him to look closely at the published accounts and draw his own conclusions. His verdict was: 'The disclosed net tangible assets of the company were of the order of 20p [per share]. Even if the figure of 300p were merely a target it was completely unrealistic. Any management being unrealistic should be sold immediately – so I did.'[25]

But he does not deny being the author of a letter to a financial journalist 'on behalf of all public schoolboys bullying Philip Green', thanking the writer for his comments on the Amber Day shares which had given him 'the chance to sell more shares'. He signed the letter E.K.[26] (Cawkwell was believed to operate under the assumed name of Evil Knievel.)

So the theory that Philip Green was the victim of a conspiracy of public school boys has some support. But the problems at Amber Day were much more deep-rooted, and while the bear raid sparked off the initial decline in the share price it was the great rumour mill of the City that kept it on a downward path well into the summer of 1992. When Philip Green flew to Sri Lanka in January, his fellow directors and the company's auditors and financial advisers had held a secret emergency meeting apparently at the instigation of Graham Coles.

This was the culmination of months of rising friction between the new directors appointed to please the City, Coles and Warman, and Green. At issue was the conduct of company business. Publicly listed companies such as Amber Day are bound by what is known as the Yellow Book procedures laid down by the Stock Exchange. These, in the opinion of Coles and Warman, were not being properly followed.

Take the matter of board meetings. They were not part of Philip Green's way of doing things: he was too busy running the day-to-day affairs of the company. With the arrival of Coles and Warman on the scene a compromise had been hammered out. As a gesture towards Green's wish to run Amber Day as an entrepreneurial company, it was agreed that informal mini-board meetings consisting of Green, Coles and Warman would be held once a month. But pinning down the busy Green to even such a modest commitment proved all but impossible.

Matters had come to a head in January 1992 when Coles chose to bring some new concerns to the auditors, Coopers & Lybrand, while Green was in Sri Lanka. He had just discovered apparent irregularities in the accounts. Green had bought in a large stock of feature films on video in a bid to boost pre-Christmas sales, but had been left with a large overhang of unsold stock. So he had shipped them to Stephen Kay, the video king, who had put his own money into the company when Green took control. Coles was concerned that the videos had been supplied without any documented agreement as to when they were to be paid for and, if extended credit was part of the deal, just what rate of interest would be charged on it. To compound the problem, Kay had just bought 400,000 Amber Day shares, which had helped put a brake on the fall in the share price after Christmas. Coles's concern was that Kay had in effect been given indirect financial help by the company to buy its own shares, assistance which would have been illegal.

At the meeting were David Caddy of Coopers & Lybrand, the firm's auditor, Sir Laurie Magnus of the company's merchant bank, Samuel Montagu, Leslie Warman, the non-executive director, and Graham Coles. It was agreed that Philip Green should be flown back from the Far East to explain just what had been going on. But this never happened. Green spoke with Sir Laurie Magnus by telephone and persuaded him that all the questions raised would be answered by him when he got back.

On his return he agreed that Kay owed Amber Day money for the videos but the sum was now less than £1 million and would soon be paid off. As an entrepreneur used to making quick deals, he argued, there was nothing unusual about a lack of complete documentation. He and Kay had struck a deal and it would be honoured. Since this explanation had been accepted by the company's merchant bankers and its stockbrokers, the board cleared Green of any wrongdoing. But papering over the cracks in the company's boardroom proved more difficult. Green and Coles emerged from the row barely on speaking terms.[27]

Following this incident, there were some within Amber Day who were convinced that Green, for all his energy and talent, was not a person suited to run a public company because of his disregard for proper business rules and procedures. It was just not good enough to run a PLC as though it were a private fiefdom. Even those who worked closely with Green on day-to-day finance, and admired what he was trying to do, agreed that he was not at that time a person who played strictly by the Yellow Book rules. Green, however, took the view that the bureaucratic processes prescribed by the City simply got in the way of running the business.

The story of the secret meeting did not appear in the newspapers until five months later but the Square Mile is a notorious rumour mill. It was impossible to keep the rift entirely secret. The City soon became polarised between those who admired Green as a deal-maker and those who regarded him as an untamed polecat who needed reining in.

The anti-Green camp found they had plenty of ammunition in what was to become an increasingly dirty war. *Private Eye*, the satirical magazine, had begun to circulate a whole series of damaging stories about Green that had clearly originated in City circles. Mainly they were about Green's close friendship with men associated with the very public financial scandals of the time.

The first name to be linked to Green was that of Tony Berry. *Private Eye* had begun sniping at Berry and Green as early as June 1989, but until Green's star started to wane nobody took it too seriously. Berry had fallen under suspicion because members of his board had complained he had behaved as though he owned Blue Arrow instead of holding it in trust for the shareholders. The whistle had been blown in the autumn of 1988 by a non-executive director held in high respect in the City as a thoroughly upright custodian of shareholder interest. His name was Dennis Stevenson, a man who was to feature at a later stage of Philip Green's career.

In October 1988, Stevenson complained that Berry had lent £25 million to Peter de Savary, a rich property developer, without the agreement of the board. Berry protested his innocence but a DTI inquiry into the affair, completed in 1991, found against him. The inquiry also revealed the fact that Berry had also lent Philip Green money without board approval – this was the £300,000 he handed over to let Green take up his share quota at Amber Day in August 1988 (though Green had repaid the loan by the end of 1989).[28] What made the revelations more damaging was a story doing the rounds that Philip Green had Berry in mind as a possible chairman for Amber Day, a story that was eventually picked up by the newspapers, although some suggested, even more damagingly, that it was not Berry but another friend of Green, Roger Levitt, who had been in line for the job.[29]

Levitt, formerly seen as a financial wizard, had fallen from grace in 1990 when his investment company collapsed spectacularly, leaving many of his high-profile investors high and dry. The liquidators had discovered a huge black hole at the centre of his empire. Levitt himself had been arrested and charged with fraud. The DTI inquiry into Berry, completed in 1991 but not published until September 1992, was to reveal that Green had once actually recommended Levitt to Berry as a personal financial adviser.[30] Although he had yet to come to trial, Levitt had already come to symbolise the worst excesses of 1980s greed.

Green had clearly not chosen his friends carefully enough. He may well have felt that guilt by association was unfair, and that he had never been found guilty of any misdemeanour himself, but the associated bad publicity still rebounded on him and on Amber Day.

In May, it became highly personal when *Private Eye* reported that Tina Green's business, Harabels, had been put into liquidation, and that Panos Eliades, Levitt's friend and next-door neighbour, had been appointed as administrative receiver.[31] Although Green had nothing to do with the management of the company it was just another bad piece of publicity for a man already under mounting pressure.

At Amber Day, matters continued to deteriorate. On 14 June, Jeff Randall ran an exclusive in the *Sunday Times* – probably leaked to him from within Amber Day – revealing that there had been a 'boardroom row' and that Coles and Warman were to leave the company. According to the article, Coles had been headhunted by another company (which was true) while Warman's resignation was due to a disagreement with Green over a matter of 'corporate strategy'.[32] To lose one director is unfortunate; for two to go at the same time sent signals to the City that Amber Day was in deep trouble.

In the same article Randall reported that Green had had to endure a campaign of personal abuse, including hate-mail and anonymous faxes, a campaign full of innuendo and racist slurs. Randall summed up: 'It is clear that Green's controversial style has upset some in the City, but he retains the support of Amber's main institutional investors.'[33]

The article failed to capture the full drama of this new boardroom bust-up. What had it been all about? The man at the centre of the row was the independent non-executive director, Leslie Warman. Highly respected in the City as a former senior director of Lloyds Merchant Bank, Warman had finally lost patience with Philip Green, who had been dragging his feet for months over the issue of appointing a second non-executive director. The independent non-execs played the important role of watchdogs over company affairs. A full year had passed since the Amber Day board had signalled its intention to make the appointment. Warman had become convinced there would be no progress on this front as long as Green held both the role of chairman and chief executive. So at the June board meeting (incidentally the first full board meeting to be held since the rights issue in 1991) he proposed splitting the roles. A new independently minded chairman should be appointed, someone Philip Green would have to account to for the way Amber Day was being run. But when he put the plan to the board – largely made up of Green loyalists – it was rejected. Warman had no alternative but to tender his resignation there and then.

Warman's resignation was bound to have repercussions. He had been appointed under pressure from the City. There would be at least an informal inquiry by the big investors into what had gone wrong. Green's stewardship of the company would be put under the spotlight, his style of management questioned, his sometimes aggressive behaviour towards his fellow directors brought to light.

Over the following weekend, Green took steps to limit the fall-out. He decided to concede the need for an independent chairman, a conversion that was correctly foreshadowed in Randall's article. But his concession had no discernible impact. When the stock market opened on Monday the Amber Day shares fell a further 6 per cent to 58p and resolutely stayed on the floor.

Worse was to follow. Throughout July and August the number of personal stories about Green and Amber Day multiplied, with *Private Eye* delighting in running a series of snippets on Philip Green's 'dodgy friends'. As well as Berry, it revealed Green's friendship with money-lender Tony Schneider. It claimed that Schneider and his wife had held 50,000 shares in Amber Day in November 1991. It added: 'Just why a man who was featured as a target criminal for Scotland Yard's organised crime squad – he was acquitted in the 1970s on charges concerning alleged pornography and extortion – should be investing in Green's company remains to be explained.'[34]

It also drew attention to the fact that Ted Ball, whose leasing business had just crashed owing creditors £120 million, had leased Amber Day and its subsidiaries luxury items such as exclusive motor-cars and speedboats. Ball was later accused of cooking the books and was convicted of fraud. Particularly damaging were the *Private Eye* allegations that many of these friends had, in one way or another, helped Philip Green to buy his shares in Amber Day. Green, darling of the City in 1991, now found himself widely vilified and treated as a man who could not be trusted. By August the Amber Day share price had slumped further to 41p. The first of the big institutional investors, the Prudential Corporation, decided to abandon ship. The others were considering their options.

When the results of the financial year were announced in September, the profits turned out to be just £7.5 million, hardly a disastrous result on the recession-hit high street but still roughly half what the City had expected just six months previously. They were also 30 per cent below what Green himself had predicted in July.[35]

Indeed the missed forecast probably did Green as much damage in the City as the loss of the two directors. Share prices are closely related to the prospective earnings and the talk of £10 million profit in July had helped rally the share price. Now, in the cold light of day, they were bound to plunge yet again. Green had become an embarrass-ment. With pressure from his once supportive institutional share-holders mounting he was forced to quit. Jeff Randall chose to look at it rather differently. He wrote in the *Sunday Times* that Green had 'walked on the wild side, and his enemies would not let him forget it'.[36]

That was not quite the end of the story. In November it emerged that the Department of Trade and Industry had launched an inquiry into the conduct of business at Amber Day. However, nothing ever came of it.

For those who supported Green, the fall-out at Amber Day was evidence of just how short-sighted the City establishment could be. In their eyes he was a man who had beaten the recession, and even made a profit, only to be pilloried for his pains. The City took a different view. Philip Green had shown himself to be a man who could not be trusted to look after other people's money. They were glad to see him go.

Never a man for half-measures, the now ex-boss of Amber Day crept away to lick his smarting wounds. There was little doubt, in his mind at least, that he would be back to prove the doubters wrong.

Chapter 5

'LEAVE IT TO ME'

Philip Green's departure from Amber Day was a shattering experience for a man who had come to see himself as uniquely gifted when it came to running a chain of high street fashion shops. He was certainly bitter about his experience. While the City took the view that he had proved himself unfit to run a public company through his refusal to stick to the rules, he took a view that was diametrically opposite, namely that public companies and entrepreneurial flair were poor bedfellows. He swore he would never run a public company again. From now on, he said, he would take the private company route, where he and a few trusted partners would own the company, and the finance needed to improve the business would be borrowed from banks and rich private individuals. In doing this he was to become something of a trendsetter.

Green saw out the dog end of 1992 and the first half of 1993 in surprising obscurity. He agreed to stay on as a consultant at Amber Day until Christmas and then, at the end of the year, went for a three-week holiday to the West Indies with Tina and their young children, Chloë, now nearly two, and Brandon, who had been born in the spring of 1992. But being Philip Green he remained on the lookout for some new business opportunity.

This might come in two guises. The easier option would be companies that were making little or no profit but sitting on assets that could be reorganised and sold on, the classic technique of the asset-stripper. But for the moment such deals did not seem to appeal to him. For a man of Green's competitive bent the best answer he could give the City was to take over another struggling retailer and show the City sceptics just how wrong they had been.

In May 1993, a loss-making discount fashion chain trading under the name of Parker & Franks was forced into administrative receivership by its bankers after defaulting on the repayment of debt. It ran a chain of fifty-four stores, eleven of which were freehold, and catered for the same market as Amber Day, selling a range of goods, from women's fashion to children's toys, mainly in the north of England. The receivers, Leonard Curtis, set out to look for a buyer who would guarantee to keep the company going and save most if not all of the thousand jobs at stake.

Green was back in the running and had the money to hand to make a bid. Since the previous September he had built himself a nice little nest egg. First had come his leaving settlement from Amber Day, a cool £1.1 million, a sum described by one newspaper as, given the circumstances of his leaving, 'an obscene pay-off'.[1] David Thompson, who had taken Graham Coles's place at Amber Day, and was now the company's acting chief executive, explained that Green had a three-year rolling contract, and was due a deferred bonus from a previous year as well as consultancy fees.

Added to this, Green had retained a holding of 8 per cent of the company shares, and had chosen a good moment in which to sell them. In April 1993, Amber Day had produced some unexpectedly good interim results, showing profits were once more on an upward curve, leading Jeff Randall to pronounce in the *Sunday Times* that 'the bears who tried to ruin Amber Day, the discount retailer, and its former chairman, Philip Green, were confounded last week . . . No black holes, no bankruptcies, no police investigations.'[2] Green's critics took rather a different view: that the departure of the colourful chairman was the major factor behind the bounce back. Whatever the explanation, the news that profits were better than expected pushed the share price up to 86p – from a 1992 low of 27.5p. Green hurried to cash in his stake, and pocketed a personal fortune of £7.67 million.

The money was the key to the deal he now negotiated with the receivers at Parker & Franks. He would guarantee 800 of the jobs and pay some £3 million of his fortune for the company, provided it was delivered to him free of all debt – a formula very like the one he had used with the takeover of Bonanza Jeans in 1985. Although there were another eight bidders, the Green offer came closest to what the receivers had in mind. The deal was struck. In the last week of May he was able to make the announcement that Parker & Franks now belonged to him and his family: 'That is the way it is and that is the way it'll stay.'[3]

The emergence of Green as a fully fledged discount rival to Amber

Day plunged him into a new controversy. Thirteen Parker & Franks stores were in towns that sported a branch of Amber Day, making it a head-to-head competitor. It was common when a top executive left a firm that he or she would sign a legally binding promise not to compete directly against the company they were leaving for at least a twelve-month period. The Weisfelds had signed such a document when they left WEW in 1991. By buying Parker & Franks, Green might be thought to have been in breach of such an undertaking. Certainly, when the Amber Day board heard of the Parker & Franks deal they were hardly pleased. Their ex-chairman seemed to be thumbing his nose at them. The hapless acting chief executive, David Thompson, was left to tell the press: 'Mr Green did have an exclusion clause in his contract but this deal does not breach it.'[4]

But whatever the satisfaction he might have felt about putting one over on Amber Day, Green knew that turning Parker & Franks into a thriving business was never going to be easy. Although now debt-free, the chain was loss-making and there was no pool of shareholders to be called on to provide capital. He could count on some financial backing from his old friend Stephen Kay, but on the whole he would have to modernise it on his own, relying on efficiency savings and a strong cashflow to pay the bills.

There was open scepticism in the City about his chances, pro-voking a typically defiant Green response. He told the trade magazine *Retail Week* that he had already begun the task of taking out costs and finding cheaper suppliers: 'Within fourteen days we will be at break even point. New merchandise is going into the stores this week. There will be two or three months of trading to achieve a quick [turnaround in] stock.'[5] Only time would tell if Philip Green could succeed where others had failed. But one change he could make quickly. He con-sidered the name of Parker & Franks wrong for the sector. The name Xception, he believed, would have much more appeal.

By September, barely five months into the task, he opened the first new Xception format in Manchester. It embodied his latest idea, what Green described as a 'value multi-store', selling a mixture of fashions for men, women and children, as well as toys, videos and discounted computer games. He announced that three stores a week were being converted to the new Xception format and thirty-six would be refurbished by November of that year.

The problem was, as Green's friends admit, that he was easily bored. He was now in his early forties, and making a success of Xception was never going to be enough to satisfy his growing ambition, which he once described as 'bigger goals, bigger achievements . . . it's about wanting to do better'.[6]

Green was fond of saying that British retailing had lost its way because the industry lacked the entrepreneurial spirit it had once possessed. He liked to look back on the latter half of the nineteenth century as a golden age, when colourful characters had opened the great British department stores, emporiums where the shopper could buy everything they ever needed under one roof. One of the chains – Lewis's stores in Liverpool, Manchester and Glasgow, the first of which was opened in 1856 – had by the 1930s become hallowed and popular venues, crammed with food stalls, furniture showrooms, vast clothing departments for men, women and children of all ages and every depth of purse, entire floors devoted to children's toys, and even dance floors. With the attractions linked by manned lifts and great monumental escalators, these were the days when shopping had been a treat, not just a mundane experience.

Even as Green worked to make a success of Xception, he already had half an eye on one of the legacies of this great British retail tradition, a baker's dozen of department stores that were grouped under the banner of Owen Owen. It was the fifth largest department store group in Britain, and had only recently taken over the great Lewis's stores in Liverpool and Manchester to add to a portfolio of eleven others. Five years previously the group had been acquired by a Swedish venture capital group called SPP, which had failed spectacularly to generate a profit out of the behemoth. In the summer of 1993 they had appointed a new chief executive whose job, it was rumoured, was as much to find a buyer as a cure. He succeeded on neither count.

Now, nine months later – in March 1994 – SPP appointed a replacement chief executive to try a new approach. Again optimistic noises were being made. Sales had risen by 10 per cent. The company issued a 'Plan for Profit and Growth', which forecast there might even be a small profit at the end of the year. Since companies in trouble usually prove adept at turning out high-sounding strategies produced by highly paid consultants, an increasingly interested Green took such management displacement activity as just another example of a company that was going nowhere.

All the signs were that he was quietly working on his own plans for Owen Owen. At the end of September Elaine Gray suddenly announced she was leaving Amber Day 'for personal and private reasons'. In fact Green had entered into secret negotiations with SPP to remove the embarrassment of Owen Owen from their hands. In December, taking the retail world by surprise, SPP announced that Philip Green had acquired the group in a private deal. The amount paid for this empire of thirteen stores has never been revealed. They had been loss-making for some time and had little or no value as going concerns, but the buildings sat on substantial city centre sites that were mostly freehold.

That new year, Philip Green and his family went to holiday in Barbados, almost certainly staying at the fashionable Sandy Lane Resort – fast becoming an annual event for Britain's retail kings. He was already dreaming up plans for the new empire. When he returned to London in January he announced to the trade press with great confidence that Owen Owen was 'my best deal yet!'[7]

He announced too that Elaine Gray was to join him as buying director with a 10 per cent share in the company. That in itself suggests that Green did not immediately envisage selling the stores. He believed that department stores like Owen Owen and Lewis's occupied a potentially lucrative niche, and held a special place in the heart of the British public. David Thompson, who had taken over from Green at Amber Day, was to join him as managing director, also with a 10 per cent stake.

Green immediately threw his energies into recapturing the romance of shopping that had once proved such a potent crowd-puller. On Valentine's Day 1995, Green threw a huge party in the art-deco ballroom on the top floor of Lewis's Manchester store. The 300 guests, many of them important retail suppliers, were provided with pink champagne in a typical Green gesture to announce that he was back and still serious about retail. Owen Owen's nervous 3,250 staff, who had heard the stories about Green, were relieved that he intended to make a go of it. Much effort was put into developing a more child-friendly ambience, again trying to recreate the old store style. In October, marketing director Annette Brown and her team rolled out the concept of a 'Kids' HQ' in four of the bigger stores. Here were not only the latest toys but the latest styles in children's clothing, an exciting 'sports arena', a computer hall, a video theatre, a huge bike shop, even a kids' hairdresser and diner. Just how much the revamp cost was not revealed, but it could not have come cheap.[8]

Asked by *Retail Week* if he was turning into a department store man, Green gave an upbeat reply: 'I like what I am doing. This is a wonderful business that keeps me motivated. You have a multiple of businesses under one roof and I'm learning about new products every day. After all, department stores always used to be run by entrepreneurial people.'[9]

There were other signs that Philip Green was serious about making a go of Owen Owen. The presence of Elaine Gray led to better buying for the target groups, and a sharp drop in the markdowns within the stores. New retail computer systems were installed making service quicker and allowing stocks to be kept in line with the actual sales figures. In July 1995, Green could tell *Retail Week* that 'neither Owen Owen nor Lewis's need a lot of work doing to them . . . They need at least another year to get them into the right shape.'[10]

But the truth was that Owen Owen was taking up just too much time. By Green's own estimate he was spending 90 per cent of his working day on Owen Owen business.[11] As other business opportunities came along, the good intentions melted away. In January 1996, a local Liverpool reporter called Steve Brauner secured an interview with the boss of his local Lewis's store, shoe-horned into a busy day in typical Green style:

> In between taking calls on his mobile, when his patter was straight out of an episode of *Minder* being shown after the 9 p.m. watershed, Green charmed customers, sent staff scurrying in all directions and gave me a load of shtick about how he was going to turn the business round and bring back the glory days . . . Sell the freehold of Owen Owen in Chester? No plans to dispose of any outlet. Lewis's in Manchester would be smartened up and more sales space made available.[12]

Six years later Brauner complained he had been badly misled by Philip Green. The Chester store had been sold while the Lewis's store in Manchester had been leased to Marks & Spencer after its flagship store had been severely damaged in 1996 by an IRA bomb.

The first signs of a loss of focus on Owen Owen came as early as 1996 when eight of the thirteen stores were sold to Allders, raising £23.6 million. This was used to pay off all debt owed by the company. Green protested that this was not the end of his interest in big stores: 'It is my intention to maintain our presence in the department store sector, which is one of the main recovery areas in the retail sector, while, as always, retaining my interests in pursuing other opportunities as they arise.'[13] But it was the other opportunities that came to dominate his agenda.

The Owen Owen saga eventually ended nearly a decade later in 2005 when the business had been reduced to the solitary Liverpool store. Philip Green allowed himself to be bought out by David Thompson, who also picked up the 10 per cent of the business owned by Elaine Gray.

Why did the grandiose plans for Owen Owen come to nothing? Apart from the question of his health (see chapter 6), by 1995 Philip Green was fast becoming something of a deal junkie. Once he became involved in negotiating complicated deals for this business and that, he simply did not have the time to turn his mind to running large retail operations, especially something as big and as complicated as a large department store operation. In 1999, he made a rare confession of failure to a journalist when he was asked if he might bid for the House of Fraser department store group then up for sale. He replied simply: 'The department store is very specialised. I've been in it with Owen Owen and I am not going back.'[14]

Certainly, his actions in the spring of 1995, three months after he had acquired Owen Owen, suggest he was now getting more of a buzz out of buying up retail properties, repackaging them and selling them on at a profit, with little long-term input from himself. Sir Terence Conran's Storehouse, a rather ill-matched group that included Mothercare, British Home Stores and Habitat, had attempted to go into the discount market in 1994 when they launched a chain called One Up. In early 1995 a change of corporate policy led to it being put up for sale. A year previously Philip Green might have jumped at the chance to acquire some cheap extra floor space for Xception. Now he simply negotiated to buy the chain, clinched the deal and sold it on within a matter of weeks to the new and impressive 'value store' Primark, a chain that was later to emerge as one of Green's hottest competitors. It was, purely, a quick way of making money.

One consequence was that there were some in the City who were beginning to see Philip Green in a new light. There had always been those who had a sneaking admiration for his energy, vision and can-do attitude, seeing him as a 'breath of fresh air' in the somewhat stale world of retail. But now he was showing his aptitude as a deal-maker, someone who possessed an uncanny ability to sort out companies on the edge of receivership to his own and their advantage, an ability he had first demonstrated with Bonanza Jeans. His solutions often showed what his friends saw as extraordinary originality, his enemies as a display of low cunning.

His standing in the City rose a further notch or two when in April 1995 he was approached by the well-respected City merchant bank Hill Samuel, to see if he might act as a 'company doctor' and sort out an ailing firm. The firm in question was Owen & Robinson (a firm with no connection to Owen Owen). Since it was a publicly quoted company, Green must have approached the task warily, but it offered an opportunity to hone his developing deal-making skills.

There were two halves to O & R. The first was a very old business selling jewellery and losing money at a fair rate of knots. The other was a fashionable chain of shoe shops, called Foothold, which had recently been bought from the giant Sears consortium, an empire that was later to take centre stage in the drama of Green's subsequent emergence as Britain's takeover king.

O & R was threatened by receivership since it had been found to be trading insolvently, not having assets in reserve with which to settle its debts, a large part of which consisted of arrears in rent. Hill Samuel wanted to know if Green could come up with a creative solution that would pay off the company's debts without closing down the shoe business. Green came back with a plan which involved him assuming the role of banker and receiver all rolled into one.

The company's biggest debt was to the TSB bank where its overdraft had risen to some £6 million. On the other hand TSB itself owned shares in the company. So, helped once again by Stephen Kay, Green came up with £6 million cash and paid off the debt, in return for the TSB shares, giving him a 15 per cent stake in O & R. With the company now owing him the £6 million, making him the chief creditor, he could threaten to have it put into compulsory liquidation. This could be used as a bargaining tool to force other creditors to accept a deal.

The outcome was a triumph since he was able to close down the jewellery chain, negotiate a reduction in the rents for the shoe shops, and sell the business on, leaving himself with a tidy profit.[15]

This was a new, confident Philip Green dealing directly with City institutions. In the middle of the negotiations he confessed he had learnt the lessons of Amber Day: 'I am older and a bit wiser. Last time

I would have taken full control and come in as chairman. This time I am happy to act as banker and watch from the sidelines, working with existing management. Everybody tells me that for a bank to sell its debt in this way is unique. At the moment no one knows how this could end up, but I am reasonably relaxed.'[16]

For those in the City who still doubted his probity he pointedly added: 'The fact that people such as TSB bank . . . Hill Samuel [and] Storehouse have all done deals with me over the past twelve months says something. I have always prided myself on doing what I am going to do. My word is golden.'[17]

Just as one great deal was being signed off, a second, even larger deal suddenly became a possibility. Green received a call from a young Scottish entrepreneur called Tom Hunter, whom he knew well. Four or five years previously he had come across him in Glasgow when Ian Grabiner had introduced him as one of WEW's suppliers of sports shoes and sportswear.

Hunter, nine years younger than Green, was full of entrepreneurial talent himself. He had been brought up in a down-at-heel part of Ayrshire in Scotland – the old mining town of New Cumnock. His father had kept the local grocer's store. As a child Tom Hunter had attended Cumnock Academy, a good quality Scottish state school, but had made very little of his chances. Leaving school at sixteen, with no real prospects of starting a career, he helped out in his father's shop for a while and won a place at Glasgow's Strathclyde University to study marketing. But a marketing degree proved to be no passport to a job when he graduated. He applied for hundreds of jobs and got only three interviews. None of the companies concerned offered him a place. He went back to work in his father's shop.

His father, hard hit by the miners' strike of 1983–4, had taken to keeping a stall in the local town markets to supplement his income. It was there that Tom noticed the growing popularity of trainers, often more a fashion statement than a serious commitment to sport. He had a sudden inspiration. He had noticed that many big retailers had opened the door to 'concessions', renting out space to smaller companies to sell specialised products. Could he become the trainer specialist? It was worth a try. In 1985 he borrowed £5,000 from his father and another £5,000 from the Royal Bank of Scotland, and used the money to buy up a stock of shoes and a van. He then fired off letters on headed notepaper, boldly headed 'SuperShoe', to every big retailer in the country. The mail-shot brought almost instant results. One company, Peter Stores, with branches in the north of England, wrote back saying they would give him concessions in their stores if he could have the operation up and running within a week.

Hunter commenced a hectic life, driving the van with stocks up and down the country, sleeping in it when necessary, and always carrying a neatly pressed shirt and suit to make the shop visits.

It was the beginning of a great success story. Soon he had opened concessions in Burton, Fosters and a group called Concept Man (later to become River Island), where he first met Ian Grabiner.[18] In 1989, when he was twenty-eight years of age, he opened the first store of his own in Paisley, just outside of Glasgow. By 1995, his company, Sports Division, had an annual turnover of £36 million and was turning in a profit of £4 million. On paper Hunter had become a rich man.

But the enterprising Scotsman, still aged only thirty-four, had begun to consider expanding his empire dramatically by taking over a much bigger rival called Olympus Sports. When he found his way blocked he turned to Philip Green for help.

In many ways the two entrepreneurs could hardly have been more different. Green was a motor-mouth with an amazing turn of phrase and a tendency to vulgar language. Hunter was quietly spoken and invariably polite. While Green enjoyed the high life, spending his time in casinos and good restaurants, Hunter liked nothing better than a night out with his old school friends at the local fish and chip shop.

But for all their differences, each recognised in the other some outstanding qualities. Green was to act as Hunter's mentor on how to make deals and drive hard bargains; Hunter possessed the gift, rare among entrepreneurs, of building up a business organically from within and finding the sort of people he could trust to run it for him. He seemed to have more patience and, unlike Green, was universally liked. These two men forged a new business partnership in 1995, one that has lasted to the present day.

Of the two, Hunter could in 1995 claim to have the better record in building a business from scratch. He owned an empire of forty-five stores, five of them superstores on out-of-town sites, employed 1,000 staff and was worth between £40 million and £50 million. Green had an 80 per cent stake in Owen Own, owned the Xception chain and had made a considerable sum from the O & R deal. At this point it is a fair guess that they were of roughly equal wealth.

Hunter had made the first move to acquire Olympus Sports earlier that year when rumours swept the retail trade that its owner, Sears, was about to put it up for sale. The Sears empire had been put together by the legendary Charles Clore in the 1950s and 1960s, and had become by the 1990s a classic illustration of the difficulty of reviving the spirit of enterprise within a large and ageing company. On the clothing side Sears owned stores such as Warehouse, Richards, Wallis and Miss Selfridge. Their shoe shops were, if anything, even more famous, with household names such as Dolcis, Saxone and Manfield. Their mail order business, Freemans, was one of the top three British mail order companies.

Sears's problem at one level was that it had become simply too large. A position of near-monopoly had bred complacency. Now, in the much more competitive shopping world of the 1990s, it was proving to be hopelessly inefficient. In 1992, the board had appointed a new chief executive, Liam Strong, to administer the necessary medicine. He had come from British Airways where he had been director of operations. He had never held a senior position in a retail business and, outside of Sears, few gave him much chance of turning around the great tanker as it headed for the rocks.

If there was one part of the Sears empire that had given Liam Strong more than his fair share of headaches it was the shoe chains, and particularly the string of sports shops that had become the centre of Tom Hunter's attention. They were branded under the name of Olympus Sports and Olympus Outdoor World. These shops were in direct competition with new independent sports retailers such as Hunter's Sports Division and JJB Sports, companies which really understood the marketplace. Olympus could never decide whether it was in the market for sportswear or fashionwear while its critics maintained its shops were manned by people who knew very little about sport and couldn't offer professional advice on the merits and demerits of what they were selling.

If top management effort alone could have saved Olympus Sports it would have been saved. During the first three years of Strong's tenure at Sears, the company tried format after format, eventually settling for large sites on out-of-town shopping malls. Opening a new Olympus Outdoor World shop on a retail park outside Enfield in July

1994, Strong seemed confident that the new plan would pay dividends: 'The biggest opportunity is out of town. There is enough public out there for us to develop any concept we would like.'[19] But this proved too optimistic an assessment. Olympus's overheads remained stubbornly high and the prices they could charge were pushed down by competition from leaner and fitter rivals. The chain continued to haemorrhage money. When, in September 1995, Sears reported that Olympus was losing more money than ever, it sparked off speculation that the chain was about to be sold.

Tom Hunter made the first move by making a direct approach to Sears as a possible buyer. He told the authors of this book: 'I was introduced to Liam Strong by . . . one of our biggest suppliers but at the meeting [he] denied that it was for sale at all and basically sent me packing.'[20]

It is not difficult to imagine why. Not only was Olympus five times larger than Sports Division, but Hunter, a fresh-faced man of thirty-four, hardly struck them as a serious suitor. Hunter later delighted in telling journalists that 'they obviously thought I was a daft wee laddie'.[21]

Hunter freely acknowledges he now turned to Green for help. He telephoned him and explained the impasse. Could he help him out? Green had grown to love the cut and thrust of business takeovers. He jumped at the chance to take on Sears, and quipped: 'Leave it to me.'[22]

At this point Hunter had set aside £12.5 million of his personal fortune to fund the bid, but it was nowhere near enough. The rest had to be borrowed. Hunter's own bank, the Royal Bank of Scotland, had backed off. But Hunter had reason to believe another Scottish bank might give him a more sympathetic hearing. A few weeks before he had been on a private jet coming home to Scotland from Turin in Italy after watching Glasgow Rangers being soundly thrashed 4–1 by the Italian champions. The plane belonged to David Murray, chairman of Rangers F.C., and a friend of Hunter. On board was Gavin Masterton, a former treasurer of the Bank of Scotland. The banker, never a man it seems to miss a business opportunity, had indulged in a bit of 'tapping up', asking Hunter if he had ever thought of banking with the Bank of Scotland. Hunter, as always the gentlemen, had politely replied that he was happy with the RBS.

But now that the RBS had cold feet, Hunter felt he was justified in looking elsewhere. He and Green were introduced to one of the Bank of Scotland's rising stars in the field of corporate finance, Peter Cummings. It was the coming together of three men who were later to work together to change the face of the high street. For Cummings proved to be a most unusual Scottish banker. While many were known for their canniness and a certain aversion to risk, he seemed keen to embrace it.

Cummings, like Green and Hunter, had left school early. Perhaps it helped cement the friendship between the three. Cummings listened as they explained why a takeover bid for Olympus made perfect business sense, with Olympus being strong in the south of Britain and Sports Division a force in the north. Hunter left the meeting with Cummings confident of the backing of the Bank of Scotland for any bid he might mount for Olympus Sports. Now it was up to Green to deliver.

Green conducted the negotiations at Sears with his customary panache. It was rather like taking toffees off a child. He found that Strong and his team were indeed anxious to rid themselves of the Olympus millstone. Sears's big shareholders were demanding it. Green allowed himself to be talked up to a figure of £20 million. But this was misleading since Sears threw in various incentives to sweeten the deal, including the huge stock of sportswear held by Olympus. Industry analysts later claimed that the whole deal had cost Sears some £35 million.

According to Hunter, Green kept his biggest surprise to last, as Sears did not know who the real buyer was: 'When we went down for the completion meeting, I walked in and they said, "Who's this?" Philip said, "He's the guy with the cheque, you'd better let him in." '[23]

Hunter was both delighted with the deal and confident he could turn Olympus around quickly and make a healthy profit. As a reward for his help Green was given a 13 per cent holding in Sports Division and the position of chairman. But although Hunter respected the older man's judgement and entrepreneurial flair, and would frequently telephone for advice, it soon became clear that the final decision rested with him. For instance, Green had argued that they should retain the Olympus name, much better known in England than Sports Division. Hunter disagreed. He had already judged that the Olympus brand was seen by his target customers as rather boring and unexciting. Shortly after taking over control, he converted all the Olympus outlets to the new Sports Division format, a fresh new identity that made it a national leader in the sporting market, with nearly 250 outlets nicely spread across the whole of Britain.[24]

To underline where the power lay Hunter had the head offices of the integrated empire located at Dundonald in Ayrshire, his own back yard. There he was joined by Ian Grabiner, who served as commercial director. Within less than a year, the loss-making former Olympus shops were turning in a healthy profit, demonstrating just how important good leadership and a strong business focus can be.

Sports Division was, of course, a privately owned company. Provided that the Hunter and Grabiner team could make a success of it, there was a built-in escalator that could multiply the wealth of the owners many times over. Philip Green's 13 per cent could grow and grow. In many ways it was a dry-run for some of Green's later audacious exploits.

CONAN THE BARBARIAN

P hilip Green's involvement in Sports Division's bid for Olympus Sports marked a milestone in his career in more ways than one. It reawakened his interest in making a bid for the Sears empire itself, a course he had first mooted six years earlier, in 1989.

Charles Clore, Sears's owner, had become something of a business hero for Green. He had pioneered the hostile takeover bid, a concept that, in the 1950s, alarmed both the City and the British government, although, by the late 1960s, it had generally come to be seen as a valuable tool of economic reconstruction and renewal. But Clore could never quite throw off his reputation of being Britain's most accomplished asset-stripper, a man who would buy up poorly performing companies, strip them down, sell off the parts and make a huge profit in the process.

In some ways Clore and Green were very similar. They both arose from Jewish immigrant stock and came from well-to-do if not wealthy parentage. Clore, like Green, relied as much on intuition and gut-feeling as on rational analysis when he decided which businesses were ripe for takeover. And Clore's formula for sorting out businesses he had taken over could almost have been written by Green: 'Stabilise management, increase margins, increase the profits.'[1]

What Green admired most in Clore were his qualities as a visionary businessman. In the 1950s he had recognised that many firms were grossly under-valued on the stock market. His first target for a hostile takeover was a shoe retail chain belonging to a company called J. Sears and Co. This chain, Freeman Hardy and Willis, became the basis of Clore's great shoe empire, one that grew to control a quarter of all the shoe shops in Britain under its various brands: Freeman Hardy and Willis, Saxone, Dolcis, Manfield, Trueform, Cable and Co, Hush Puppy and several others.

Clore rationalised the business, sold off surplus property and made himself very rich. But he was not simply out to line his own pockets. He had a keen sense of how businesses could be brought together to produce synergies. At a time when governments were striving to rationalise much of British industry to make it more competitive – think British Leyland and GEC – Clore showed them how it could be done. Nor did he stop with shoes. He set himself up as a rival to Lord Wolfson's GUS mail order business by buying Freemans, Britain's third biggest catalogue sales company. And he expanded the Sears empire to include some of the most famous names in women's fashion – Wallis and Miss Selfridge, to name but two – and the Adams childrenswear chain. He took special pride in having organised a takeover of the Lewis's Group in the 1960s, which then included Selfridges in Oxford Street.

Clore had flourished because he saw that many firms were being run by out-of-touch management with no entrepreneurial insight. Left alone, companies ossify, don't keep their business practices up-to-date and sink into bureaucratic inertia. Ironically this is exactly what had befallen the Clore empire after his death. By the 1990s Sears had become the sick man of the high street, laden down with increasingly uneconomic shoe factories, shops that failed to keep up with changing fashions and a surge in competition. The rise of out-of-town shopping centres and of big supermarkets selling clothing and footwear only added to the gloom.

Since 1992, Liam Strong and the Sears board had struggled to revive the stumbling empire, but the shareholders were increasingly restive as they saw the share price slump. In the ten years from 1988 to 1998 the share price of Marks & Spencer had tripled while the Sears share price fell by 40 per cent.

In August 1995, the board decided that to stop the slide they would need to sell most of the old Clore shoe business. Rumours of the change of policy had soon surfaced in the trade press, so when Green became involved with the Sears board in the takeover talks for Olympus Sports in November 1995 he was already aware that much of the Sears shoe empire was already up for grabs.

Yet Green was uncharacteristically slow to respond to the opportunity. One reason would have been the state of his health. In the latter half of 1995 he had been taken ill with chest pains. Aware that his father had died of a heart attack at a fairly early age, Tina had rushed him to hospital where tests showed two of his coronary arteries were partially blocked. He was lucky. As his wife confirmed in June 2005, 'He got the right drugs in time to avoid a full heart attack.'[2] What she did not say was that her husband also apparently underwent surgical treatment. There were reports that he had two stents – springy little tubes that held the blood vessels open – fitted to two of his coronary arteries.[3]

The heart scare took him out of action for a while, but he now had an anxious wife, worried about his work rate and lifestyle. She later admitted that the heart scare 'was difficult'. They argued 'about how he lived his life, the smoking and what not'.[4] Under pressure, Green made the gesture of switching to Marlboro Lights and taking his foot off the pedal, at least for the moment.

But even had he been fit and well Green might have found little joy in talking to Sears. The group had entered into negotiations with Green's only rival in retail for the title of most flamboyant entrepreneur, a northerner called Stephen Hinchliffe.

Hinchliffe, who was at forty-five two years older than Green, was from Sheffield. He had begun to move into fashion retailing in a big way in 1994 when he first bought Sock Shop, then Red or Dead (a chain that sold itself on a rebellious image) and then the more respectable Oakland Menswear. But his greatest coups were still to come. In August 1995 he had begun secret talks with Sears over the acquisition of 245 shoe stores – the Freeman Hardy Willis, Trueform and Manfield retail chains.

When the deal went through, Hinchliffe could boast of presiding over an empire of 750 shops, employing around 5,000 people. Green, who at this point owned Owen Owen and Xception, lagged some way behind. A hint of the rivalry between the two men was reported in the *Retail Week* gossip page in January 1996. Hinchliffe had apparently telephoned his congratulations to Green on the Olympus deal, telling him he had 'out-Hinched the Hinch'.[5]

Hinchliffe did not mention that he was lining up a further deal with Sears, buying up another 134 Saxone and Curtess shoe shops in February 1996. News of the mass sell-off of the stores and the rock-bottom prices he paid led some in the City to turn their fire on the hapless Liam Strong. Analysts denounced the deals as bad for Sears's shareholders. One of them, Neil Darke of Collins Stewart, scathingly commented: 'I don't think Liam Strong can spell shareholder value, let alone enact it.'[6]

The convalescing Philip Green may have been out of the loop for a while but it was not long before he was back. In February, Mark One, a highly regarded chain of discount fashions for teenagers and young adults operating mainly in the south-east of England, went spectacularly bust. Only two years before, the chain had delighted industry observers when it had announced it planned to double its size in just two years. As so often happens, the pace of expansion had outrun the capacity of the management to maintain its competitive edge. The company's banker pulled the plug.

Green pounced. The receivers, who had been called in to manage the failed chain, accepted his offer of around £4 million for the ninety-four-shop chain, after he had become involved in a bidding war with another rag-trade entrepreneur, Shami Ahmed, founder of the cut-price Joe Bloggs discount jeans. With victory secured, Green told a *Financial Times* reporter that he now intended to draw in his horns. The buying spree was over: 'It's time to consolidate. There are some interesting things around, but we have to make the stores we already have work.'[7]

It was probably a wise thing to do. Conditions on the high street remained tough and not a week passed without the opening of some new out-of-town shopping centre or 'factory outlet' – huge discount warehouses where the surplus stock, including seconds and last year's styles, could be flogged off very cheaply. Turning Mark One into a profitable business was never going to be easy. It offered its dis-counted fashions on the high street, cheek by jowl with the big high street chains, meaning its rents were comparatively high. Such shops could only hope to make profits on very high volume sales. Green brought Elaine Gray over from Owen Owen to help him do it. She was later to take over as managing director. To help motivate her, she was given performance bonuses and a share in the business.

But while he laboured to make a success of Mark One, a quite unexpected train of events turned his interest back to Sears. In June 1996, without warning, Stephen Hinchliffe's Facia group dramatically collapsed, owing its creditors an estimated £50 million. A week before the collapse, rumours had swept the City that there was something fishy about the company's accounts and that Hinchliffe had had 'a run-in' with the DTI and Companies House.[8] Three weeks after the company went bust, Hinchliffe was told that the DTI would press for his disqualification as a director of a public company. It was the beginning of a seven-year process that ended with his pleading guilty to conspiracy to defraud and being given a fifteen-month jail sentence suspended for two years.

It was not only embarrassing for the Sears management, which had seen Hinchliffe as a trusted ally, but it blew a huge hole in the Sears accounts. It emerged that Facia still owed millions for the stocks of shoes Sears had supplied them, and millions more in unpaid rent to Sears as the landlord of many of its premises. Sears was forced to repossess some 380 shops and sell them on where it could to third parties. When the total bill arising from the Facia collapse was totted up it was calculated that Sears had lost a staggering £265 million trying to clear up the mess.

In the City the Hinchliffe collapse was seen by one analyst as 'the last nail in the coffin for Liam Strong'.[9] The beleaguered Sears boss did not immediately succumb, despite an angry shareholders' meeting in late June. But he was fatally wounded. It was thought his departure would only be a matter of time.

Meanwhile, Green's potential to mount new raids on what remained of the Sears shoe empire was being strengthened by the strong performance being put up by Tom Hunter in turning round the old Olympus Sports business. Ironically much of this success was down to the Sears policy of building up its chain of Olympus Sports World supermarkets in out of town retail parks where the boom in casual sportswear had continued, fired up by the huge promotional expenditure injected by global brands such as Nike and Adidas. Under the new management, the former Olympus stores moved from loss- to profit-making. Green was reported to be willing to sell his share in the business. It could now yield him as much as £15 million.

At this stage, the Sears shoe empire had shrunk somewhat, but it still owned Dolcis and Cable & Co and had pumped money into two new chains, Shoe Express and Shoe City. Both these newcomers were meant to be modern, one a self-service shoe shop concept in the high street, the other a set of out-of-town retail park superstores. In November 1996, some analysts concluded that this was madness. The costs of this new strategy were pushing Sears's footwear deeper and deeper into the red. The only sensible policy, they argued, was to pull out of the shoe business altogether.

Then, in January 1997, Sears took another step that was to land it even deeper in the mire. Strong had been chief executive now for five years and was under heavy pressure to do something to please the disillusioned shareholders. He announced that he would sell the Sears catalogue business, Freemans, for over £400 million to one of its competitors, Littlewoods Mail Order. In the event, this promise could not be kept. Strong and his team shelved talks with Littlewoods in favour of talks with another mail order company, Manchester-based N. Brown. When N. Brown pulled out in April, Strong was left high and dry.

The failure of the scheme to sell Freemans proved to be the last straw. A month later, it was announced that Strong was to go, although strangely not until August. When he left he would carry with him a £500,000 compensation package.

With Strong a lame duck chief executive, the lead was now taken by Sears's chairman, Sir Bob Reid. Reid was a respected City figure, but his expertise lay in running railways and oil companies rather than shopping empires. His strategy was to break up Sears into manageable business units and then dispose of most of them to raise cash for shareholder handouts. Freemans would be sold to Littlewoods after all. The great Selfridges store in Oxford Street would be hived off as a separate concern and floated on the stock market. And, biting the bullet, all the remaining shoe shops, about 500 in all, would be sold.

To mastermind the great shoe sale Sears hired a 'company doctor' called David James. A fifty-nine-year-old fitness fanatic and opera-lover who started each day with 200 press-ups, 100 sit-ups and a 3-mile run, James had worked for years with the leading City firm of liquidators, Cork Gulley, helping to find a comfortable last resting place for insolvent firms. He was to be paid £700,000 to negotiate the best deal he could manage. For Green, the coming of Mr James re-opened the takeover game. But would the urbane Mr James be a match for the shrewd and ruthless Mr Green?

As it happened, Green himself had been going through difficult times. The discounted fashion market was proving tough as the big retailers set up their own discount shops or factory outlets to dispose of surplus stock. In January he had decided to abandon an uphill struggle to keep Xception alive, closing it down with debts of £13 million mainly owed to himself. But despite this setback Green could still find the cash he would need to do business with Mr James. Bank Leumi, which had helped him out with Bonanza Jeans in 1985, was still supportive and Peter Cummings at the Bank of Scotland would certainly be interested.[10]

Taking up his post at Sears at the end of May 1997, David James was in no hurry to rush the shoe stores to market. He spent the summer assessing the properties and doing what he could to talk up their value. By the autumn he was ready to talk to anyone who would take the shoe chains off his hands at least cost to Sears. Only one piece of Sears's footwear was actually making a profit, a small chain of twenty-four upmarket shops operating under the name of Cable & Co. In an unguarded moment James later told a reporter on *The Times*: 'A cynic might say that Cable has benefited because it has had the fewest number of bright ideas applied to it.'[11] Green was not interested in Cable & Co. Instead he had fixed his eyes on Shoe Express. He saw that many of Shoe Express's shops were in high streets where Mark One, his remaining fashion chain, had yet to establish a presence. He could afford to cherry pick the best sites and, as he had done with One Up in 1995, find a buyer for the ones he did not want.

After weeks of negotiation in late 1997 a complicated deal emerged. Green would acquire 185 Shoe Express shops for a payment of just £8.3 million. That would leave 136 Shoe Express shops in the hands of Sears. Green was concerned that Sears would use them to sell off its shoe stocks at fire sale prices, destroying the market for the Shoe Express shops he had just bought. An ingenious solution was found. James agreed that Green would manage these shops to allow him to sell off the stock and then return them to Sears for final disposal.

James seems to have assumed that Green would hold on to the shops he had bought and help preserve the jobs, a cause he knew was dear to the heart of Sir Bob Reid. But when the deal was done, Green almost immediately announced that seventy-five of the shops would be converted immediately to Mark One. He was cagey about what he would do with the others merely saying, 'We then want to see if the rest are viable as a small stand-alone chain.'[12]

Green was in upbeat mode in January 1998 when he took part in an auction at a ball for the retail industry's charity for the old and the infirm, Cottage Homes. He made the highest bid for a Rover Ascot car donated by Andersen Consulting, a mere £7,500, and immediately redonated the car to the charity to be re-auctioned. It was bought by Tom Hunter for £8,000. This appears to be the beginning of Green's regular appearance as a high-profile bidder at charity auctions.

It was not until March that he announced his next move. The rest of his Shoe Express stores (some 110 shops) were to be sold to the independent shoe chain Stead & Simpson for about £20 million – far more than the £8.3 million he had paid for the whole package of shops. Sears, commented one observer, 'will be severely embarrassed to see Green making a sizeable profit only four months after selling it to him'.[13]

But while Sears might have seethed at the fact that Green had bested them for a second time in just thirty months, the Greens had by this time other matters on their mind. Tina had been wanting to move to a life in the sun for some time. In March she got her wish. Philip and she rented a large penthouse apartment overlooking Monte Carlo harbour and moved themselves and their children there before the month was out. From now on Philip Green would commute by air from Monaco to London on Monday mornings and fly back on Friday afternoons.

The Greens have always protested that their move was for reasons other than the avoidance of British taxes. Tina Green, in her first ever published interview, told the *Daily Mail* in 2005 that there were two major reasons for the move. The first was Philip's heart problems of 1995. At least in Monaco he could relax at weekends with the family, playing tennis or chilling out aboard the luxury yacht he was soon to buy. The second was an incident which took place in 1997, outside their large London home in St John's Wood: 'It was a Sunday afternoon and Philip had wandered outside to wave goodbye to a friend. He had walked out to the gate, turned right, and there were three guys, one of them with a great big sword, which he held to Philip's throat. He handed over his watch and he was fine, but the police said we were very lucky. I just thought, what are we doing here? I wanted a new life, a nice life.'[14]

The real balance of motives is not easy to gauge. But the fact was that Philip Green had now joined the Monaco set and broadened his acquaintance with some of Europe's richest men. Every spring Tom Hunter would fly in with friends such as Peter Cummings and Jackie Stewart, the former racing driver, to watch the Monaco Grand Prix. Other wealthy businessmen spent much of the year in the principality. Of these none were to prove more useful than a pair of identical twins who built up a huge fortune over the years away from the spotlight of publicity: the Barclay brothers.

Sir David and Sir Frederick Barclay (knighted by the Blair government in 2000) were born in Glasgow in 1934 of humble stock (their mother kept a sweet and cigarette shop). Brought up in the shadow of London's Olympia, their father died when they were twelve and they left school at fifteen to take jobs in the accounting department of General Electric. But it was not for them. They soon left to set up their own painting and decorating business. Working on properties in prosperous West London may have sown the idea that they could make a living as estate agents, a profession that required no qualifications. Dealing in property was the making of them. By 1970 they had become the proud owners of London's landmark Ritz Hotel.

They lived in a mock gothic castle (built for them by the anti-modernist architect Quinlan Terry) on the island of Brecqhou, part of the British Channel Islands, but they also had a home in Monaco and indeed spent much time there. Despite their dislike of publicity the brothers had become famous for their complex property deals, shrewdly buying up businesses and flogging off the separate parts to make them more than a tidy profit.

They had been attracted, as many rich men are, to the idea of owning newspapers – a policy that reached its zenith when they acquired the London-based Telegraph group in 2005. One of their earlier ventures had been the *Sunday Business* newspaper. Needing a sharp business journalist as editor, they had recruited Jeff Randall from the *Sunday Times*. By instinct they were very private people. Had it not been for Randall's personal introduction they might never have met Philip Green. It was a timely encounter.

When Green first met the Barclays in 1998 he was at a turning point in his career. So far, by wheeling and dealing on the margins of the retail clothing and footwear industry, he had made himself a moderately rich man. Despite his other retail failures, he was also making a success with Mark One, a real achievement in the very competitive high street of the 1990s. Although he had often dreamt of mounting a takeover bid for the whole Sears empire, he had never had the financial resources to do it. An alliance with the Barclays could provide not only the money, but also the credibility.

There was no doubt in his mind that the once mighty Sears was now more vulnerable than ever to a lightning takeover. The shareholders were rapidly losing faith in the ability of the existing management to handle even the sell-off strategy they had embraced. Since the departure of Liam Strong nothing had gone well. The renewed attempt to sell the Freemans mail order business to Littlewoods had run into a brick wall when the proposed merger had been referred to the Monopolies and Mergers Commission by the incoming Labour government in 1997. The commission eventually ruled that the proposal was against the public interest, throwing Freemans' management and staff into uncertainty once again.

The second arm of the new strategy, the plan to float off the Selfridges emporium in Oxford Street as a separate company, was also faring badly. In order to make it attractive to investors, its new chief, a showman of an Italian called Vittorio Radice (who liked to call such stores 'cathedrals of consumption'), had embarked on an expensive upgrade of the store, that initially reduced profits.[15] This, along with declining profits on actual sales, had affected investor sentiment. Hoping to raise £500 million from the sell-off, Sears had to settle for just over £300 million when shares in the new company were floated in August 1998.

The result was that Sears ended 1998 in an even more vulnerable position. With Sir Bob Reid at the helm, not a man renowned as a retailer, it was open season for anyone to have a go at making a bid for the whole group.

The future of Sears must have been a topic of conversation between Green and the Barclays. Sears offered real scope for making a killing. It had its own financial services company, built around the group's various store-cards and estimated to be worth £150 million. Its property arm, run as a separate business, was conservatively valued at some £140 million. On top of this the sale of Freemans would probably raise around £150 million (down on Sears's original estimate but still a substantial sum). There remained the clothing businesses, which might be worth another £200 million. Yet the Sears share price in October valued the company at only £250 million.

In London shareholder sentiment had firmly turned against the regime. In October 1998, Reid found himself under fire when the company produced its annual results and announced that the sale of Freemans – mooted now for eighteen months – had once again been postponed. The mail order business had slumped badly into the red and was too 'fragile' to be put to market, a claim dismissed as 'pathetic' by Richard Ratner, a prominent retail analyst. He declared: 'The current share price is a sad indictment of what the City thinks of

Sears's management.'[16] (It stood at just above 160p a share.)

On 5 November, the mail order firm N. Brown mounted an ambush, offering to buy Sears for some £400 million, a bid that valued the shares at 255p. Reid and the board rejected it outright. Green was now ready to move. Perhaps because the Barclays were yet to be convinced that there was much money to be made out of the deal, Green's first approach in mid-December was made by a special acquisition vehicle company, called Medinbond, in which Tom Hunter was a partner. Earlier in the year Hunter had sold his Sports Division empire for £290 million (bringing Philip Green a very useful 'dividend' of almost £38 million) and he was now flush with cash. But the bulk of the money would come from interested banks, chief of which was the Bank of Scotland. Peter Cummings had come to be a great admirer of Green's business ability, and was ready to join the party.

Green used the bid techniques he was later to perfect. He did not want to make the bid formal, since that would entail following the procedures as laid down by the Stock Exchange Takeover Panel. This would have meant hiring expensive lawyers and accountants and eroding the potential profits. So Medinbond put in its bid wrapped up in conditions, describing the offer merely as 'around 300p' a share. It could not turn this into a firm bid until Sears provided more information on the latest trading figures at Freemans, a statement on the value of its property assets and on whether a price for its financial services business had already been agreed with a prospective buyer.

Reid and the Sears directors, who had no reason to be well-disposed towards Green, gave the bid short shrift. It was too hedged about with conditions and not in the best interests of shareholders.

Meanwhile, Green had lined up the Barclays. A new takeover vehicle – appropriately called January Investments – now made a bid. The Barclays put around £100 million into it, Tom Hunter an amount that has never been disclosed and Green £20 million. Although the Barclays were the major partners, Philip Green was to act as chief executive and chief negotiator, with Aidan Barclay, Sir David Barclay's son, as managing director. Tom Hunter also had a prominent role. It was a formidable team that had the backing of Peter Cummings at the Bank of Scotland and a clutch of other banks, providing an additional fighting fund that topped £400 million. Everything was now in place for the killer strike.

Green, although based in Monaco over Christmas 1998, kept in constant touch with a team of London advisers and stockbrokers. He knew Reid would remain hostile to any bid he was likely to put forward in January. It was time to go beyond the Sears board and attempt to engineer a shareholder rebellion. The biggest of the shareholders was Philips and Drew, which held 22 per cent of the shares. As the New Year came in, an intensive lobbying campaign was set in train, master-minded by Green himself from the Dorchester Hotel in London. By mid-January the walls of the citadel had begun to crack: Philips and Drew gave Green assurances that they would commit themselves to accepting a cash offer of 340p except in the unlikely event of a larger bid appearing from elsewhere. Other big shareholders were wavering. On 14 January a new offer arrived on the desk of Sir Bob Reid. Unlike the previous offer, this was to be a firm cash offer pitched at 340p a share and valuing Sears at around £520 million.

Reid and his board were no longer able to dismiss the bid out of hand. One newspaper, picking up the story, put the truth in stark terms: 'After all, cash is the only language Sears shareholders under-stand. They have lived on empty promises for too long.'[17]

Reid must have known that the game was up. But there was one last service he could perform. A positive board recommendation would guarantee victory for Green. On 21 January he got in touch with Green and held out the carrot of board approval if the bid could be raised. A day of intense negotiation followed, concluding with an agreement. January Investments would raise the bid from 340p a share to 359p a share, increasing the value of the whole bid to £548 million. In a statement, Reid gave the bid his final seal of approval: 'The increased cash offer of 359p per share represents a fair deal for shareholders and is in line with the board's strategy to return value to them.'[18]

Green and the Barclays had wrested Sears out of the hands of a hostile board. The majority of the shareholders, predictably, accepted the deal. Revealing his delight at the outcome, Green told an enquiring journalist who phoned him on his yacht in Monaco: 'I've done my homework and I've backed my judgment. The banks and the Barclays have backed my judgment. It's been a fascinating campaign and it has been a long haul to get it on the runway. I get a target in my mind and I stay with it.'[19]

Green's business instincts had again proved themselves. It was a dry run for further takeover battles to come. But the great question was, what would Green and the Barclays do with Sears? Would it be a question of breaking up the empire to release the assets, or would Green set out to show the world that he was, as he had always claimed, a master retailer who could breathe new life into badly run companies? As Richard Ratner told *Retail Week*: 'All eyes will be on Green to see if his deal-making audacity will be matched by retail flare.'[20]

It did not take long to find out. Within a month, Freemans was sold to the German mail order company Otto Versand for £150 million, and the Sears financial services to the French group Galeries Lafayette for £140 million. The property portfolio was poured over by Aidan Barclay and put up for sale.

Green then turned his attention to the clothing chains, Adams Childrenswear, Wallis, Outlet, Miss Selfridge, Warehouse and Richards. The first was easily dealt with. The Adams management had already put in train the first steps towards funding a management buy-out. It eventually raised £90 million that went straight into the coffers of January Investments.

In the middle of February Green called a meeting of all the top managers of the remaining clothing chains. It lasted six hours, during which Green gave them all a dressing down. They did not enjoy it. Someone in Sears management described the meeting to *Retail Week*: 'He treated them like school kids and told them to get their acts together or get out the door . . . Heads will definitely roll among the £100,000 a year personnel.'[21]

It was for some a bruising encounter. It suggested that Green was intent on turning the shops around, to show the sceptics that he knew how to run the retail side of the business. For one thing, he emphasised to the meeting that there was to be a squeeze on suppliers' margins, following the Green dictum that prices had to be what the customer was prepared to pay, not what the producer thought a garment was worth.

But Green's commitment to the Sears clothing chains proved very short-lived. He was under pressure from Tina not to spend so much time away from the family. Perhaps he considered the challenge too much even for a man of his talents. Or, again, it may have been that the temptation of making a great deal of money very quickly by selling off the parts was just too hard to resist.

For some weeks, in the late spring of 1999, Philip Green and a clothing group called Arcadia were locked in talks about the future of the Sears companies. Arcadia owned some of Britain's best-known names in fashion clothing, including Topshop, Topman, Dorothy Perkins, Evans and Burton. Philip Green and the American chief executive of Arcadia, John Hoerner, spent a month haggling over the details but on 8 July announced to the press that a deal had been agreed. Wallis, Warehouse, Miss Selfridge and Richards were to be bought by Arcadia for £151 million. The news was welcomed on the stock market where Arcadia shares rose by 7 per cent in a day. Green was pleased to add to the receipts of January Investments, taking them above the total paid for the Sears group, with the valuable property assets still in hand. They would be sold for at least £300 million.

For the staff of the Sears shops it was a shock. They had regarded Arcadia as the enemy. Some complained to *Retail Week*: 'We would never have willingly sold ourselves to Arcadia.' But it was a coup hailed by analysts such as Seymour Pierce: 'Hats off to Philip Green again. He certainly knows how to cut a deal. Credit to him that he should have spotted the opportunity and is making money. It's a sort of indictment on Sears.'[22]

Green and his friends had pulled off a remarkably lucrative deal. It was a classic case of asset-stripping. The takeover team had paid £548 million for the consortium, sold the parts for around £800 million and thus pocketed approximately £250 million in profit. All for a few months' work. Seizing and dismantling the once-mighty Sears had made Green, the Barclays and Tom Hunter look remarkably shrewd.

It was an especially symbolic moment in Green's own career. He had won a hostile takeover of the retail empire created by the legendary Charles Clore, and made a fortune in doing so. On three separate occasions – over Olympus Sports, Shoe Express and now the rest of the group – he had run rings around Sears's management. Still a relative novice, he had outmanoeuvred one of the business giants of the era. As one commentator put it at the time, 'each time Green bought from Sears, he has royally legged them over'.[23]

It was this deal that was to earn Green the nickname 'Conan the Barbarian', the man now seen in some quarters as a business predator, an opportunistic hit-and-run operator who may have enjoyed a mixed record when it came to running companies but had found a remarkably successful way of making money none the less. Sears was by far his most significant deal to date. He had watched how the Barclay brothers operated and how they made money and, as a result, learnt a lot that he was to put to use later in his career. The deal had also strengthened his reputation in one area where it mattered most – the City – and in the process brought him to the notice of a number of powerful businessmen and bankers. In doing so it set him up for a new offensive on the high street. Who, the retail world wondered, would be next in line for the Green treatment?

Chapter 7

PROJECT MUSHROOM

F or most people, the weeks leading up to New Year's Eve 1999 were dominated by preparations for the millennium celebrations. For Philip Green, the transition from one century to the next was the last thing on his mind.

He emerged from the Sears deal not only seriously rich, but brimming with confidence. Even if others had their doubts, he was convinced that he had the Midas touch. In only a few years of frenetic business activity he had become a man who was being closely watched by both his retail peers and institutional investors. In the autumn of 1999, the City was rife with speculation about where the arch deal-maker, now awash with cash, would go next.

The ambitious Green was convinced that most of the big names on the high street were living on borrowed time. One of his oft-repeated jokes is how he used to check out Oxford Street shops in the 1990s to see how the opposition was faring: 'You could walk into a shop with a machine-gun, fire off a whole clip of ammunition and you wouldn't hit a customer.' He called it the Kalashnikov test. He was now in a position to buy some of those under-populated shops

He was careful to pick his targets. If the experience of Owen Owen had taught him anything, it was that department stores were much too complicated an operation for a quick fix. So he dismissed the tempting prospect of bidding for the ailing upmarket House of Fraser group. Storehouse, owners of Mothercare, British Home Stores and the Blazer menswear chains, had been underperforming for years and he briefly discussed the possibility of a bid with the Barclay brothers. But these were small fry and Green was setting his sights on much bigger fish.

The two companies he settled on were Sainsbury's and Marks & Spencer, worth £8 billion and £11 billion respectively. Both companies had been losing ground to competitors and were beset by sharp falls in their share price. When he looked at them he saw retail dinosaurs, companies wedded to an out-of-date business model that did not meet the needs of the new marketplace. Of the two, it was M&S that Green really wanted. For a man obsessed with the rag-trade, there was no greater prize than seizing control of what was then, and arguably still is, the crown jewels of British retailing. It was a prize he now thought was within his grasp.

Only two years earlier, in May 1997, champagne had been flowing at the company's Baker Street headquarters in the West End of London. M&S had announced that its profits for the previous trading year had exceeded £1 billion for the first time in its history. And the architect of this record was the volatile and domineering Sir Richard Greenbury.

M&S had had a tradition of autocratic bosses, one continued when the egocentric Greenbury had taken over the reins in 1991. His arrogant and insular style did not seem to matter so long as he was delivering record profits. There is of course nothing especially unusual about overbearing company bosses and that year Greenbury had been voted the country's second most impressive chief executive. In October 1997, the share price had hit 664p, another all-time high. The company was then worth £19 billion, making it Britain's largest retailer and ninth largest company. It proved to be a peak in the company's fortunes.

Eventually Greenbury's management style started to work against the interests of the company. His top directors knew things were beginning to slip, that the clothes and stores were slowly losing their appeal. But Greenbury was one of a declining number of business leaders who held both posts of chief executive and company chairman (shades of Green at Amber Day), and his underlings, many of whom had come to loathe their boss, were frightened to take him on. Nobody had the power or boldness to unseat him.

From then on it had been all downhill. Two years later, sales had slipped and profits had halved. Following months of internal conflict, a subdued Greenbury was effectively forced to stand down as chief executive in November 1998. Peter Salsbury, a senior manager, took over as chief executive while Greenbury stayed on as chairman, but Salsbury could barely disguise his intense dislike of his predecessor and the two were soon at war. Throughout 1999, beset by internal bloodletting, a succession of profit warnings and concern about its strategic direction, the share price plunged. In little more than two years, the value of the company had almost halved. In June Greenbury was finally forced to resign as chairman, and was replaced as a short-term fix by one of the non-executive directors, Brian Baldock.

Salsbury and Baldock now had to arrest the decline. Baldock, a former director at Guinness, was viewed as a heavyweight in the City and had been taking the lead on the tricky problem of who should take over from Greenbury. He had also witnessed at first hand the destructive internal jostling for the succession as it became clear that Greenbury would have to be eased out. He was certainly not a man to trifle with.

Green meanwhile had been watching events closely from the sidelines, a leopard waiting for the moment to pounce. The winter of 1999 seemed exactly the right time to make a move. Greenbury was gone. Baldock was an interim chairman. Salsbury had been in post barely a year. And although plans were afoot to cut costs the problems ran deeper. The company was dogged by an ideas-resistant culture. At the beginning of November, the company revealed another collapse in profits. At one point in that month, the share price fell to 238p, an eight-year low. Barely a year after his appointment, Salsbury was now being seen as a mistake. In the words of one City analyst, he was going around the country 'spreading inertia'.

The struggling company was in need of a blood transfusion and Green saw himself as the man to supply it. Despite a lingering suspicion about his business methods in parts of the City, Green had overcome some of the negative reputation gained during the Amber Day period and was now confident that he could find backers willing to fund a bid. At least to some in the City he was now seen as something of a business guru who was able to unlock the hidden value that had proved elusive to others. Armed with his new reputation he initially approached Bob Wigley, a top executive at Merrill Lynch, one of the giant American investment banks that had come to dominate City institutions in the previous decade. Green wanted Merrill Lynch to take the lead role on banking advice and was disappointed when the prestigious bank declined. Green next approached Sir Laurie Magnus, who had acted for him at Amber Day. Magnus was now a director of another American investment bank, Donaldson, Luftkin & Jenrette. DLJ stepped into the Merrill Lynch shoes and Green had the satisfaction of bringing the rival bank back on board as a secondary source of advice.

Green still required someone to provide the lead finance. He found that in the dynamic American Robin Saunders who now headed the London office of the German banking group WestLB. Green had already been introduced to Saunders and the two got on well. She enjoyed working with what she saw as maverick entrepreneurs, men with huge reserves of energy and drive who were not unnerved by apparently high-risk deals. Like Green she had plenty of bottle herself. Born in North Carolina and a classically trained dancer she had started to make a successful banking career in Britain in her early thirties. By 1998, at the age of thirty-six, she had built up an impressive team of merchant bankers at the Deutsche Bank's London head-quarters. She then took a gamble by upping sticks and moving herself and her team, lock, stock and barrel, to the relatively small and obscure regional German bank WestLB. It ranked as one of the largest City mass defections ever seen and it paid off. Virtually single-handedly she turned the firm's London office into one of the capital's raciest deal-makers.

Described by *Newsweek* as the 'City's glamour girl, a pin-striped Claudia Schiffer', she had earlier helped Formula One boss Bernie Ecclestone by putting together more than £1 billion in loans to refinance his company. No one else in the City wanted to know. The rescue deal, a bold and risky operation at the time, helped to turn Ecclestone into a billionaire and simultaneously raised millions in fees for her bank and pretty handy bonuses for herself in the process. Saunders specialised in securitisation – a complex device by which a company raises a large sum by selling bonds which guarantee bond-holders a regular return from the cash income of the company.

Although neither of his lead advisers, DLJ nor WestLB, were perhaps in the premier league, Green was confident they had the firepower he needed to mount his assault on his unsuspecting target. In early December, three weeks before the millennium celebrations, Project Mushroom, the codename used for the potential bid, was under way. To preserve secrecy, M&S was designated 'Campbell' in all the planning documents. Meanwhile a number of international backers were being approached informally for finance. Knowledge of the bid was not yet public and initially Green decided to make informal soundings to M&S.

He was already acquainted with sixty-year-old Sir David Sieff, then the last remaining member of the founding Marks family on the board of Marks & Spencer. Born in 1939, he was the great-grandson of Michael Marks, the Polish immigrant who had founded the business as a bazaar stall in Leeds in 1884. For its first 100 years, M&S had been controlled by the intermarried Marks and Sieff families. They may have been dictatorial bosses, but they had also achieved legendary success. Sir David was, in 1999, the last link with that past. His grandfather, Israel Sieff, married into the company through marriage to Rebecca Marks, and had run it in the 1960s before handing over to his son and David's father, Marcus Sieff, later Lord Sieff of Brimpton.

David had begun his lifelong career at Marks in personnel at the age of eighteen and by 1999 was a non-executive member of the board. He had first met Green a few years earlier in his role as chairman of the British Retail Consortium, a high street pressure group. The two men could hardly have had more contrasting personalities. Sieff – urbane, cultured and respected – had been born right into the heart of the British retailing establishment. An opera buff, he was a trustee of Glyndbourne. Green – brash, irascible and unorthodox – preferred pop music, casinos and football. Sieff was a member of White's – the establishment club favoured by leading businessmen and the aristocracy – and played by the rules. Green's inspiration came from breaking them.

Green rang Sieff in early December and was as blunt as ever. Could he broker an introduction to Brian Baldock? The following afternoon Sieff popped into Baldock's office to let him know that Green was interested in M&S. The acting chairman was dismissive. He had never met Green but was well aware of his reputation as the hit-and-run merchant of the retail sector. Determined to keep Green at bay, he believed a meeting would serve no purpose. He asked Sieff to pass on his refusal to meet.

Green was not a man to accept no for an answer. A few hours later, and completely out of the blue, he rang Baldock and attempted to charm him into a meeting. The flattery did not work. Baldock was blunt – if Green was contemplating a takeover, he would have to put his plans down on paper. Green knew that taking control of the high street chain was not going to be as smooth an operation as it had proved in some of his earlier ventures. Nevertheless, this was to be the first of many snubs he was to receive at the hands of the directors of M&S, and it did not go down well.

Baldock, who had direct experience of hostile bids, may have been a stopgap leader, but he hardly wanted to be labelled the man who handed over the precious company to the Johnny-come-lately Green. Following Green's call, the acting chairman called an immediate board meeting. To those who knew about these things, the fifteen-strong board would not have inspired a great deal of confidence. Its members had been with the company for an average of twenty-four years and had presided over the worsening fortunes of the company. Even so, the meeting was unanimous. Green's overtures were rejected out of hand. The board wanted nothing to do with him.

Its motives were mixed, however. Green had already developed a reputation as a corporate raider who took no prisoners, so some of the directors feared that they would lose their jobs. He was also viewed by others as not the sort of man they wanted to be running the still rather snooty M&S empire – he was simply too brash, too much the barrow boy. The company was still in the throes of a stormy transition from the old company run on traditional family lines to one with a more modern business outlook. But even those who were pushing for modernisation thought that a ship run by Green was a step too far.

Above all, although the overtures from Green were not welcomed, they were also not seen as too much of a threat. As David Sieff commented after the event: 'We didn't take Green that seriously. You have to understand the M&S culture. We may not have been having a good time, but we were not down and out and we're a heck of a lot bigger than you . . . After all, at that stage, Philip Green had not made a big name for himself.'[1]

Maybe, but Green was not going to go away and could not simply be ignored. Baldock took personal charge of M&S's defence. He created a war cabinet of the company's advisers – the giant American investment bank Morgan Stanley, the Queen's stockbroker Cazenove, the top corporate law firm Slaughter & May, and the influential PR company Brunswick. On paper, this was a formidable advisory group. Although Green's thwarted approaches were not known outside a very small circle of insiders and advisers on both sides, the City, a leaky institution at the best of times, was awash with rumours about the possibility of a takeover bid against M&S. In early December, financial correspondents, bloodhounds without a clear prey, started to specu-late about the possible contenders. Former Asda chairman Archie Norman, and Kingfisher, the owner of B&Q and Woolworths, were among those said to be interested. The Barclay brothers were also known to be hunting for acquisitions at the time.

Tesco was looking closely at M&S, too. Indeed, senior executives had even undertaken strategic planning exercises in case it bought the business. The attraction for Tesco was that a deal would have enabled it to expand its non-food business in the face of mounting competition from Wal-Mart, the new owner of Asda. A merger with M&S would also have enabled it to reap big savings by combining the two food businesses. Their powerful chief executive, Terry Leahy, was certainly tempted, but knew that a bid would prove highly contentious among his shareholders. Some of the bigger investors had quietly warned him that a bid would be viewed as corporate arrogance. M&S was still seen as something of a 'national asset' and not to be lightly tinkered with.

Philip Green, of course, had no such qualms and was identified by several newspapers as having been spotted in the City where, a year after completing his break-up bid for Sears, there was keen anticipation of his next trick. The linking of Green's name with the Barclay twins led to a frenzy of further speculation. On 9 December, M&S issued a statement denying they were in bid talks, a move that served merely to fuel the rumours.

The next day nearly 100 million M&S shares were traded amidst growing speculation about an imminent bid. The share price rose 14 per cent to 300p. Three days later, on 13 December, Green was approached by the Takeover Panel, the industry body which sets rules, ensures fair play and acts as an arbiter during takeovers. The body, as required, had already been informed of Green's potential interest. Because of the risk of damage to M&S from the growing speculation, the Panel demanded that Green made his intentions public. Green issued a terse statement confirming publicly what insiders already knew and most City watchers had guessed – that he was weighing up a possible offer. Under the Panel's rules, having declared an interest, he had another eight weeks to clarify his intentions.

M&S was, by now, not just attracting excitement at home. Fuelled by the prospect of quick takeover profits, some opportunistic US fund managers had started buying shares in the retail giant in December. By the beginning of the New Year, Brandes, a San Diego company specialising in what it considered to be 'undervalued' companies, had acquired 6 per cent of M&S shares making it the single largest investor in the group. Another company, Franklin Resources, had taken its stake to 5 per cent. The interest was part of a highly significant phenomenon – the increasing ownership of well-known British companies by American investors, a trend that was to play a key role in later events. One effect of the entry of Brandes and Franklin into the market was to fuel expectations that a bid was likely since they were certainly not investing on the basis of performance.

M&S bosses may not have been too disturbed by Green's interest initially, but events were not moving as they would have liked. Hanging over them was the uncertainty of who would replace Baldock, who had been searching for his own replacement for months. A number of top names had been approached but had declined. Other candidates simply sparked off a new bout of internal wrangling on the board. Rumours also spread that M&S's trading performance had continued to deteriorate, especially in the weeks running up to Christmas, the single most important period in the retail calendar. To the City this was another signal that the management team of Salsbury and Baldock had yet to prove their worth.

M&S was at this point as embattled at it had ever been in its recent turbulent history. It had just come out of a prolonged period of very public boardroom infighting over internal attempts to ditch Sir Richard Greenbury and the serious falls in profits. The company was locked in yet another internal power struggle concerning the appointment of a new chairman and how to respond to declining sales. Against this backdrop, M&S could not be certain that they would be able to fend off the persistent Green, a man who already had a series of successful, if less significant, takeovers to his credit.

In mid-January, M&S announced its seasonal sales figures – a 9 per cent fall in non-food sales – amongst the worst on the high street. Salsbury knew that unless he could halt the slide he would be out. So far, all his efforts at a radical overhaul had proved marginal at best. He had introduced television advertising, reversed the long resistance to outside credit cards, turned to cheaper overseas suppliers and shaken up senior management, all without noticeable effect. Patience amongst the bigger shareholders was wearing thin.

Salsbury was now pinning his hopes on the new fashion collection to be launched at the end of January. Masterminded by Salsbury himself, the spring range was the first to introduce designer names such as Betty Jackson, while prices on average had been cut by 5 per cent. This was an implicit acceptance that they were being outsmarted in the style stakes by chains such as Next and Gap, and losing out on price to rivals such as Matalan.

None of this was enough to prevent continuing speculation about other bidders. Online investors started to place bets on a gambling website, www.bluesq.com, about the future of M&S. Although the firm favourite was that Marks would remain independent with odds of 4/7 on, the board knew they were far from secure. Tesco, despite its continuing denials of interest, was the favourite outsider with odds of 5/2. Green was rated at 9/2, not especially long odds, and Nomura, the Japanese investment bank, a longer shot at 10/1.

Matters for M&S were not helped by the fact that although Baldock had finally found a man to replace him as chairman, he was proving hard to get. Luc Vandevelde, a cool and cultured Belgian retail star who spoke five languages and oozed charm, could claim to have transformed the performance of the French supermarket group Promodes, but had just lost his post as number one when its bigger French rival negotiated a successful merger. Vandevelde was not happy about being forced into the number two role.

If Baldock could secure the services of Vandevelde, he was convinced it would move the balance of advantage in M&S's direction. But Vandevelde would not be hurried. It was another three weeks of anxious waiting before a deal could be struck. The announcement that Vandevelde would be joining the company was finally made on 24 January. News of his appointment was met with the usual brittle comment from Green: 'They need a striker and they have hired a goalie.'[2] To Green, of course, the best striker in town was himself.

While M&S was continuing to struggle, Green's team was busy trying to get the financial support needed to launch Project Mushroom. Even with the fall in the share price since 1997, M&S was still one of Britain's largest companies. Buying it would cost more than £10 billion, making the potential bid amongst the highest ever attempted in Britain. Nevertheless, progress was being made. By the end of January, Green had secured agreement from several leading retail figures to join him as senior managers if his bid was to succeed. Most prominent was his friend Allan Leighton, who, with Archie Norman, had helped to turn round Asda. Bringing Leighton onside was a real coup for Green since he was just the sort of experienced and successful retailer that would attract other top names and, equally importantly, City investors.

The rest of the Green team would also have been welcomed in City quarters. Terry Green, no relation, the man who had led the revival of Debenhams, agreed to head up the clothing side of the business. Richard North, then finance director of Bass but formerly of Burton, agreed to take on the role of head of finance. Most significantly, Green had persuaded Rupert Hambro, the well-connected British banker, to be chairman if the bid was successful. It said much about Green's persuasive powers – and the pulling power of M&S – that men of such calibre, all of whom already had lucrative jobs at top companies, were willing to take the risks associated with such a project. For the moment, though, Green kept the names under his belt. When approached all four firmly denied any involvement.

Towards the end of January 2000, with Vandevelde finally in the bag, M&S moved to the second phase of their survival strategy. They were by now taking Green pretty seriously and had been undertaking their own investigations into him and his past business record, looking for evidence that they could use against him. As part of this 'hunt for dirt' they issued a series of '212 notices' under the section of the Companies Act that gives companies the right to find out who owns their shares. On 28 January, Green received his own notice: did he own any M&S shares? A few days later, similar notices were sent to Donaldson, Luftkin and Jenrette, and to Allan Leighton, Terry Green and Richard North, the three key members of Green's prospective management team. In a tribute to how leaky the City can be they were already dubbed the 'Three Musketeers', despite their denials of involvement. The issuing of notices against the three was a deliberate move to flush out Green's team. They all claimed they had no shares but their names were now in the public domain, not something they exactly welcomed.

Green replied promptly, through his lawyers, Allen & Overy and Titmuss Sainer. This revealed that although Green had no shares, his wife Tina did. She had bought no less than 9.5 million shares in M&S over three days in early December just before her husband's announcement of his interest in the company. At a cost of £23 million, this had given her a 0.33 per cent stake. The reply gave no clue as to how his wife had raised the money for the shares. Green had always tried to keep Tina out of the limelight of his business activities. She lived in Monaco and was an infrequent visitor to Britain; he was the one who jetted weekly between London and his Monaco home. In fact, she had been integral to his business affairs ever since he was forced out of Amber Day in 1992.

Within twenty-four hours of Green's purchase of Shoe Express in 1997, for example, ownership was transferred to Tina, just a few months before the couple moved to Monaco in March 1998. From that point, involving Tina in his business affairs became an established pattern. In July 1999, Green transferred a 53 per cent shareholding in Owen Owen to her name. In September 1999, she became a share-holder in Northworld, the parent of the successful Mark One chain. Now she had built up a sizeable stake in M&S. Since she was a Monaco resident, any income she received in her own name was, quite legally, free of British taxation.[3]

Of course, the Greens could argue that the business arrangements were not about tax-efficiency and that Tina was a successful business-woman before meeting Philip and understood the retail business, but this was something of a fig-leaf. Tina's joint business dealings, however, may help to explain how she was able to finance the M&S share purchase, which she did through offshore accounts in the Channel Islands using no less than fifteen nominee names and which enabled the identity of the purchaser to remain secret.

There was nothing wrong with buying shares in the way Tina Green had. It is relatively common practice for individuals to buy shares in order to gain a toehold and potential voting power in a company for which they are considering launching a bid. Indeed his wife's purchase was part of a perfectly legitimate plan by Green to secure a reasonable stake in the company. But the law is clear. Shares can only be bought in advance of a bid if the buyer is acting as a recognised 'concert party', City jargon for a takeover consortium. Under such an arrangement shares are handed over at cost price to the bidding vehicle in the event of a bid being launched. This is to ensure that individuals don't profit personally from the usual rise in the share price following a bid.

In fact, in November 1999, Green had visited the Takeover Panel with his legal advisers before the purchase of these shares. At the meeting the Panel had accepted that Tina Green qualified as a 'concert party'. The Greens were thus not guilty of any legal impro-priety over the purchase and they knew it.

M&S, of course, were not aware of such a prior agreement and remained convinced that, as one of their team puts it, they had 'struck gold'. Their suspicions were fuelled by the way in which Green had chosen to word his reply. While acknowledging that Tina had bought shares it added: 'She is the sole beneficial owner of those shares.' M&S's solicitors, Slaughter & May, assumed that this implied that Tina was acting as an individual and not as part of a concert party. If so, as Green's wife, she could have been privy to inside information. It appeared to the lawyers that Green had been caught red-handed, thus providing the M&S board with a golden opportunity to discredit the predator in the eyes of the public.

Armed with this potential bombshell, M&S went straight onto the attack. Unknown to Green and his team, who assumed the matter had been cleared, M&S's advisers rang and arranged a meeting with the Takeover Panel on 2 February. It was a bitterly cold day. After lunch, three men arrived at the Stock Exchange building in Threadneedle Street in the heart of the City and took the lift to the twentieth floor. One was Graham Oakley, the company secretary. The others were Piers de Montfort from Morgan Stanley and Andy Ryde from Slaughter & May. The three men expected that this would prove the decisive meeting in the battle to ward off Green. They not only wanted to raise the matter of the shares, but to press the Panel to force Green to move formally with a bid or withdraw – 'to put up or shut up'. Their argument was that Green had been stalking the company for close to eight weeks, had announced his interest, but had yet to make a formal bid. This was creating enormous and unhelpful uncertainty for the company.

The refusal to make a formal bid was a classic Green tactic. His preferred method was to approach companies privately and indicate the size of his offer, and in this way was able to keep his costs down. But the three men knew that their desire to force Green's hand would cut little ice with the Panel, which, in earlier takeovers, had usually taken a relatively lenient line over timing. Although the eight-week deadline was about to elapse, they knew that with Christmas intervening since the announcement, Green and his advisers would be able to argue that more time was needed.

But the trio from M&S now played what they still considered to be their trump card – Tina's share purchase. The Panel agreed to look into the issues involved and rule on the matter within a few days.

Two days later, on 4 February, the Panel informed M&S that they could see nothing wrong in the purchase since they had accepted

Green's account that his wife was part of a 'concert party'. This was a blow to M&S, but their lawyers, Slaughter & May, were loath to let the matter drop. They argued that, even if insider dealing had not taken place, under the rules Green should have informed M&S that his wife's holdings were part of a concert party and that, having failed to do so, he was guilty of providing misleading information and was thus technically in breach of the strict rules governing takeovers. The issue at stake was whether Tina's involvement in a concert party should have been declared properly and not fudged as it appeared to have been. It was a legal technicality but one that M&S believed they could still exploit to the full.

That evening, M&S and their professional advisers Morgan Stanley and PR agency Brunswick met to decide their next move. Following the meeting and in full knowledge of the implications, Green's 212 reply was leaked to a number of Sunday newspapers. As one of their advisers put it: 'This has been going on for long enough now. We are moving onto the front foot.'[4] Journalists were informed not only of Tina's purchases but that M&S was going to refer the matter to the Department of Trade and Industry and to the Stock Exchange's Market Supervision Department. The journalists were told that either Mrs Green was involved in insider dealing or Mr Green's reply was misleading and thus a breach of the takeover rules. M&S were hoping that the negative publicity would rebound on Green. It would not be the last time that what some people saw as questionable tactics would be used in the battle for ownership of M&S.

Indeed, Brunswick was well practised in the art of destroying the opposition. They had advised ICI when Lord Hanson had tried, unsuccessfully, to take them over in the early 1990s. Amidst allegations of dirty tricks, Hanson had been forced to back off when details of his lavish personal and corporate lifestyle were leaked.

The tactics against Green were a textbook example of how to use the press to manipulate public opinion against a predator. One member of the M&S defence team described the tactics to Susanna Voyle of the *Financial Times* as a 'surgical procedure'.[5] They were certainly carefully plotted and clinically enacted. Whether they were ethical was another matter.

Alerted by a series of calls from journalists on the Saturday, Green, who did not retain a full-time PR company, contacted his lawyers. A series of three-way and sometimes heated conversations then took place between Green, his lawyer and journalists in which the Green side tried to kill the story by explaining that he had stuck by the letter of the law. Despite this, several Sunday papers carried versions of the story on 6 February including the *Independent on Sunday*, the *Observer* and the *Sunday Times*. The *Independent on Sunday* ran it under the headline, 'M&S STALKER'S WIFE "SECRETLY BOUGHT SHARES" '.[6] The *Sunday Times* put the story on the front page under a large banner headline, 'TYCOON FACES INSIDER DEALING ROW OVER M&S SHARES'. The opening paragraph began 'A potential bidder for M&S is at the centre of insider trading allegations . . .', thus carrying the suggestion that the Greens had been acting illegally. The front-page spread had been written by the paper's business news editor, John Jay, but the headline had been written by a sub-editor. The article's contents had also been subbed before publication.[7]

The day after the allegations, Sir Laurie Magnus of DLJ approached the Takeover Panel for clarification and was told they were satisfied with the way Green and his wife had handled the share purchase. On Monday evening, 7 February, Green issued a statement that he had done nothing wrong and that he and his wife had complied with 'all the relevant laws and regulations'.

But it was too late. M&S knew only too well that the mud would stick. Whether Green's ambiguous response to M&S on the issue was merely a clerical error or a technical and deliberate sleight-of-hand, the newspaper coverage did serious damage to Green's aspirations. Apoplectic about the leak, he knew that the revelations would provide an opportunity for the old stories around Amber Day to be revisited, reinforcing prejudices against him and making it more difficult to win round an already sceptical City. They could also not have come at a worse time. They raised doubts not merely in shareholders' and the public's mind, but also in the minds of some of those that Green had been courting to put together a financial deal.

In fact, some weeks before the newspaper allegations broke, top executives at DLJ had been having second thoughts about Green. His past reputation was only too well known in the City, and had returned to haunt him again, quite possibly as a result of deliberate rumour-mongering in financial circles. The bank's bosses were sufficiently jittery to have taken the extraordinary step of commissioning Kroll Associates, the world's largest corporate detective agency, to investigate their own client. Kroll had once been famously hired by the government of Kuwait to trace Saddam Hussein's worldwide assets in the aftermath of the first Gulf War, uncovering a complex web of Swiss bank accounts and hidden investments held by the Iraqi dictator.

In January a team of investigators from Kroll had begun to check Green's history, corporate dealings and activity. The exact findings of the Kroll report on Green have never been revealed, though the report is believed to have referred to some of his business history, including his earlier business relationships with men such as the discredited Blue Arrow boss, Tony Berry, and the fraudster Roger Levitt.

This was not the only concern of the American bank. There was also anxiety that Green was becoming too greedy. He had put together an impressive plan for M&S – to concentrate on the UK market, to bring a much-needed 'wow' factor to clothing, to sell some properties including the Baker Street head office and to sell off M&S's overseas businesses. Green knew that M&S could not be dismantled in the way Sears had been and would not yield the same kind of rapid takeover benefits. Although there was potential from its large property port-folio, financial services arm and drastic administrative savings, he was aware that he would have to play a long-term game. Indeed, in order to challenge his reputation as a 'bottom-fishing' opportunist who simply preyed on the weak, Green was quick to emphasise that M&S needed better management not dismembering.

But in return for putting the plan together, Green also wanted a large chunk of the financial gain. Some in his advisory team argued that he wanted too much, more than the City would be prepared to accept. According to one adviser: 'The financial terms were so hope-lessly greedy, his own take so enormous. He wanted to be creator, owner and driver.'[8] There was not only concern about Green's apparently excessive demands. His explosive and abrasive manner grated with many of the more traditional City types at DLJ and Merrill Lynch. On one occasion, it was reported that 'Margaret Young, a key member of the team, returned to the office in floods of tears following a difficult meeting with him.'[9] His candour may have been seen as refreshing in some quarters. In others it was viewed as bullying.

A few days after the newspaper revelations, executives at both the New York and London office, with the Kroll report in front of them, held an international conference call. Within an hour the executives agreed to pull the plug. It was an extraordinary decision, one triggered by multiple concerns. Shortly afterwards, Martin Smith, the chairman of DLJ in London, went to see Green in the office suite he kept at the Dorchester Hotel in Park Lane to break the news. True to form, Green 'pleaded, cajoled and lost his temper'.[10] But it was too late – the decision had been taken. The verbal outburst fell on deaf ears.

Green's hopes were crumbling. His and his wife's propriety had been questioned, his top financial backers had, unexpectedly, pulled out. The next day, 10 February, he accepted the inevitable and withdrew his bid.

Green liked to present his reason for pulling out as down to the underhand tactics of M&S and the barrage of negative press publicity they had so cleverly orchestrated. The reality was that once his banker had pulled out, he was left with little choice. His personal manner, one that clearly alienated some of those he needed on his side, had not helped.

As in the case of Amber Day, Green complained bitterly of 'old boys' clubs' and City bias, and it was true that he had never won the backing of the mainstream City players. On the other hand, his detractors could point out, he had never made a formal bid so his stalking was something of a phoney war. In fact, Green's raid was more substantive than M&S liked to claim. Shortly after he pulled the plug, Green claimed that he had been close to being able to mount a formal bid – that he had both a management team and the financing, a mix of cash and shares, in place. Indeed, WestLB confirmed that a consortium of banks, including Barclays Capital and the Industrial Bank of Japan, had raised close to £6 billion at that stage with the remainder to come from a share offering.[11] To have won backing on this kind of scale meant that he had been able to persuade the supporting banks that he had more than a few spreadsheets supporting his radical plans for M&S.

He told the *Independent* on the day after he pulled out, 'It is my prerogative to play or pass, and I don't need to stress myself with all this. I want to wake up in the morning feeling happy. I was waking up feeling grumpy.'[12] Green liked to claim he was shocked by the ferocity of the campaign against him, that while he expected a dirty war, he was surprised it came before a bid was on the table. Such complaints had to be treated with a large pinch of salt. Although Green employed no PR firm, he was neither naive nor innocent in the matter of spin and counter-spin. Nevertheless, it proved an experience that further soured Green's attitudes towards the City, and, as he put it, 'their whispering campaigns . . . people talking off-the-record in their posh accents'.[13]

Green was right about the whispering. At the time of the bid, rumours had been spreading in some small circles that Green was friendly with a woman called Aida Hersham, an attractive and elegant thirty-eight-year-old who was the divorced wife of a Mayfair estate agent called Gary Hersham. At this time she was living in a smart house in fashionable St John's Wood.

It was not until two years later that this was revealed in an article in the *Mail on Sunday*. According to the newspaper, Mrs Hersham had built up a significant personal holding in M&S in the weeks after Green had declared an interest. At one stage the stake was said to be worth some £200,000.[14] Although there would not have been anything legally untoward about such purchases, the revelation of the friendship and her dealing would undoubtedly have been embarrassing at such a decliate moment in a takeover bid.

Then, some fifteen months after the first article appeared, the *Mail on Sunday* returned to the issue with an article in which Green was quoted as saying that his friendship with Aida Hersham 'was a story that was known by my wife three years ago. I said I had a friendship . . . My wife is standing here. She knew about it. What's the issue?'[15]

The relief felt by M&S at their success was palpable. They had won the prolonged duel more easily than they might have hoped. But the mood of celebration could not disguise the fact that the company's more deep-seated problems could not be so easily dismissed.

To make things worse, one effect of Green's withdrawal was to push the share price down. Indeed, by the end of the day on 10 February, the share price had fallen 20p to finish at 233p – its lowest level for nine years. This put a valuation on the company of only £6.7 billion. Since reaching an all-time high of 664p in October 1997, M&S shares had dramatically underperformed the FTSE All Share index. Salsbury may no longer have had Green breathing down his neck, but he knew he was running out of time to deliver.

Brunswick emerged a little tarnished by the deal and ended up more in the spotlight than they would have liked. Alan Parker, Brunswick's boss and founder, refused to be drawn about his business in public, but privately he dismissed the allegations of dirty tricks and smear tactics. 'Brunswick fights tough but not dirty,' he said.[16] While the 'Three Musketeers' may have continued to deny any association with Green, they still had some tough explaining to do to their respective employers – Wal-Mart, Debenhams and Bass.

The lawyers acting for the two sides continued to wrangle for weeks over the way in which Green and his advisers had replied to the 212 notices, though mainly amongst themselves in an exchange of increasingly acid memos mostly about legal technicalities. In one letter, Slaughter & May wrote to Titmuss Sainer, 'Section 204 . . . requires disclosure where there is an agreement between two or more persons. You presumably accept that Mr Green is a person and that Mrs Green is a separate person?'[17] Titmuss Sainer were eventually forced to admit that 'the matter is not free from doubt'.[18]

The story did not end there. Green complained that both he and his wife continued to feel shocked and distressed by the high-level public allegations against them, which continued to rumble in press and City circles. Tina later described those days as amongst the worst days of her life. A few weeks later in March, she launched a libel action against the *Sunday Times* for defamation.[19] The paper recognised that the story had been overblown, accepted that Tina had done nothing wrong and agreed to issue an apology and correction, which they duly did on 23 April. Green had not been consulted and was livid with rage over the wording of the apology, which he claimed was inadequate and insincere. He was also incensed by the fact it was placed at the bottom of page two of the paper when the original article was carried prominently on the front page.

To make matters worse, Green's lawyers had found that the original article was still, inadvertently, being carried on the paper's website, despite the company accepting responsibility for the error. This made Green even more determined to press on with the legal action, according to one participant, to 'take the paper to the cleaners'. The matter dragged on for over a year with the two sides unable to agree on the level of damages, which Green had promised to give to a charity of his choice.

Then suddenly, in the early summer of 2001 and apparently out of the blue, the Green camp moved from their bullish stance to wanting a settlement. Green eventually settled in July 2001 for a sum in the region of £100,000, much less than the sum he had been seeking. (He also settled with the *Observer* around the same time.[20]) As Green's legal costs would have been close to this amount, he would have been able to give barely anything to charity in the way of damages, and thus achieved little or nothing financially for his eighteen months of litigation.

Chapter 8

THE STEAL OF THE CENTURY

The day after Green pulled the plug on his attempt on M&S, there was little left to do in London, so he abandoned his suite at the Dorchester Hotel and returned to Monaco. You can understand why. The Mediterranean principality has a lot of attractions, and not just the climate. For those who can afford it, it is only a short helicopter ride from Geneva, Paris and Rome. The mountains on the Italian border are close enough to allow a morning's skiing. With its vast marina, its private clubs and expensive restaurants, it has become a playground for the super-rich, who as Monaco residents pay no income, wealth, capital gains or inheritance taxes. There are few better places in the world to flaunt your wealth and Green had plenty to flaunt.

Waiting for him was his £8 million hilltop penthouse apartment overlooking the Mediterranean, his £20 million custom-built Benetti yacht, *Lionheart*, and a navy Bentley (Tina had a matching baby-blue model). This helped to distinguish them from the Rolls-Royce owners which are often seen in the daily traffic jams that clog Monaco's small streets. He was also able to indulge his love of gambling in one of the most famous, and stylish, casinos in the world – Monte Carlo. Since the Greens had moved to Monaco two years earlier in 1998, they had built up a range of friends, mostly fellow members of the super-rich club. Chloë and Brandon attended a local international school. Green played tennis with Prince Albert of Monaco and enjoyed lunching with other new economic exiles such as David and Simon Reuben, the billionaire metal traders. A committed Tottenham fan, he was also sometimes seen with Irving Scholar, who also had a Monaco home. Tom Hunter, who had a house in nearby Cap Ferrat, was another frequent visitor.

One of Green's popular haunts was the nineteenth-century Hotel de Paris, conveniently situated opposite the casino, and an elite hangout for the new and old rich alike. When they were not hiding from the world in their fortress on the tiny Channel Island of Brecqhou, the Barclay brothers were also lunchtime regulars at the hotel where they always chose the same table, rarely talking to anyone as they sipped coffee or aperitifs, read the English newspapers and listened to the hotel's pianist playing Frank Sinatra hits from the 1940s. Green also liked to lunch at superchef Alain Ducasse's Michelin three-star restaurant, Le Louis XV, where meals cost upwards of £1,000. It was also a favourite restaurant of Monaco's ageing ruler Prince Rainier before he died.

Apart from the obvious attractions, there is another reason why Monaco, a mini-state with its tiny population of 60,000, has become a magnet for millionaires and increasingly, billionaires. It is one of the world's most accessible tax havens. As one long-term British tax exile explained, 'Monaco has style, grace and charm – Marbella does not. Besides, where else is there to go? Switzerland is too cold, the Bahamas too far.' The mini-nation is crawling with international banks and financial and tax experts to help the rich get around international tax laws.

The French have started calling Monaco '*le rocher Anglais*' – the English rock – because of the estimated 5,000 Britons who have chosen to live there. They are now the third biggest group of foreign nationals after the French and the Italians and close in numbers to the 6,000 native Monegasques. There are seventeen flights a day from London to Nice airport and then it is a one-hour drive along the hair-raising coastal road, or a ten-minute helicopter ride. Although the British residents include a number of famous names such as Shirley Bassey, Roger Moore and Ringo Starr, known locally as Ringo Monaco, most are new quick-rich British businessmen who simply fly into Britain for a day or two a week to run their companies and then fly back.

Green spent February and March of that year in Monaco, playing Monopoly and table tennis with his family and brushing shoulders with other residents. But he was far from inactive. He does not enjoy reading and is not the sort of man to lie around on a sunlounger longer than necessary to maintain his tan. Between attempts to break the bank at Monte Carlo, trips in his yacht and entertaining his friends, he was plotting his next move. M&S may have been the asset Green most wanted to acquire, but this did not prevent him looking elsewhere. This time he settled on British Home Stores.

The high street chain was not in the same league as M&S. It had 154 stores compared with 375 and less than a fifth of its turnover. It had never achieved anything like the same level of national esteem. With its dowdy, uninspiring reputation it had always had to live in M&S's shadow. Nevertheless it was Britain's fifth largest retail chain with some £800 million in annual sales and enjoyed 2.1 per cent of the clothing market. The store had been founded in 1928 in Brixton in south London where it sold light fittings and food. Conveniently, its headquarters in Marylebone Road was only one block away from M&S headquarters in Baker Street.

For Green it would have been an acceptable consolation prize. In 1986, it had become part of the Conran group when Sir Terence Conran acquired the store and Mothercare and renamed the trio – Habitat, Mothercare and BHS – as Storehouse. Under Conran, however, the chain suffered a declining market share, the result of the changing shopping habits of its core customers who had been steadily seduced by the newer arrivals. Despite his proven skill at design, which he used to improve the look of the stores, Conran failed to develop a successful strategy for a pile-it-high-sell-it-cheap business. The increasingly aware British shopper did not want to be seen with a BHS carrier bag.

Always a slightly odd jumble of stores, Conran later kept Habitat but sold Mothercare and BHS in 1996. Alan Smith, a former M&S director, became chairman of Storehouse. But the combination of Mothercare and BHS proved a nightmare to run, and BHS's somewhat bland reputation was difficult to discard. In the six months to October 1999, the stores incurred losses of £8 million. As one retail watcher remembers, 'BHS looked as if it had no future. It was heading down the toilet, had become a tarnished brand, and with the cost base he inherited, Smith couldn't make it pay.'[1]

BHS was hardly the only under-performing high street retailer at the time. The second half of the 1990s had proved something of a watershed for British retailing. While Tesco, Asda, Next and Matalan were leading the way, other more established and less adept retailers were struggling. These included not just Storehouse and Marks & Spencer but also House of Fraser, Sainsbury's, Safeway and Arcadia. The nation's big-name retailers had been the victims of a lethal mix of over-capacity, price deflation, intensifying competition and increasingly fickle customers. Although the new-blood retailers were breathing down the necks of the once dominant old guard, the typical response had been boardroom complacency and arrogance, which simply added to the problems. This attitude was perhaps exemplified by M&S where there was, as Sir David Sieff once put it, 'a creeping culture of arrogance and too many egos at play'.[2]

BHS was a classic example of the type of business Green liked to stalk. It was under-performing, and successive management teams had been unable to make it work. Most of the despairing shareholders were only too happy to see it go at the best price they could get. Again Green spotted the opportunity to buy it on the cheap, strip it down and make a killing.

Knowing that BHS, now rebranded Bhs, was ripe as a takeover target, the Storehouse board decided in November that the best strategy was to split the group, retaining Mothercare but selling Bhs. It effectively put the store up for auction and in the New Year began discussions with several potential bidders. On 17 March 2000, Smith took the day off to celebrate his fifty-ninth birthday, confident that, with the negotiations proceeding, a deal was just around the corner. But his optimism was premature. A few days later, the two principal bidders, Iceland, the grocery chain, and Brown & Jackson, owner of the Poundstretcher discount chain, both pulled out of takeover talks, partly because they had become nervous after scrutinising the books.

Green, meanwhile, was watching events closely. It is at such moments of vulnerability that he likes to strike. He had had his eye on Storehouse for years, and despite once dismissing it as a 'dog', had indeed considered moving on the group the previous year before settling on M&S. It had a key asset that appealed to Green – a large property portfolio in prime high street locations.

Green knew Smith and on 22 March, less than six weeks after he had been effectively forced to drop his interest in M&S, he phoned him from his yacht on the Côte d'Azur. At that time Green did not fly back and forth between London and his home unless it was strictly necessary. He was not yet in the private jet class. Another of those he had contacted was Robin Saunders at WestLB. In the months since they had begun working together on M&S, her reputation had continued to grow. She promised she could put a deal together in days.

Green now had a personal fortune of around £140 million, most of it tied up in his existing stores like MK One but up to £40 million of which had come from his piece-by-piece break-up of Sears. He was prepared to put some £20 million of his own money into the deal. The rest he planned to borrow, some from WestLB and some from Barclays Capital. His old friend and partner Tom Hunter also agreed to commit a small stake. As good as her word, Saunders completed the financing package for British Home Stores in seventy-two hours. For management back-up, Green once again approached Allan Leighton and Terry Green, two of the former 'Three Musketeers' with whom he had stalked M&S. Both agreed to be part of the management team if the deal came off.

One of Green's own golden business rules is that you should always meet the opposition on home ground. At the time, that meant the Dorchester. The week after his first phone call from his yacht, Green met Alan Smith at his suite at the top Mayfair hotel. Green liked to conduct the principal negotiations himself, as one of his aphorisms went: 'Do not leave two lawyers in a room on their own – they will only have an argument.'[3] The deal proved a lot more straightforward than his bid for M&S. Green was blunt with Smith from the outset. He offered him a take-it-or-leave-it deal of around £200 million and a deadline. Smith had four days for his reply and Green would not wait a minute longer.

This did not prove to be an issue. Smith and the principal shareholders regarded Bhs as a millstone around the Storehouse neck and were eager to sell – maybe too eager. Smith grabbed the deal with open arms, agreeing to sell the business for the sum on the table. The deal was sealed in mid-May 2000, barely four months after the M&S bid had been aborted and less than a year since Green had dismantled Sears. British Home Stores had been a public company for seventy years but was now being taken private.

Green held 94 per cent of the equity while Tom Hunter had a 5 per cent stake. Robin Saunders had also invested some of her own money in the deal and held a 0.5 per cent stake, as did another colleague at WestLB.

The deal may well have been welcomed by the Storehouse board, but others had serious concerns, not least the 14,000 staff. Green was widely expected to pull the same trick as he had at Sears, splitting the company up, selling the stores and making off with a quick and easy profit. But this was not what Green had in mind. He had in fact reassured Smith that the store and the staff would be safe in his hands. Green was now out to demonstrate that he had a nose for retail, that he could run as well as dismantle a business. He was in effect putting himself to the test. Could he turn a loss-making chain around in a ferociously competitive mid-market with Matalan to the left of him and M&S to the right? The whole retail trade would be watching closely with as many willing him to fail as wanting him to succeed. Proving his detractors wrong was the sort of challenge in which he revelled.

Green made it clear that, for the first three months, he would run the store himself, giving him time to study the operation before moving in new management. Of course, he had done the same with Sears. So he bent over backwards this time to give reassurance that he had no plans to dismantle the company: 'It's a matter of evolution not revolution.'[4]

Like most of his deals, this one was quick. Other onlookers may have written Bhs off, but Green was confident that he had got a bargain even though he always claimed he had bought it 'blind', that he knew little about the company and its operation and had only visited two of the stores. 'The deal was done on bits of paper,' he claimed. It may have been a typical Green gamble – it was making a loss on its most recent trading – but it was also a calculated one. He had put up only a limited amount of his own money and the banks would have borne most of the initial risk. The deal also came with an effective 'exit' strategy – if things went badly wrong the stores could be sold to pay off the liabilities.

Wherever Green moved, of course, the sniping would soon follow. His purchase of Bhs was no exception. Green's detractors had rubbished his attempt on the Marks & Spencer citadel. For them, it was bad news for any chain to fall into his hands. While his deal-making and asset-stripping skills were legendary, a big question mark remained over what he would make of a chain as a retailer.

Takeovers often bring plenty of surprises for the new owners. This one was no different. When Green walked into the store's Marylebone headquarters shortly after he had bought it, he realised why Smith was so eager to clinch a deal. The trading situation turned out to be worse than he had expected. He announced that the store was overloaded with stock and many of the fashion lines were proving hard to shift. It sounded like a ready-made excuse for failure.

Green arrived with a reputation as a difficult boss, a cost-cutter who would not hesitate to unload what he saw as surplus or under-performing staff. Despite the assurances he had given, however, the staff – from shop-floor sales to middle management – were inevitably apprehensive about what Green had in mind.

They would soon find out. As he wandered round the flagship Oxford Street store on his first day as the new boss, staff were shouted at and the clothes dismissed as 'utter rubbish, like fancy dress and that's being unkind to fancy dress'.[5] Green threatened to tear the garments off the racks and shred them. It was too late to do anything about the existing stock, but he was determined to do something about the clothes on order.

Soon after arriving, he found that a £6 million order was shortly to be delivered. Green phoned the supplier, inviting him to meet the new boss and bring sample items from the range with him. When the somewhat nervous supplier arrived, he was asked to display the clothes around the boardroom. With garments strewn across the room, Green turned to the man, 'Right, we're going to buy it all over again.' The supplier responded, 'What do you mean? You've already bought it.' To which Green responded, 'Yeah, but just for a bit of fun, let's buy it again.' Green inspected the items one by one and turned to the supplier, offering him an unenviable choice: '"Look, this is where we think we are. You deliver the £6 million of goods, you get a cheque and don't come back. Or let's get in the real world and help me understand why I would pay, for instance, £9 for something that's worth £4." So we went through it all again. We got some discounts, we got some money back. We got a more intelligent understanding of the way forward.'[6]

This was characteristic of the way Green likes to do business – his way or not at all. Taking on the suppliers was critical to his strategy. 'Discipline' was how he sometimes put it. Green's view, according to one expert, was that 'he'd regard a contract made under the previous management as one he was not bound by and as the master of negotiation, he would be convinced he could better it'.[7] When asked, Green did not accept that he had crossed the line between being a tough negotiator and a bully. 'Do I use my seat to bully people? No, I don't. Would I phone someone to get a better price? Yes, I would. I don't phone all the time. If you phone occasionally, it's more likely they'll accommodate me for the sake of ongoing business.'[8] Now suppliers and staff both knew what Green's arrival meant. Such behaviour may be questionable but it is not that uncommon for new proprietors to renegotiate contracts that have already been agreed. Other stores under new management have followed similar practices, and supermarkets, in particular, have a long history of bullying their suppliers. Green certainly never feels bound by rules and being tough with suppliers is part of the reason for his success. As one close associate admitted: 'You don't get where he is without being a bastard.'[9]

By June, Green was proclaiming that the chain still had £60 million worth of summer frocks left. 'We had 10,000 little dresses – the sort of thing Pocahontas would wear. We couldn't sell any of them.' Even massive discounts only shifted some of them. The pre-purchased autumn and winter stock was not much better. Green found, for example, that the previous buying director had bought masses of coats in green and burgundy, ordered nine months earlier: 'It was stuff that wasn't good enough for floor mats.' Green certainly liked to portray the company as in a mess and the task to turn it around as an uphill struggle involving endless long days and nights, 'an assault course, six months of torture'.[10]

Green is a hands-on boss but when he found out the state that Bhs appeared to be in, he quickly called on trusted colleagues to help. Elaine Gray, chief executive of MK One, was asked to help review the business. He also brought in a new finance director, Paul Coackley, who had previously spent eleven years at Sears.

Green soon started his expected shake-up of Bhs's top management. As the truth about the state of the store and the saleability of the stock became apparent, few of them survived. New buyers were poached from Arcadia and River Island. In October, Saunders and Hunter were both made non-executive directors of the company along with a senior executive at Barclays Capital. In the same month, Terry Green, one of the 'Three Musketeers', left Debenhams to become chief executive. Then, in November, another of the 'Musketeers', Allan Leighton, stood down as the successful chief executive of Wal-Mart Europe, the owner of Asda, to become chairman.

Allan Leighton and Terry Green were seen by Green as his retail 'dream team'. Both had strong track records helping to revive the ailing Asda and Debenhams respectively. On the other hand, Leighton by then had become known as a serial director – he had several other directorships on top of Bhs. Although he denied he had 'spread himself too thinly' he was also chairman of Lastminute.com and on the boards of BSkyB, Leeds United, Scottish Power, Dyson and several others.

More importantly, the three now running Bhs were all men with giant egos and robust temperaments. As one who knew all three put it, 'I can't see how it will last. Terry and Allan are used to running their own shows. If Philip was in partnership with God, God would have to play second fiddle.'[11] Initially, however, the trio worked well, though clashes were inevitable and it was Allan Leighton who often had to play the role of referee. Despite the epic rows, which Philip always won, the three men presided over a massive shake-up in the way the company was run.

Although Green likes to deny it, Richard Caring, one of his closest friends, also played a central role in the attempts to transform Bhs. If Terry Green and Allan Leighton ran the business, Caring was Green's key adviser on the products. He was brought in the moment Green acquired the chain, given a desk at Bhs headquarters and handed the crucial role of helping with a series of 'range reviews' with buyers.

As the owner of International Clothing Designs, a huge international network of clothing factories, Caring is known as the 'Mr Sourcing' of fashion, and has been one of Bhs's principal suppliers of women's clothes. He also supplies M&S and Next and is amongst those who have had the most influence on what the British wear. A highly private man, he is little known outside the rag-trade, however. The *Sunday Times* Rich List 2005 estimated him to be worth £300 million.[12] He lives in Hampstead with his wife Jackie and two adult children in a mansion described by estate agents as the 'most expensive new home in Britain'; it includes a cinema, a ballroom, a thirty-seat dining room, a vast wine cellar and a lake in the two-acre garden. He also has homes dotted around the world. Like Green, Caring has a strong work ethic, inherited from his father, and Green was said never to have made a move in retail without Caring's backing. Some say the two were inseparable.

Green's primary emphasis at the new Bhs was on cutting costs, and having spent a good deal of his business history running discount stores, he knew how to do it. One retail insider tells the story of how, when he knew that Green had clinched the chain, he popped into his local Putney branch of Bhs a week before Green took charge and then again a week later. Unsurprisingly, nothing had changed apart from one thing – the lighting had been turned down. As he described the store, 'It seemed as if a third or more of the lights had been turned off. You couldn't see. It was like a morgue.'[13]

Neill Denny, then editor of *Retail Week*, said he would not have been surprised if this was the case: 'Green would be looking for ways to save money and, with his attention to detail, would have looked at all the operating costs for potential savings. He might well have turned down the lights, or even the heating a fraction to save £10,000 a year.'[14] There was certainly no shortage of cost-saving measures. Changing the coat-hanger supplier, for example, saved the company as much as £400,000.

Green also set out to improve the previously slow and cumbersome decision-making process. This was made easier by being the country's largest private retailer. As a result he didn't have to defer to shareholders and could move more quickly than his rivals. Green spent a good deal of time on the shop floor himself, masterminding the changes, getting to know the stock, talking to customers and sometimes bawling at staff.

Within a year of taking over, with the last of the old stock sold or cleared and the new merchandise in place, sales and turnover started to pick up. In May 2001, Green announced that profits had increased to £31.5 million. 'The steal of the century' was how he described it. A year later, in May 2002, Green made another highly public announcement that profits had risen threefold to reach £100.2 million, the highest level in the company's history, while all the loans had been paid off. Green had, apparently, done it again. He had bought what proved to be an undervalued company – but one locked in what he called 'the Dark Ages' – re-mortgaged a handful of stores, repaid his backers in full and pocketed a pretty handy profit. This time there was one crucial difference. He had kept the company intact.

Being forced to pull out of M&S may have been galling at the time, but it appeared to have done Green a big favour in the wealth stakes. In his early thirties, Green's CV added up to little more than a string of failed businesses. By his early forties, he was worth a few million pounds through the sale of Jean Jeanie and the cashing in of Amber Day shares. Now, just a month after his lavish and much derided fiftieth birthday party, he was declared by the *Sunday Times* Rich List to be the thirteenth richest person in Britain with a fortune of £1.2 billion.[15]

This was as a result of the near five-fold increase in the potential selling price of Bhs. For Green, this was the best birthday present of all and a firm answer to his critics. He could bask in the glory of being a member of a very exclusive group – the British billionaire's club, a mix of aristocrats, entrepreneurs and tax exiles with a membership of only twenty-one people in 2002. Other members of the 'club' included the Duke of Westminster and Earl Cadogan, both of whom own acres of prime urban land in the heart of central London; Bernie Ecclestone and his wife Slavica, the owners of Formula One motor racing; Hans Rausing, the Swedish businessman who made his fortune from his global milk and food carton business, Tetra Laval; and Lord Sainsbury, the supermarket chain owner and Labour minister.

Moreover, Green had moved from a few million to a billion in less than a decade. This was not only electric speed by both contemporary and historical standards, it was the fastest billion in British history. Green first made an appearance on the Rich List in 2000 at 216th place with an estimated personal wealth of £140 million. In 2001, he leapt fifty-seven places to reach 159th position with an assumed fortune of £200 million.

Over the next year, Green's fortune was estimated to have increased sixfold (at least on paper) and in the process he leapfrogged a number of well-known members of Britain's wealthy elite. He was, for example, now richer than Richard Branson, Viscount Rothermere and the international steel magnate Lakshmi Mittal. He had also outstripped some of his former business colleagues, including the Barclay twins and Tom Hunter, and most of his Monaco neighbours, too.

One of those he had passed on the way up was Alan Sugar, another fast-talking, direct, wheeler-dealing north London Jewish entrepreneur who had also left school at sixteen. He had made his money largely out of computers and property. Sugar and Green were not exactly bosom pals, but they knew each other, had a common interest in Spurs as well as being fellow members of the rich club and, according to Sugar, used to have a 'chinwag' when they bumped into each other.

In June 2002, Sugar wrote a somewhat petulant article for the *Evening Standard* suggesting that he was now being snubbed by the Bhs owner: 'Recently when I bumped into him at the Dorchester, I got a very regal down-your-nose look and was then ignored. This must be because he is worth £1.3 billion and feels he does not have to talk to anyone unless they are in the top thirty of the *Sunday Times* Rich List.' In the same article he also criticised Green for his public

announcement of Bhs's profit levels. Being a private company he
certainly didn't have to do this:

> Why, one asks, does anybody who dislikes the pomp and circumstance
> of the City so much publicly announce company results when he does
> not have to? . . . One can only assume this is a way of letting his fans or
> hangers-on know what a great businessman he is. Phil, take it from
> this East End boy and all of your north London groupies: we love
> what you have done, we got the message a long time ago you are
> shrewd, you are a dealmaker extraordinaire, we are all proud of you . . .
> If you see me out next time, at least give me a nod, put out your hand
> for me to kiss and spare a thought for us mere fractional billionaire
> mortals.[16]

The turnaround at Bhs was certainly a spectacular business success
story. And Green loved to crow about it. As he repeatedly pointed out,
his rivals and City critics may have sneered at him for buying Bhs, but,
even if the financial risk to him was smaller than he liked to imply, he
was the man who took the gamble and made it work. He was particularly forthright about company chief executives: 'The fundamental
difference between me and all those tossers running public companies is that I invest my own money. I stand or fall on my decisions.'[17]
Of course, luck played a part. Smith chose to sell Bhs just a few months
before the withdrawal of Dutch group C&A from the UK. C&A was one
of Bhs's principal competitors, especially in womenswear, and its
removal provided a gaping hole in the market which Bhs was well
placed to fill.

The rise in profits, however, could be explained mainly by two
critical factors: firstly, through Green's ability to wring better deals
from suppliers; and secondly, by a dramatic shake-up in the way Bhs
sourced its goods. Green cut out the wholesaler and started buying
from suppliers directly. BHS had been one of a declining number of
stores to continue to rely heavily on middlemen, which greatly added
to costs. Green, of course, would have known before he bought the
group that there would be plenty of potential for cutting the costs of
supply. Retail consultant Robert Clark calls the return to profitability
'an easy win' because of the significant cost reductions from buying
direct.[18] Green had been one of the first retailers to turn to direct
contact with cheaper overseas suppliers and had built up connections
around the world. But Green got very annoyed by any implication that
turning round Bhs had been easy. On the contrary, he liked to protest,

trading was dire when he bought it and recovery had required a huge amount of effort and skill.

Together with his new hirings, he negotiated new relationships with suppliers, especially in Central and Eastern Europe, and also some in the UK, focusing on those that could deliver new orders much more quickly than the company's traditional suppliers. This enabled Bhs to make much quicker buying decisions instead of second-guessing the market up to nine months in advance, and enabled faster turnover. Gradually a whole range of new clothes started to displace the stock he had inherited. There were fewer items more carefully displayed. Green was targeting Bhs's core middle market of women aged forty to fifty-five with new fashionable but traditional ranges aimed at a mass rather than what he saw as a series of minority fashion markets. Within eighteen months, sales in womenswear – which crucially accounts for a third of all Bhs sales – had risen. Sales elsewhere, on the other hand, were not nearly so impressive.

The shake-up also showed his undoubted rag-trade skills. He liked to describe the business jokingly as 'the second oldest profession' of which he was a master. He liked to boast that he knew everything about the business from 'buying the fabrics to putting the zippers in'. He claimed that at Bhs he knew the origin, cost and sales of every item on every rack. He certainly impressed his staff at all levels with his depth and spread of knowledge. As one who knows him puts it, 'He does his homework. He visits the suppliers, gets to know them, knows what's going on.'[19]

He was also always quick to respond to customer whims. If he spotted a bad line in the sales figures, he would put them on offer the next day. New internal layouts and window displays were introduced. Bhs was the first store to ditch clothes from the window and replace them with large posters of clothes and prices. The new layouts, designs, special offers and even the numbers on the price tags were all influenced by Green. He was sometimes spotted helping shelf stackers during closing hours, and occasionally used to visit his Oxford Street stores after midnight, occasionally with Tina, demand to be let in by the security guard to check if everything was in place, and would even move displays and racks around: 'You get a different perspective when the shop's empty.'[20] If there was anything untoward he would be on the phone at 8 a.m. the next morning to the store manager or the section head. On one occasion he found a cushion wrongly marked with a reduced sticker. The culprit was found the next morning.[21] Tina has also acted as a kind of 'mystery shopper', popping into stores to check if mistakes had been rectified.

Although the steady transformation of Bhs had Green's finger-prints all over it, he also relied heavily on his managers, designers and buyers. Both Leighton and Terry Green, along with some of the senior managers he brought in, played a big part in the recovery. Of course, attracting able retailers was no flash in the pan – it was a sign of just how much his currency had risen since Amber Day.

Although he likes to get involved in the range reviews for most of the 5,000 lines sold in the store and certainly has a real feel for many products, he is not a style guru. When it comes to fashion trends, he generally relies on his buyers. One reason Green has proved popular with some staff is because he has given them responsibility at a relatively young age. Green is happy to delegate decisions about taste but insists on final approval of most of the clothing products. He does of course sometimes overrule his teams. He is also the one who clinches the deals with suppliers. On non-clothing items, he is happy to delegate and Tina has helped with homeware.

Not only did Green move swiftly to alter the supply arrangements, he did a lot of the negotiating himself. He was, according to Neill Denny, the 'master of smart buying', a skill he had built up pains-takingly over nearly two decades in the trade. Denny describes Green as 'the best at what he does, and what he does is market trading on a giant scale. He sources the goods as cheaply as possible, and sells on at the best margin. He's the purest natural retailer I've dealt with. He buys cheap and sells expensive.'[22]

He also rewards success. He expects his staff to follow his culture of aggressive buying, to achieve tough targets, and rewards junior managers and the top tier accordingly through a generous bonus scheme.

On joining Bhs, his two top henchmen, Allan Leighton and Terry Green, were on highly incentivised deals. When Green was asked how much Leighton was being paid, he replied: 'He's working for love.'[23] When the first accounts were published, however, it was revealed that director remuneration had more than doubled from £2.9 million in 2001 to £7.3 million in 2002. Leighton had been paid a total of £1.6 million, most of which was a performance-related bonus.[24]

But although his top executives were well paid they still knew their place. In March 2002, Eric Musgrave, editor of *Drapers*, had written a flattering editorial about Green's achievements at Bhs: 'His abrasive attitude and colourful language may not be to everyone's taste, but credit where credit is due. The man knows his clothing and that is the heart of his success . . . Green's success is his feel for the product, attention to detail and single-minded drive to get the business where he wanted it to be.'[25] Musgrave's reward was to be invited over to lunch with Green at Bhs. The two men were joined by Terry Green. Musgrave recalls the lunch as being highly revealing about the men's relationship. 'Philip dominated the conversation, and Terry said virtually nothing apart from, "Yes, no, you're right, Philip." It may have been different behind the scenes, but in public, for someone with Terry's tough reputation, he came over as somewhat overawed by his boss.'

As some predicted, this dream team could not last. After a year in post, Leighton announced that he was scaling back his involvement. In late 2001, Terry Green, who had missed out on bonuses at Debenhams by leaving to join Bhs and was now in search of his own fortune, offered Green a £700 million buy-out for the business with the backing of a venture capitalist company. But Green did not want to sell, even though it would have made him a tidy profit of £500 million for a little over a year's work.

It was not a real surprise after this that Terry Green left somewhat prematurely, in June 2002. Although the departure was said to be amicable, some commentators believe that Philip had changed his mind about Terry. True or not, he still left with a generous £909,000 pay-off.[26] A few months later, he negotiated a deal to buy Allders and took it private. Paul Coackley, Green's trusted finance director, took over as chief operating officer.

Green's methods may have brought results but they also continued to surround him in controversy. When record profits were announced in May 2002, he seized the opportunity to pay a record dividend alongside them – a total of £175 million. Green's share of this was £164.5 million, Hunter's £8.8 million and Saunders's and her co-investor at WestLB, £1.7 million between them.

The payout earned Green the nickname 'the £500,000-a-day man' but it also raised eyebrows since the dividend greatly exceeded the actual profit. Had this been a public company the shareholders would have questioned it. This, of course, is why Green made Bhs a private company. The gap would have been even greater if Green hadn't sold a number of properties, which netted a profit of some £65 million. The properties were sold to Carmen Properties Ltd, an offshore company owned by his own family, and then leased back to Bhs. In this way Green and his family received rental income (of some £12 million in 2003) from the deal. He had in effect arranged a sale and leaseback deal with himself, meaning that he held on to the asset while the income flowed between his own firms.[27]

Ever since his successful legal action against the *Sunday Times* and the *Observer* over Tina's share dealings in M&S, Green had loved to brag how he had taken money off the papers and more recently, the *Independent on Sunday.* Despite his litigious reputation, the *Guardian* newspaper decided it was time to put Green's claims to the test. Was Bhs really worth £1 billion? Was the miracle turnaround as great as it looked?

The paper asked Ian Griffiths, an accountant and former City editor of the *Independent*, to take a look at Bhs's published accounts. Because of their somewhat opaque nature, the paper's financial editor, Paul Murphy, who knew Green, rang him with some queries. Green exploded with rage. As Murphy recalls: 'I received a torrent of expletive-ridden abuse over the phone. It went on the whole day. Green kept ringing back, refused to co-operate, threatened to sue the paper and reminded me that he had taken money off other papers. And it didn't end there. It went on for another three days with Green continuing to ring, hurling abuse and issuing more threats.'[28] It was extraordinary behaviour for such a high-profile businessman.

Despite the threats, the *Guardian* proceeded to publish an article by Ian Griffiths. In a somewhat technical analysis, he found that Green had certainly performed an impressive turnaround of the company but raised some important queries about the way the accounts were presented, about the declared level of profits and about the actual value of the company. As well as Griffiths's sober analysis, the paper also published detailed extracts from the telephone exchanges with Green, some of which had been recorded.

In one exchange, Green said: 'I don't want to deal with some dickhead, ex-*Independent* journalist that can't read . . . Jesus Christ. Robin Saunders and Chris Coles are on my board. Allan Leighton is my chairman. I've got a fucking audit committee that I am not on. And Ian

Griffiths, some old c**t from the *Independent*, knows more than all these people. Please. Go and write about someone else.'[29]

To make matters worse for Green, during the exchanges, he had laid into Paul Murphy, saying: 'He can't read English. Mind you, he is a fucking Irishman.' In fact, he was born in Oldham and raised in Portsmouth. This comment was also splashed all over the front page of the paper and eagerly repeated elsewhere. Irish newspapers and the London-based Irish Centre demanded an apology from Green while threatening a boycott of his stores.

The morning of publication, Green was being interviewed by the BBC's news presenter Michael Buerk at a high-profile retail conference. Needless to say, the question and answer session was dominated by the *Guardian* articles. It might have been thought that Green would back off and attempt to limit the damage, but no. He continued to rail against the paper openly. Continuing to attack the press in this way was perhaps not the best way to defuse the controversy. An individual who knew him well commented at the time, 'He's started to love his own profile.'[30]

Behind the scenes, his close colleagues and friends tried to calm him down and urged him to draw a line under the affair. But Green would not let it drop. It was typical Green. As Murphy explains, 'He seemed to believe everybody was on his payroll.' The paper kept the story going with another front-page splash the following day with a photo of Green and the caption, 'Threat of consumer boycott leads to Bhs owner issuing apology to the Irish.'

Green was left with little choice but to issue a series of embarrassing climbdowns for his remarks, and spent the best part of a week ringing a widespread group of Irish acquaintances looking for advice. It might be wondered why Green doesn't appoint PR advisers to do this for him, but he has always resented the fees PR companies and City firms charge.

Those he turned to for help included Eddie Jordan, Arthur Ryan, the boss of Penneys, Dermot Desmond, the veteran financier and chairman of Celtic football club, and his Monaco neighbour Michael Smurfit, the owner of a Dublin-based international packaging business. It was an impressive list. What they also had in common, of course, was that they were all multi-millionaires. When Green added that 'some of my best friends are Irish', others were quick to point out that what it really meant was that some of Green's best friends were rich.

'My PA is Irish, my driver is Irish, my security staff are Irish, I am not a racist,' cried Green to the *Sunday Tribune*. Many of those he contacted jumped to his defence, including Ryan, one of the most successful figures in Irish retailing: 'I could not speak highly enough of the man, he is a wonderful, exceptional character . . . a legend in retailing.'[31] High praise indeed but then Green had sold sixteen stores to the retailer two years before when Ryan was expanding his Primark chain in the UK.

Green eventually issued an apology to representatives of the Irish community in Britain but refused to speak to *Guardian* journalists for months. By questioning the true value of Green's empire, the newspaper certainly seemed to have touched a raw nerve.

Journalists were used to being at the end of his temper if he did not like their stories. He once asked a national newspaper journalist, 'How old are you, son?' to be told he was twenty-three. 'If you want to live to be twenty-four, you'd better stop writing like that about me.'[32] And on another occasion: 'Don't you think I know where you journalists get your stuff from? Tell that lanky streak of piss that if he spreads any more of this stuff around, I'll come round and see him.'[33]

In the drawer of an antique cabinet he keeps in his office at Bhs is a batch of black T-shirts with the caption 'You are the weakest link – Goodbye.' 'I sometimes get them out at buyers' meetings,' he tells visitors. 'They concentrate the mind.'[34] All this is typical Green. To his supporters it is just part of his DNA; to his detractors it is uncouth, vulgar and counter-productive.

Such behaviour is something of a shock to those with no previous dealings with Green. Those who know him, on the other hand, have learnt that this is his own way of putting things. One senior financial journalist who has been on the receiving end of Green's ire a number of times describes his own ticking-offs: 'I've never really felt threatened, it's just the way he behaves. He's usually quite jovial about the fact he's never going to get anything very positive out of me. It's not really on the Maxwellian scale.'[35]

Green may have put fear into some, but he also has a mischievous side with a schoolboy sense of humour and a fondness for pranks. He often used to ring rival retailers in London from his yacht in the French Riviera and tease them with remarks such as, 'Still working, then?' He certainly had a quick sense of irony. When asked in May 2002 after the profit announcement if he planned to float Bhs to raise some cash, he quickly replied, 'Milkmen have floats.'

Green also induces mixed reaction amongst staff and colleagues. Some senior staff like his infectious enthusiasm and his relentless energy, or at least claim to. Romney Drury, brought in from Arcadia as the Bhs marketing manager, has said, 'I'd heard all the rumours. He was seen as being a bit of a scary character, but he's really not turned out that way. He's very straight, you get answers right away and get on with it.' Managers certainly liked the passion he brought to the business and the speed with which he took decisions, launching promotions without delay and making commitments to product lines. He is also a 'brilliant motivator' according to one colleague.[36] He is also widely admired for his memory, his recall and attention to detail.

Others have been more critical. Some senior staff have complained that he runs Bhs like a medieval barony, threatening to fire people and shouting at them, and that his mood is unpredictable. Sometimes he is funny, generous and very good company, almost childlike in his delight at small triumphs. But when things go wrong he can be explosive. One former senior executive at Bhs says working for him was a nightmare: 'It took me twenty-four hours to realise that he took all the decisions. He's probably the best retailer there is but he's a monster, totally politically incorrect. We had board meetings but they were just a formality. Nothing was decided then; that all happened day to day with Philip. It's like doing business with Conan the Barbarian – he always gets what he wants.' Another manager commented: 'He puts the fear of God into me but everything he says makes perfect sense.'[37] He once took an under-performing store manager aside and told him, 'I want you to look in the mirror every day and call yourself a c**t.'[38]

Green's style was certainly not for everyone at Bhs. Only about 25 per cent of head office staff there when he arrived were still there two years on while about 40 per cent of the supply chain had changed as well. It is the survivors who sing his praises, of course.

Although he likes to take the mickey out of others and gives the impression that he doesn't give a fig about what people think, he in fact has a pretty thin skin. One journalist explained that over lunch on one occasion he 'spent the whole time telling me how brilliant he was. I'm good at product, I'm good at property, I'm good at finance, I can put deals together. Nobody else can do all that.'[39] Under the tough exterior is an apparently deeply insecure man who is highly sensitive to criticism. Despite his claims to the contrary, he seems to care deeply what people think of him. His constant need to prove himself – as an entrepreneur and a retailer – is also, of course, the source of much of his formidable drive.

Despite the heart attack he had suffered in 1995, and his attempts to ease off a little after it, with the takeover of Bhs Green found himself working harder than ever. He seemed to thrive on long days and gruelling hours. He had few other interests and, apart from some sport, watched little television. Work was his relaxation. In the harness at Bhs he could manage on four or five hours of sleep a night and was an early riser, often up at 6.30 a.m., checking the papers and then making contact with head office to get the overnight sales figures. A typical day would be endless meetings about strategy, sales and products with senior managers, and tortuous negotiations with suppliers, interspersed with back-to-back phone calls and several packets of cigarettes.

The telephone dominates Green's life. He refuses to have a computer in his office and rarely uses email. His desk is usually full of papers, stock figures, profit summaries, refit plans. When asked why he doesn't use a computer he points to his head – 'It's all up here.'[40] During the day, he tries to fit in a store visit, usually unannounced. He rarely goes out to lunch, mostly taking a light meal of chicken or salmon and water with no alcohol or bread. Once asked if he went to the gym he replied, 'I work out on the phone.'[41]

His near-instant success at Bhs helped to earn him an enhanced reputation as a man who could turn round a tired company, despite the remaining question marks about his unorthodox methods, his explosive temperament and about the way he presented his figures. He certainly demonstrated a rare combination of personal skills – a determination of steel, an encyclopaedic knowledge of the industry built through years of hands-on experience and sheer hard work and commitment and a genuine instinct for the market.

Of course, Bhs was small beer compared with M&S. As one retail analyst told the *Sunday Times* at the time, 'If Bhs closed tomorrow, would anyone care except the little old ladies who buy their fish and chips in the café?'[42] But the success had put him on track as a major high street player. In March 2002, he was awarded Retail Personality of the Year at the retail equivalent of the Oscars sponsored by the trade journal *Retail Week*. It was a coveted prize and won him a standing ovation from most of the 1,500 guests gathered at the Grosvenor Hotel in London's Mayfair. Even the normally cool Green could not hide his delight at the accolade. As the winner was picked by a panel of influential retail chiefs, it was an indication of how highly he was regarded by his peers.

Two questions remained. Could he sustain the success story? The turnaround had been achieved mainly by better cost and inventory control, more efficient buying and sourcing. Maintaining that improvement in an increasingly competitive market might prove more of an uphill struggle.

The second question was: where would he go next? Many analysts – a group once dismissed by the former chancellor Nigel Lawson as 'teenage scribblers' but powerful none the less – had expected Green to struggle at Bhs. They had been proved wrong. Now they took the view that the takeover of British Home Stores was merely a small part of a much more ambitious plan by the new billionaire. Few expected him to stop there. Green, a man who likes to keep his plans close to his chest, admitted as much, confirming at the time that he bought it that he had other retailers in his sights. 'It doesn't rule anything out,' he said.

Chapter 9

THE GIANT AND THE ANT

Despite his success and his tycoon lifestyle, Green was not a man capable of standing still for long. He was always on the lookout for the next challenge. A mixture of triggers was at work. Some suggested that his mission to prove himself after being ousted from Amber Day by the City would never be satisfied. Green denied this, but in an interview for the *Sunday Times* in September 2002, he said, 'Fuck the City. They don't like me. Look, I didn't start with any money. I started from zero with one shop in 1979. I've had to go the hard way, get a shovel, knock on doors, take big risks.'[1]

Some suggested the search for his next target was because the improvement at Bhs was not sustainable. He also denied this but still seemed determined to build on the billion he already had by buying up more businesses. Partly this was a matter of his desire to win big. But money was only part of the story. One of his inner circle suggested at the time, 'Green is no longer motivated by money alone. It's not the money any more, a lot of it is in the game.'[2]

For Green, building a fortune and a business empire had also become an addiction. He is what business academics like to call a serial entrepreneur, a relatively rare breed for whom once is not enough. This type of entrepreneur, according to one management expert, is 'an obsessive runner of companies who needs to continuously prove themselves'.[3] Green is a deal junkie. As one retail analyst put it, 'For every deal he does, he probably looks at ten.'[4] He was always on the prowl. After buying Bhs, he was rumoured to have eyed up Mothercare, House of Fraser, Littlewoods and several others. Some supermarket bosses began to wonder if they might be next. At one stage in 2002 he reportedly talked to Mohamed al Fayed about buying Harrods. There was something of a gap between what al Fayed was looking for and what Green was prepared to pay, and the two did not hit it off.

In April 2002 Green rang Gerald Corbett, the former Railtrack boss now running Woolworths and a businessman in the same mould – headstrong, self-confident and voluble. The two had never met before and Green admitted to not having been in a Woolworths' store for years. Green's pretext for the call was to enquire how a former employee was getting on, but the two started chatting about business and agreed to meet for lunch on Green's home ground – his Bhs office, a second-floor corner suite in London's Marylebone Road.

Tina had taken responsibility for its decoration and layout soon after he moved in. It was decorated with gilded antiques and dominated by a large glass-topped table in the centre of the room. On a wall hung a contemporary painting of a cheetah. There were, of course, plenty of ashtrays. Over lunch Green puffed away on his low-tar cigarettes and Corbett on his cigars while they mused about clothing and retail. Corbett was open about some of the problems facing the business.

Six weeks later, Green had still not set foot in Woolworths but was phoned by Ken Costa, vice-chairman of UBS Warburg, the investment bank working for Woolworths. Costa proposed a merger with Bhs. Green agreed to a meeting with Corbett and his advisers on 22 May at the Dorchester Hotel. At this stage the talks were top secret and had not yet leaked to the press. A few days before the crucial meeting, Green visited Woolworths' flagship store on the Edgware Road in central London. He had gone to buy a package of goods to compare with his own products but was spotted by a business journalist from the *Sunday Telegraph*, Richard Fletcher. Fearing his spying trip might have been rumbled and would be all over the press the next day, the quick-thinking but slightly embarrassed Green told Mr Fletcher, whom he knew, that he was keeping an eye on his competitors. It is doubtful if any other retail boss would have been spotted on such an exercise. It says something for Green that it was expected he should conduct such an exercise himself even if he had an army of less conspicuous staff who could have carried out the task.

Despite improvements made by Corbett in the year he had been in the job, Woolworths was in a mess and Green knew it. The multiple had one endemic problem – it was finding it difficult to know just what it should be selling. Analysts were fond of commenting that if the chain didn't exist, nobody would want to invent it. Woolworths hoped that a merger would bring in Green's expertise in tackling its persistent problems such as supply and over-stocking. The day of the meeting also coincided with Bhs's announcement of record profits, figures that highlighted the differences between the two. Bhs made twice the profits on much lower sales. At the meeting, Corbett suggested a reverse takeover in which Green would end up owning nearly a third of the enlarged company and be paid £500 million in cash for giving up Bhs. He would also have had to play second fiddle to the chief executive, Trevor Bish-Jones, the former boss at Currys and Dixons.

Although the meeting had only been attended by four people, word soon leaked out and Woolworths' share price started to climb. Corbett was seen in the Square Mile as a safe pair of hands. His stewardship at Railtrack, the privatised company owning stations and tracks, may have ended in disaster, but the City preferred to judge him by his stints as finance director at the blue chip Dixons and Grand Metropolitan. He had degrees from the London Business School and Harvard, and was credited with making a difference at Woolworths in less than a year. The two men were hardly a natural fit, however. Green was proud of his self-taught career and his lack of business qualifications. Corbett would have been too establishment a figure, too much part of the old boy network for Green to stomach. This would also have been an opportunity for Green to return to PLC life after a decade out of the public-company arena. It was of course unclear whether such a return would have been embraced by a still sceptical City, or by Green himself. Woolworths after all was not M&S.

It was not, in the event, to be put to the test. The talks soon collapsed in acrimonious name-calling. Green scathingly labelled the Woolworths management 'amateurs'. And he added, 'Fortunately I woke up from my slumber and decided swapping good money for Woolworths' toilet paper wasn't a good idea. At least Ronnie Corbett got paid for being a comedian.'[5] Corbett, in contrast, wisely kept his own views to himself. Green and Bish-Jones, who would have stayed as chief executive of the combined groups, were also chalk and cheese, and it is difficult to see how Green could have reported to a man he nicknamed 'Bish-Bosh'.

An ever restless and driven businessman, he now decided to return to an earlier hunting-ground, Arcadia, the parent company of Topshop, Topman, Dorothy Perkins, Miss Selfridge, Wallis, Evans and Burton. Less than three years earlier he had sold four of these chains –

the remnants of the Sears empire – to Arcadia, a deal that was highly profitable to him at the time.

Green had sold the shops to John Hoerner, who had ambitious expansion plans, but the deal loaded the company with new debt, the plans could not be fully realised and the share price plunged. In November 2000, Hoerner had been ousted and replaced by Stuart Rose.

Rose had begun his career as an M&S management trainee, rising to become a commercial director of the European division after seventeen years at the store. He then moved on to Burton, working for Ralph Halpern as the buying and merchandising director. When the company was split in 1997, he was bitterly disappointed not to get one of the top jobs and he quit, although he walked away with a comfortable £600,000. Nevertheless, this failure made him more determined than ever to get to the top.

He next joined Argos as chief executive in the middle of a hostile bid battle from Great Universal Stores. He failed to fend off the bid, but won plaudits from the City for managing to force up the price GUS had to pay for the acquisition. Rose walked away with £540,000, all for three months' work. He continued his upward surge in the wealth stakes when he went on to run the somewhat down-at-heel cash-and-carry chain Booker, saving it from collapse and netting £2.6 million in options when it merged with supermarket chain Iceland. He rejoined Arcadia as chief executive in November 2000. He had certainly proved to be a master of timing and developed a perhaps unfair reputation as a serial chief executive who seemed time and again to have hit the pay-off jackpot. It was a reputation that Green, who at that time counted Rose amongst his friends, was later to exploit mercilessly. Like Green, Rose's rise was not a simple rags-to-riches story. He spent his childhood in Tanzania where his Russian émigré father worked for the overseas civil service. In his early teens he was sent to Bootham, a Quaker boarding school in York. After finishing school with few qualifications, he blew a £3,000 inheritance living it up in London. His mother committed suicide when he was twenty-four and her early death seemed to have a galvanising impact.

Rose owned a house in Suffolk and an apartment in Mayfair. He had two children and was separated from his wife Jenny, though they had a 'cordial relationship'. He may have run Arcadia but he was not the sort of man to buy his clothes at Burton and was rarely to be seen in anything other than a Savile Row suit. He was suave, measured, unruffled. Unlike Green he rarely lost his rag. He was once described as a 'corporate James Bond'.

At Arcadia, Rose inherited a ragbag of thirteen brands, and although it enjoyed sales of some £2 billion, second only to M&S, it was deep in the red and buckling with debt. He culled the less profitable brands such as Racing Green and Principles to focus on six chains – Topshop, Burton, Evans, Dorothy Perkins, Wallis and Miss Selfridge, which together had over 2,000 outlets.

Despite Arcadia's problems, the company was starting to improve, the result of measures put in place by Hoerner and the return of consumer confidence after the crash of 2000. Topshop, for example, was in the process of being turned from a teen shop to a high fashion store frequented by stylists and even celebrities. Arcadia's share price was down to 50p when Rose arrived. Within eighteen months of his arrival it had soared to 400p. Although much of this improvement was down to Hoerner's recovery plans, Rose was quick to claim credit for the extraordinary rise. Many thought he was lucky to pick it up when he did. As Neill Denny puts it, 'Hoerner had been through the pain barrier and Rose had benefited from it.'[6]

That, of course, was why other retailers were circling the group. Rose had already survived one bid. In February 2002, the Icelandic retailer Baugur, which already owned 20 per cent of shares and operated the Topshop and Miss Selfridge franchises in Iceland and Scandinavia, had made a takeover bid with an initial offer of 280–300p a share. Ironically, Baugur was finding it difficult to fund a deal and turned to Green in search of a possible joint bid. But in subsequent months, Arcadia's share price passed 400p and out of range. Then, in July, the share price dived in response to sharp market falls across the world. Baugur approached Green for a second time. This time he took up the offer.

Once again Green turned to Bob Wigley at Merrill Lynch to put together the finance. He wanted to repeat the Bhs trick and move the company private by buying out all the existing shareholders. There was no question of part financing through an equity launch. The plan was a joint bid with Baugur, the largest shareholder. Baugur was keen to acquire a couple of the younger fashion brands, possibly Topshop or Miss Selfridge, in return for their 20 per cent ownership. Wigley put together a package worth some £700 million with most of the loan coming from HBOS – the Anglo-Scottish bank formed from a merger between Halifax and the Bank of Scotland in 2001. Green's own contribution was, as at Bhs, likely to have been modest. His usual stalking tactics in the past had been to make an offer and then rubbish the company and its management. But Arcadia was different from his earlier conquests – it was neither a basket-case nor did it have a vulnerable management. The usual Green strategy simply wouldn't work.

In early August, Rose had just finished one of his regular central London jogs when his mobile rang. It was Green calling from his yacht in the Mediterranean to say he was minded to make an offer. Philip and Stuart had known each other for years and, of course, Rose had been a guest in Cyprus. But they were more professional acquaintances than close friends, a 'business-peer type of friend rather than a best friend'[7] as Rose described their relationship, although he also said, 'He's immensely funny, a great guy and hugely talented. I never come off the phone to him without laughing.'[8]

The news of a potential bid soon leaked, putting the business press pack on full alert. Rumours spread around the gossipy City that Green's twelve-year-old daughter, Chloë, had asked him if he would buy Topshop. During telephone discussions with Rose he is even said to have passed the phone, jokingly, to Chloë to negotiate on his behalf.

In their next conversation, Green informed Rose that a formal offer was on its way, and then started singing, 'If I Were a Rich Man'. Rose was used to Green's sense of humour and took it in fun. Green had no doubt spotted further potential efficiencies over and above those achieved by Rose, and offered 365p a share or £690 million. This was a premium of some 53 per cent over Arcadia's closing share price of 267p the day before. On the announcement, the share price started to rise.

The next day, Arcadia held a full board meeting. It lasted thirty minutes and was unanimous – the offer was rejected. Arcadia was not going to cave in quite as easily as Bhs. Rose told Green he had undervalued the store. Green joked privately that he would revise his offer – downwards.

Green and Rose had some things in common. They had both lost a parent at a young age. They had both gone to religious boarding schools, Jewish and Quaker respectively. Both were shrewd and tough negotiators. They both liked the good life and Rose was a regular at celebrity restaurants like The Ivy. For leisure he owned a single-engine four-seater private plane, a Rockwell Commander, which he liked to take over to France to lunch. Above all they both had huge egos. Otherwise, they could hardly be more different. Rose was tall and lean; Green was short and hardly fit. Rose was a smooth, urbane and polished performer, and a master of manners; Green was still the brash rag-trader, with an intimidating, sometimes aggressive manner, whose idea of small talk was a string of abuse. The trade magazine *Retail Week* once suggested that if the two were reincarnated, Rose would return as a fox and Green as a bulldog.[9]

Now the two alpha males were head to head in a major business confrontation. For two years Green had been boasting about having bought Bhs for a giveaway price and Rose was determined not to end up as the next Alan Smith who, as Rose put it himself, 'has never been forgiven for selling the crown jewels for nothing'.[10] The last thing he wanted was to be added to the list of those who had handed a company to Green on a plate. But Rose stood to make more than £20 million through share options if Green succeeded. Other directors also stood to do well. Either way Rose could hardly lose.

He certainly gave the appearance of a remarkably unflustered boss, willingly giving interviews to the press in a relaxed, feet-on-the desk mood at his office in Berners Street and always quick to deny he was interested in becoming rich: 'I'm not motivated by money. I'm a different sort of animal to Philip. Philip is the sort of guy who's made a billion and he's still hungry to make another. I don't do that sort of lifestyle.'[11] By most people's standards, Rose was already rich. Thanks to his earlier pay-offs and cashing of share-options, he was a multi-millionaire, although he liked to present his money as small beer compared with Green, which of course it was. 'I'm an ant on a hill compared with Philip Green,' he told the *Observer*.[12]

The difference in their levels of wealth reflected their contrasting career paths. Both had pursued similar careers in retail. Both had made it to the top of their chosen paths, enterprise on the one hand and corporate management on the other. But the man who took the entrepreneurial route was now a billionaire, a giant in the wealth league. The man who chose the perhaps safer path was a multi-millionaire, a mere ant by comparison. So this was now a battle between an ant and a giant.

Both sides went through the appearance of the usual takeover hostilities. In fact what was being played out was something of a phoney war. What was at stake was not the deal itself, but the price. Rose had to avoid the impression that this was going to be a pushover for Green, but there was also a strong element of bluff that was needed for public consumption. Behind the scenes, Arcadia let the City know that they might sell for 425p a share. It meant they would be happy with something nearer 400p.

Green spent the August bank holiday weekend with his family on his yacht. Between bouts of sunbathing – Green these days rarely looked anything but tanned and healthy – he was also plotting his next move. On Tuesday, 27 August, he flew back to London for a top-level meeting with his Merrill Lynch advisers. Although the City bank was closely involved, Green had a natural dislike of bankers and especially their fees. In his career he had done a lot of deal-making himself, making his own calculations and drawing on his own highly tuned hunches about the value of his potential targets.

After the meeting with Merrill Lynch, Green met Rose face to face and asked him point blank why the company was worth more than his initial offer. The next day Green and Bob Wigley together stitched up a higher bid. At 7 a.m. the next morning he rang Rose again with a revised offer – 408p per share. It was, he said, his 'final proposal'.

The deal, as expected, included £75 million in options for Arcadia's senior management. The same morning the board met to consider the offer and a deal was about to be struck when Green received an urgent phone call from one of his press contacts. It was not good news – Baugur's offices in Reykjavik had been raided by the country's fraud department. The company, which denied the charges, had been accused of improper financial dealing. Green was incandescent that his carefully plotted plans had been thrown into chaos and that he had only heard the news second-hand. The raid threatened to scupper the biggest UK retail deal of the year.

When Green met a group from Baugur that evening at Bhs, he was trembling with fury. The Icelanders were apologetic and certainly not prepared for a Green-style outbust. 'Don't you sorry me!' he told them. 'You have left me standing on a ladder that is getting kicked over. I wish I had never met you. I don't know where Iceland is and I don't care. So far as I know there are not that many people in Iceland. How unlucky can I be that of the four that I meet, three are under a fraud investigation.'[13] The meeting continued in the same vein and the Baugur team asked for a break. They reconvened in Green's hotel suite later. This time the Icelanders brought a lawyer with them. Green pulled out a chequebook and offered to buy their shares on the spot. He was one of the few people in Britain who could afford to do so. Two hours later, the Baugur team, which Green had now started to refer to as 'The Vikings', crept away.

As Green flew back to Monaco for the weekend, the future of the deal was still uncertain. A still fuming Green was minded to ditch his tainted partners. But if he did so, he would have to scratch around to find the extra cash. For the next week Green was locked in lengthy and heated negotiations to salvage a deal. The meetings went on way into the early hours, the ashtrays filling and the temperatures soaring. An increasingly fraught Green at one stage shouted at a Baugur adviser from Deutsche Bank, 'Get your jacket on and get out of the building.' Eventually, dismayed by the continuing uncertainty surrounding the fraud allegations, and the difficulty of reaching an agreement, a frustrated Green dropped Baugur and decided to go it alone. As he told the *Daily Telegraph*, 'It's been torture with a capital T. I'm feeling weary. I've had five hours' sleep in three days, but in the end we couldn't get there. There's been twenty to thirty lawyers in my Marylebone offices for days. They must have mowed down eighteen forests with the amount of paper they produced. My office looks like a bombsite.'[14]

Green now had to hunt around for the extra cash, around £200 million. He phoned Peter Cummings, managing director of corporate banking at the Bank of Scotland, now part of HBOS, and the man who had put together the loans for some of his earlier deals including Sears. According to Green, it took just four hours to stitch together the extra money with the lion's share coming from the bank. While Green was getting the additional funding in place, Arcadia's non-executive directors were weighing up the bid. Three days later, in the first week in September, Arcadia accepted the offer. Chloë had got her wish; Topshop was now family-owned. Her dad had extended his real life Monopoly board once again.

Rose's official position was that he 'was saddened' by the sale. That was not how it looked to others. Jeff Randall, now the BBC's business editor, bumped into him as he left the board meeting when the deal was agreed. According to Randall, although he was not actually singing 'If I Were a Rich Man', his body language gave it away. 'His smile was as wide as an Evans extra-large pantie-girdle and his gait was unmistakably that of a man about to have £25 million shovelled into his bank account.'[15] Arcadia's other two main directors were to get £13 million between them.

The deal cost Green close to £900 million after fees. He owned 92 per cent of the holdings, while HBOS had bought a small 8 per cent stake. Although the deal had taken a month to seal, largely because of the unexpected hitches over Baugur, it was still quick by the usual takeover standards.

It was only some six months previously that Green had held his extravagant birthday party in Cyprus, which some sections of the press had portrayed as 'an orgy of excess'.[16] It might have been thought that the rumpus created would make Green wary of repeating the experience, but apparently not. He now decided to go for a re-run in early October.

The invitations this time went out in the form of a jiffy bag. Inside was a DVD containing excerpts from *PG50 – The Movie*. Green had had the entire Cyprus party recorded by a TV crew and now wanted to relive the experience. Again guests were flown out at his expense, this time to Monaco where they were put up in the plush Meridien Beach Plaza Hotel, where the dinner party was held on a Friday evening. Prince Albert of Monaco again put in an appearance, as did Stuart Rose and Allan Leighton. For a second time, Earth, Wind and Fire were brought over from the States. Perhaps because of the row over the first party, guests were reluctant to talk about it.[17]

With the securing of Arcadia, Green was now one of the biggest players on the high street. In less than a decade he had risen from obscurity to dominance. His empire had swollen overnight to 2,500 shops and some 40,000 staff. With his fourth, and the largest by far, pay-off in as many years, Rose was now seriously rich. Despite his declared lack of interest in money, for a while he became known as the 'Million-Pound-a-Month-Man'. The only downside was that, having agreed to stay on for a few months, he was now reporting to Green.

Most of the players were happy with the deal. The institutional shareholders took Green's cash, the banks his fees and, by making the business private, Green stayed well away from the stock market. Baugur, of course, missed out badly. Moreover, while most analysts thought that Green had paid a fair price, several fund managers who held shares in Arcadia warned that Rose was selling out to Green at too low a price. They were later to be proved only too right.

It was of course another gamble for Green. Could he squeeze more out of the company, enough to pay off his debts and make some money on the deal? Would he be able to exploit the potential of greater economies of scale and increased buying power through a combined Bhs and Arcadia? Would he enhance his new and carefully built reputation as an inspired retailer?

There was no doubt about how Green felt. As he told the *Financial Times*, 'I have created Britain's biggest private retail company. Look back in history at all the great entrepreneurs. People talk about those like Hanson as great empire-builders. But that was all done through stock market money. I have done this as a solo artist.'[18]

Green could certainly never be accused of humility.

Green's acquisition of two public companies reflected a new trend – an acceleration in the number of public-to-private deals. In the late 1990s, Debenhams, British Home Stores, New Look, Selfridges and Arcadia had all been run by corporations. Now all had been taken into private ownership. After Amber Day, Green had sworn he would avoid the public arena and, apart from his flirtation with M&S and Woolworths, had been true to his word. He was now by far the biggest private presence on the high street. This was a significant development. Private companies are required to provide much less information about their activities, sales and profits, do not have to answer to shareholders and are much more difficult to scrutinise. Green's companies are listed offshore and owned through a Channel Islands holding company, Taveta Investments Ltd, incorporated in Jersey. What information is available about them is almost exclusively at his disposal.

A few weeks after the deal Green received the accolade of Entrepreneur of the Year in the annual business awards sponsored by the *Daily Telegraph*. He was the unanimous choice amongst the judges – a panel which included Jeff Randall of the BBC and Lord Stevenson, the chairman of HBOS and Pearson. 'Love him or hate him, that man is an entrepreneur. He puts his money where his mouth is' was how one of the judges described him. Randall was a close friend, of course, and Stevenson was his principal banker. On the other hand, even his detractors would have accepted he was a strong candidate. The *Telegraph* described the award as a 'runaway victory'.

Fortunately for Green there were fewer nasty surprises awaiting him at Arcadia than there had been at Bhs. The company was in better shape and had a first-rate team of managers. Now he had the opportunity to test his skills on a much bigger enterprise. Under the deal, Rose was to leave on Christmas Eve 2002, taking his jackpot with him. He was to be replaced by Ian Grabiner who was to come in as chief operating officer. Ian was the cousin of Lord Anthony Grabiner QC, the newly appointed non-executive chairman. Anthony Grabiner was Alan Sugar's lawyer when he ran Spurs. Ian had of course worked with Green at Amber Day and had joined Tom Hunter as commercial director of Sports Division, in which Philip Green held a 13 per cent stake. He was another of the respected, loyal managers Green had collected on his route to the top.

Green came to Arcadia with a reputation as a 'slash and burn' entrepreneur, a man determined to squeeze every last ounce of performance out of a company. He also had a pretty unique way of running a business – with very short reporting lines. He was also widely seen as an autocrat, as a man who couldn't delegate and who liked to be in control.

Green's acquisition of Arcadia did not initially go down well with the company's 24,000 staff, especially the managers. The expectation was that jobs would be slashed and he would rule with a rod of iron. Senior staff knew that at Bhs there had been a cull of top managers, most of whom left or were forced out. The personnel director spoke of the fear of 'rape and pillage' as Green tried to make the finances work.[19] This fear was not borne out.

What Green did was to take out the top layer of central management, such those who used to interface with the City, and give the next tier of store-based senior managers more authority. Many head office functions were cut, and each brand was to be run as a separate entity with responsibility devolved to the eight existing brand directors in charge of the individual chains. He set each of them aggressive targets, with generous bonuses, and at least to some degree left them to get on with it, working closely with them when necessary to sort out snags. Unlike at Bhs, he certainly let the brand managers have more freedom, especially Jane Shepherdson, the director of Topshop, the most successful of Arcadia's range. In the end, fewer than 100 lost their jobs. All the brand directors were kept on.

Arcadia's 200 suppliers fared less well. One of his first acts was to demand a 1.25 per cent discount. The suppliers had little choice but to comply with the retrospective diktat. Large retailers wield enormous power over their manufacturers. Of course, autocratic decisions such as this are deeply unpopular and controversial. Green also insisted on paying less for repeats of successful styles than for the original orders. He also ensured that he would get the best price for a garment. As one of his brand directors, Frances Russell at Burton, put it, 'He helped sharpen our pencil and he helped our suppliers sharpen their pencils.'[20]

Changes came thick and fast. Managers could call him on his mobile and were often able to get immediate decisions. Green had stripped bureaucracy out of Bhs and was now doing the same at Arcadia. He introduced a more rigorous system of inventory control and faster turnover, and aimed to get merchandise into his stores more quickly than many of his rivals. If ponchos were suddenly all the rage, he would order loads, get them made quickly and have them in store in weeks.

'Fast-fashion' was now the name of the retail game, especially in the trend-setting stores like Topshop. It meant that stores needed to cut product lead times dramatically, a development that had been initiated by the newer stores like Spain's Zara and Sweden's H&M. Speeding up the supply chain also helped to reduce markdowns and increase margins. Green knew that to match the competition, clothes now mostly had to be designed, manufactured and in the stores in weeks not months. He insisted on lines being kept in stores for much shorter periods, even in menswear, to satisfy customers' growing obsession with newness. At Burton, for example, suits were in store for an average of twelve weeks, down from twenty. At Topshop, Jane Shepherdson describes fashion speed as close to immediate: 'Ten years ago you had collections every six months. Now it's six weeks. People are seeing things in celebrity magazines and they want to have the same thing instantly.'[21]

As at Bhs, Green liked to get his hands dirty. He checked the profit-and-loss account by brand and product line for each of his stores at the end of every week. There was little that he didn't know about the business. With his usual eye for detail, Green soon found that the window displays were being sent by DHL to the stores, while the clothes were being delivered by their own logistics department. Green ordered the clothes to be sent with the displays and saved £1 million a year as a result.

Although he gave his brand managers a lot of freedom he insisted on seeing the ranges himself. Managers would parade their collections in his office and he would divide them into what he termed 'the good, the bad and the ugly'. Although he allowed autonomy he showed from time to time that he had an 'intuitive eye' as Frances Russell puts it. On one occasion, Russell showed him some outerwear including a knit-sleeve puffa jacket, for which the store planned to place an order for 6,000. Green told her to back it, they upped the order by another 15,000 and it became a bestseller. Green certainly has good instincts. As one fashion journalist comments, 'You wonder how he can live in Monaco and have a feel for what a thirty-four-year-old woman with three kids on a council estate in Barnsley wants, but he appears to do so.'[22]

He was again able to apply his undoubted skill in sourcing goods cheaply – which some of his main competitors, such as M&S, were still struggling with. He insisted on reacting quickly to what was selling and what was not, clearing out and discounting in recognition of customers' capricious and rapidly changing tastes. Managers soon discovered that Green liked to visit stores unannounced. His first port of call was usually the sweet display, 'the one perk of the job', he liked to quip. He would insist on changes and return later to check they were in place.

The Bhs formula was repeated. One year on, in October 2003, Green announced a near doubling of operating profits to £227 million. Bank debt had been reduced from £808 to £400 million, three years ahead of schedule. Green liked to joke how his banks complained that he paid off his debt too quickly. To celebrate, Green called a breakfast meeting of his top 200 managers. After the news, the team was treated to magnums of Laurent-Perrier. The profit figures meant that Arcadia – which Green had paid some £900 million for – was now believed to be worth around £2 billion. Green had, apparently, turned round another retail company.

The profits rise was, as at Bhs, the result of a mix of cost-cutting, supplier squeezing and a general retail recovery rather than a selling miracle. 'Cost-cutting' is a phrase that always rattles Green who sees it as a somewhat pejorative way of defining what he prefers to see as improvements in efficiency. Green had certainly generated extra cash through better profit margins. Such savings are important and can be sustained but there is also a limit to the extent to which margins can be improved. Above all, higher profits were not being driven by faster sales growth. In the year to 20 August 2003, 'like-for-like' sales grew by 2.6 per cent, in the right direction but hardly outstanding.[23]

Although the results surpassed most City expectations, not everybody was impressed. Some analysts concluded that much of it would have happened anyway under Rose. Unsurprisingly, this was a view shared by Rose himself. Speaking in 2004, he claimed that the improvement achieved by Green at Arcadia was down to two things: a retail market that grew more rapidly than expected and Green's management for short-term results: 'I don't deny he improved the sourcing and this and that, but I was there as a public company chief executive and I had to manage two, three, four years out and make sure we were under-promising and over-delivering . . . He wanted to show, for a completely different reason, that he could squeeze it like mad to show the banks he could pay down the debt. His objective was: "Christ, I've borrowed £800 million and I've got to pay it back." '[24] Whatever the reasons, Green had almost certainly taken Arcadia 'further, faster' than Rose, as Robert Clark put it.[25]

The *Guardian* again questioned the scale of the success, returning to a theme they had begun only a few months before in their analysis of Bhs accounts. According to the paper, 'progress is not as dramatic as first reported'. This was because 'accounting and not just acumen has its part in the reported success'. The paper claimed that accountancy devices had apparently been used which put a gloss on the profits and debt repayment figures.[26] Some of the reduction in bank borrowing, for example, had been achieved by re-mortgaging Topshop's flagship building in Oxford Street, which raised around £200 million. Such sale and leaseback, pioneered by Charles Clore, has become an increasingly common practice in business and Green had made similar changes at Bhs.

Green also changed the arrangements governing the chain's storecard. Arcadia was one of the big players (along with M&S, Debenhams and John Lewis) when it came to in-house credit cards, and the contract with GE Consumer Finance, which supplied the cards, was due for renewal. The deal with these cards is that the profits – which can be substantial – are shared between the store and GE. The normal arrangement is that these profits flow on an annual basis, but Green re-negotiated the deal so that Arcadia was paid a one-off lump sum of £73 million upfront, in lieu of payments in each of the next thirteen years of trading. The effect of the new deal was to boost the cashflow now at the expense of subsequent years, in effect mortgaging the future profit flow. Although some of Green's undoubted success in improving performance at his two companies was certainly down to retailing prowess, some of it was also the result of clever 'financial engineering'.

Nevertheless, although question marks remained over the scale and roots of the turnaround, even the most critical of analysts couldn't argue with the overall improvement in cashflow at Bhs and Arcadia. Green had taken two companies, at least one of which was previously poorly managed, and presided over a pretty rapid increase in efficiency, margins and profits at both. It may have been achieved with the application of ruthless business behaviour, and some re-jigging of the finances to improve the short-term position, but much of the improved cashflow was real. Richard Hyman, chairman of the retail research consultancy Verdict, calls the turnaround of the two stores 'outstanding in scale and speed. I can't think of any kind of comparable achievement from anyone in modern times in retailing.'[27]

Green, of course, got pretty steamed up about the sniping, but as a public figure who sought the limelight, he could hardly complain if his claims became the subject of public scrutiny. None of the carping affected his relentless climb up the wealth ladder nor his personal gravy train. In 2003, he sanctioned a further round of Bhs dividend payouts totalling £214 million, financed by a new five-year bank loan. Green's share was some £203 million on top of his payment of £164 million the year before. This meant that in the two years since he had bought Bhs, he had personally recouped nearly double what he had paid for the chain.

In 2002, he had been rated the thirteenth richest man in Britain by the *Sunday Times*. In 2003, he moved up to sixth place with estimated wealth of £1.85 billion. In the 2004 list, he climbed another two places to stand at fourth with a fortune of £3.6 billion.[28] He had made his first billion in a decade, no mean feat in itself. He had now added another two and a half billion in just another two years, tripling his fortune as a result of the revaluation of Bhs and Arcadia under his ownership. It was a remarkable climb, a level of wealth accumulation achieved at unprecedented speed.

Those investors who had warned that the company had been sold too cheaply liked to claim that they had been proved right. They may have been cursing, but Green had demonstrated once again that he had a remarkable nose for a deal. Arcadia could now be added to the long list of purchases that had subsequently proved to have been a bargain. How much of this was down to skill, impeccable timing and instinct and how much to fortune and accountancy wheezes has long been the subject of debate amongst retail watchers. Not everything had gone right in his business career. He had a string of failures in the first fifteen years of his entrepreneurial career. In his failed attempt on M&S, his opponents proved smarter than him. But Green was now starting to get it right. He had also come off best in most of his dealings with other businessmen from Bob Reid to Alan Smith. Now Stuart Rose could be added to the list.

Green's success was not his alone. Without the trust and pulling power of people like Bob Wigley, Peter Cummings and Robin Saunders, he would not have raised the money. He also benefited from a number of key and loyal managers at both Bhs and Arcadia. One of Green's business rules was to work with a tight team. In Bhs and Arcadia's case the two senior lieutenants were Paul Coackley and Ian Alkins, both managers he had inherited when he bought the Sears empire in 1999. Richard Caring, the owner of International Clothing Designs, was still playing a central role.

The two men have been involved in a number of joint ventures, including the takeover of Whistles, the upmarket women's fashion shop in 2001. One of the many things they have in common is a taste for expensive parties and presents. Hence Caring's fiftieth birthday present of a Ferrari. When Green cut payments to suppliers on taking over Arcadia there was much friendly speculation as to whether Richard Caring had been included in the cuts. Green and Caring have often been seen bidding against each other at charity auctions. In July 2003, Caring paid £195,000 to dine with Elton John in support of the singer's AIDS Foundation. He was up against Hugh Grant and in the end the two men paid £390,000 for a joint supper. Few of the guests at the celebrity white tie and tiara gala dinner – which included the Beckhams, the Duchess of York, Kylie Minogue and Sir Michael Caine – were previously aware of who the publicity-shy Caring was.

By 2005, however, Caring appeared to be playing a lesser role in both Green's empire and the fashion business. Caring had been withdrawing slowly from the clothing trade, selling off some of his own businesses and diversifying into other activities by buying Wentworth golf club and a number of upmarket restaurants including

Philip Green, then aged 29, launches Joan Collins Jeans outside his Conduit Street shop in April 1981. The star of *The Bitch* and *The Stud* does the honours while Green's girlfriend Viviane Ventura is on hand to lend support.   *Alan Davidson*

A delighted Green looks on as the glamorous Collins cuts the first slice of the celebratory cake. Unfortunately the jeans did not sell well to a less than adulatory British public.

Alan Davidson

Tony Berry (right) with Alan Sugar, Paul Gascoigne, Terry Venables and Gary Lineker. Berry owed his position on the Tottenham Hotspur board in part to Philip Green and went on to help Green take control of Amber Day. *Mirrorpix*

Sir Jackie Stewart with Tom Hunter at the opening of the Stewart Grand Prix HQ in 1998. By then Hunter had – with the help of Philip Green – become one of Scotland's richest men. *Mirrorpix*

Vera and Gerald Weisfeld, the couple who built up the successful What Everyone Wants chain. Their near-miss with death on a DC-10 opened the way to a Green takeover of WEW.   *Mirrorpix*

The Barclay twins are knighted in 2004. Their support gave Green the financial muscle he needed to become a takeover king.   *Empics*

Philip Green with Stuart Rose on the announcement of Green's acquisition of Arcadia, October 2002. The two men were to later become bitter rivals when Rose became chief executive of M&S in June 2004 after Green announced his second takeover bid.

Alan Davidson

Richard Caring and his wife Jackie. Caring has been one of Green's closest friends and, until recently, one of his leading suppliers. *Dominic O'Neill*

Philip Green with Terry Green. The latter had been hired by Green as chief executive of Bhs but left after barely 18 months to buy Allders. *Draper*

Philip Green with singer Beyoncé at the 'Fashion Rocks' benefit in aid of the Prince's Trust, Royal Albert Hall, October 2003. The singer and her platinum-selling group Destiny's Child were hired to perform at Brandon's bar mitzvah, the Jewish coming of age, a three-day celebration that cost £4 million.   *Alan Davidson*

Philip Green with Jane Shepherdson, brand director of Topshop, at a reception. Shepherdson took the prestigious number one spot in the 2003 *Drapers'* top 100 most influential people in fashion.

Dominic O'Neill

The Ivy and Le Caprice. The principal reason seems to have been the declining role played by the intermediary as stores including Bhs, Arcadia and M&S sought to cut costs by sourcing their clothes directly from the factories. Insiders claim this may even have been a source of tension between Caring and Green.

Despite his success at Bhs and Arcadia, Green's ambitions appeared to remain unfulfilled. In January 2003, he had joined the race for the takeover of the supermarket chain Safeway. Interestingly it was Stuart Rose who had been lined up to help run the supermarket group if Green had succeeded.[29] Others in the running for the £3 billion business included Morrisons, Sainsbury's, Wal-Mart and Tesco. It was Green's remarkable success of course that had enabled him to compete in such company.

Green's interest in Safeway was curious. After all, he had no track record or expertise in food retailing. Some experts speculated that his interest was primarily in Safeway's property empire. Green's inner circle included a number of high-level property dealers such as the Barclay brothers and Irving Scholar. Green had made a killing from the sale of property in a number of his earlier deals, including the sale of the Shoe Express shops and the break-up of Sears. Some insiders suggested that in pursuing Safeway Green had in mind another Sears-type deal in which he sold off the stores, used the cash to pay off his debt and then sold the company on, netting a tidy profit. Green later scotched that rumour by promising the Office of Fair Trading that he planned to run the supermarket chain as a going concern if he were successful.

Others saw the move as a sign of Green's changing mindset, of a man who now felt his ambitions had no limit. His opponents saw this as a signal that Green had become arrogant, apparently seduced by his own propaganda. Courted by journalists, City grandees and the glitterati set, Green was certainly not a man plagued by self-doubt. Whatever the driving force, what Green almost certainly had in mind was to use Safeway to expand his clothing lines to compete with Asda and Tesco.

Green was up against both some tough rivals and a Competition Commission inquiry concerned to ensure that any takeover of Safeway would not reduce overall competition in the grocery market. As a result, the takeover of Safeway proved to be a long drawn-out affair.

Green eventually withdrew. Eleven months later, the Commission ruled against Tesco, Asda and Sainsbury's, leaving the way clear for Sir Ken Morrison, himself a formidable retail entrepreneur who had built his supermarket chain from a single market stall in 1952.

Safeway was not the only supermarket Green was contemplating. In May 2003, when the outcome of bids for Safeway remained uncertain, he also approached Sir Peter Davis, then chief executive of Sainsbury's, with an offer which valued the ailing supermarket group at around £6.5 billion. The offer was rebuffed by the board.

Despite, or perhaps because of, his success, Green remained a controversial figure. He was certainly not a wider retail team player. When he bought Bhs it was a member of the British Retail Consortium, a collective and powerful retail lobby group. Sir David Sieff, who was then chairman of the Consortium, lobbied Green hard to stay a member but he refused. He also let Arcadia's subscription lapse when he bought it. As Green put it to Sieff, 'I don't need the BRC. What can they do for me?' Sieff sees this as typical of Green's attitude: 'He has skills, but he is arrogant. He's now a success, but he doesn't always stop to listen to what other people say, which doesn't endear him to some people.'[30] He also refused to contribute towards the cost of Oxford Street's famous Christmas lights, one of central London's great traditions. When the story was published in the *Financial Times* under the headline 'GREEN MAKES OXFORD ST BLUE', the organiser of the Oxford Street Traders' Association got one of Green's notorious ear-bashings.[31] In 2004, though, Green paid up.

The issue of the BRC was certainly something Green was sensitive about. He once rang up Neill Denny, whom he had met on numerous occasions, about an editorial he had written on the subject. 'I got a call from Katie, his secretary, and she's got Philip on the line and the phone goes dead. Then Philip comes on and the first thing he says is, "You c**t, what you fucking doing writing this?" And I said, "What's the matter, Philip?" And he says, "It's the leader, it's bollocks. Why didn't you ring me up and ask me first?"'[32]

On this occasion, Denny had got something wrong in the editorial. Green had displayed a flash of anger – which is his way – but in common with his dealings with most journalists, it did not mark a breakdown in their relationship. From that point on, Denny always called Green when writing opinion pieces that affected him, and Green mostly returned his calls.

Green was unpredictable. He blew hot and cold, and his dealings with his own staff – junior and senior – have always been legendary. He has sometimes found it difficult to hang on to staff for long. Despite this, he has enjoyed respect amongst his management teams for his drive, enthusiasm and skill. When he spotted talent he was careful to nurture it. Part of the reason for the loyalty of some of his senior staff is that he pays well, often over the odds, which is something of an incentive. When Ian Grabiner, who prefers to keep a low profile, was asked what he was being paid when he started at Arcadia he replied, 'Loads.' According to the accounts, the highest-paid director was paid £1.5 million in 2003.[33]

Although Green can rule by expletive, he can also be 'informal and engaging' according to Malcolm Storey, a long-standing brand director at Dorothy Perkins: 'He'll plonk himself down, have a fag and chat.'[34] Despite his fiery reputation, Green likes to see himself as an approachable boss. 'People know they can come and see me about anything and I'll help them. I don't stand on ceremony, they haven't got to book an appointment, my office door is open.'[35]

Green certainly likes talking to staff and customers and can also listen and stay attentive. But he can also be short, impatient and gets bored easily. It is not unknown for him to walk away mid-sentence. Some say he is very fair-minded, others a bully. Although he has a loyal following in some powerful quarters, others question his judgement, his inability to control his temper, the size of his ego.

Despite his brushes with colleagues, journalists and pundits and the doubts about the extent of the Green miracle, he continued to add to his collection of business accolades. In March 2003, he was awarded the Retail Personality Award by *Retail Week* for the second year running. No one had received it two years in a row before. As the then magazine's editor, Neill Denny, says, 'He was then something of a hero to many retailers. If you're a racing driver you'd vote for Schumacher, you'd vote for the best in the field, and at that stage Green was arguably the best single-handed retailer in Britain.'[36]

Green may have liked taking awards himself but, despite his claims to a hands-off approach in letting his brand directors run their own show, he seemed less enthusiastic about his staff winning accolades in which he did not have a hand. Six months later, in November 2003, *Drapers* published the second of its annual listings of the Top 100 'most influential people in high street fashion'.[37] The prestigious number one spot was given to Jane Shepherdson of Topshop, for the reason that her store was the star performer within the year's best performing retail group, Arcadia. Topshop had recorded a 10 per cent rise in sales and operating profits of £70 million, and Shepherdson, with the most autonomy among his brand directors and known as 'Ms Topshop', was the architect of the improvement. (Green came in at number two.)

The fashion magazine described Shepherdson as 'having a zeal for Topshop that has reached epic proportions'. One might have thought Green would have been pleased for one of his top directors, but apparently not. The magazine had approached her directly without going through Green. When the magazine came out with a triple-page spread on Shepherdson, written by deputy features editor Louise Foster, an irate Green rang the magazine to complain along the lines, 'What the hell are you doing, fucking article in your magazine, what you trying to do, make her head bigger than it already is, giving me a load of grief with her and every other brand manager?'

Foster had even talked to Terry Green who was quoted in the piece on Shepherdson: 'She looks like a gorgeous woman and acts like a bloke.' This didn't go down well either. 'What the fucking hell are you talking to Terry Green for? He couldn't run a bath.'

Green would, of course, never want the highly rated Shepherdson to leave. As one fashion writer puts it, 'He needs her more than she needs him; she can do the things he can't. He may understand family retail, but he hasn't a clue about teenage fashion.'[38] She is certainly her own person. As a top competitor suggests, 'Philip would say he's taught her a lot, but that's a load of bollocks.'[39] Shepherdson also continues to speak highly of Green: 'He is actually very funny, he has some great turns of phrase. Philip came into my office the other day, offered me a Crunchie and we both sat there chatting happily about the state of the high street.'[40]

A year later, Green was the one who was awarded the top slot by *Drapers*. This time he gave the go ahead for the magazine to talk to his brand directors. During his interview, also with Louise Foster, he painted a different picture of relationships at his companies at odds with his fierce reputation: 'I think we've got a very happy ship . . . it's very calm, it's organised, there's no big explosions. Yes, there's odd moments. Things that get annoying . . . There hasn't been, touch

wood, since we bought Arcadia, one drama with anybody, not one row
. . . I want them to get their bonuses, I want them to hit their targets.'

'Who do you have rows with now?' asked Foster.

'You,' he replied.[41]

Chapter 10

UNFINISHED BUSINESS

In October 2003, Green bumped into Roger Holmes, the chief executive of M&S, at a retail dinner. Green had just banked another huge dividend and was in bullish mood. He made some abusive comments about M&S's Marble Arch store and then 'offered to help'. It was typical Green bluntness. Holmes, mild-mannered, softly spoken and much less of an extrovert than Green, was not used to such straight talking and was clearly taken aback. He did what most other people would have done in similar circumstances – smiled nervously and walked away to join another group.[1]

Holmes certainly had plenty to be nervous about. He had been promoted from head of UK retail at M&S to chief executive the previous year. Despite his success in fighting off Green in February 2000, Peter Salsbury had been forced to resign as chief executive seven months later and Luc Vandevelde took over the combined chairman/ chief executive role. The urbane Belgian knew that to make M&S secure from predators he had to bring about a drastic improvement in the company's performance following years of drift.

When Vandevelde arrived in February 2000, he was taken aback by the extent of demoralisation and chaos within the company. Over the summer he restructured the board and Roger Holmes was poached from Kingfisher, the parent company of Woolworths and B&Q. In spring 2001, Vandevelde – now known as 'cool hand Luke' – made one of his most crucial appointments. He hired George Davies, the highly creative designer who had established the winning formula for the successful Next chain of stores and was the architect of the successful cut-price George brand at Asda. At M&S he was given the right to create and sell a new range of fashionable clothes under the Per Una brand name designed to appeal to younger women. When the news leaked out in early February, the share price jumped 16p.

Other changes came thick and fast. In March it was announced that most of the store's overseas operations would be put up for sale, bringing twenty-five years of continental and American expansion to an end. Shortly afterwards the company announced it was to move its head office from Michael House in Baker Street to a smaller and much more modern new development in Paddington Basin. Vandevelde also had the portraits of the former chairmen removed from the boardroom to be replaced by blown-up photos of M&S products. These changes, unthinkable even a few years earlier and all accompanied by fierce internal rows, seemed to symbolise the struggle to move M&S on from its paternalistic, hierarchical and deeply conservative roots.

When the Per Una range arrived in the shops in September, it was a great success, applauded by the press and loved by the public. M&S at last seemed to be doing something right. Profits stopped falling and some in the City started to sing the praises of M&S again. The new initiatives continued to roll. Three new stand-alone Simply Food stores were opened to compete directly with Tesco Metro and Sainsbury Local. The new women's spring collection also went down well with the usually sniffy fashion editors. The only cloud was the news that Bhs, which Green had bought eighteen months earlier for £200 million, was now worth £1 billion.

In September 2002, Vandevelde stepped down to become part-time chairman and handed over the chief executive reins. Holmes, a universally recognised 'nice guy', had begun his career at McKinsey, one of the leading management consultancies, then went on to help turn around B&Q. M&S was now in slightly better shape at least in part due to his efforts over the previous eighteen months – costs were down, debt had fallen and there was a new concentration on core business with new ranges and designs. But the improving situation failed to last. One by one the new and widely hailed initiatives started to unravel. The Per Una range was a roaring success, but the attempt to expand into the teen market through Per Una Due came up against the perhaps predictable barrier that teenage girls don't want to be seen dead in Marks & Spencer clothes.

In an attempt to reverse the slide, Vittorio Radice, the suave and flamboyant Italian retailing whiz-kid who had made his name transforming Selfridges' Oxford Street store, was brought in to spearhead the launch of a number of new 'Lifestyle' superstores which were to sell cutting-edge furniture and household fittings. As Radice envisioned it, these stores would sweep the ground from under IKEA.

But three years on from Green's failed takeover attempt, the Vandevelde initiatives, well received though they were, had failed to deliver the magic formula that would return it to its accustomed level of profit and sales. The early success achieved when Vandevelde was in sole charge had run out of steam. By autumn 2003, when Green taunted Holmes, the company was languishing.

Everybody had their own, mostly contradictory, theories about what was wrong: it was too fuddy-duddy or not fuddy-duddy enough; it ignored the teenage market or was too wedded to it; it was too fashionable, too frumpy, too safe, too bold. But M&S's central problem was the much tougher competition from all sides, especially in the crucial area of womenswear. At the casual end, there were the specialist fashion retailers like Gap, the relative newcomers such as Zara and H&M and of course, Green's Topshop. At the discount end there was Matalan and the large supermarket chains, especially Tesco and Asda, offering much cheaper and popular ranges especially in children's clothes. In the middle was the ever successful Next and now the much-improved Bhs. Under Vandevelde and Holmes, M&S had attempted to compete with the funkier stores by targeting customers aged between seventeen and twenty-five, a strategy that not only failed but helped to alienate their traditional older customers. Even food sales, where M&S had traditionally enjoyed a major quality advantage over its rivals, had started to falter by late 2003.

One of those creating headaches for M&S, and revelling in it, was Philip Green. On the wall of his second-floor office at the Bhs Marylebone headquarters was a framed montage of cuttings and congratulations about his successful takeover of Arcadia. There was also a photo of him meeting the Queen at a Bhs-sponsored royal gala performance of Andrew Lloyd Webber's musical *Bombay Dreams*, held in October 2002. Even more nostalgic amongst the framed pictures in the office was one of a young Jimmy Greaves when he played for Tottenham, Green's team, in the 1960s. Greaves had inscribed it: 'To PG from JG, from one predator to another.'

Despite his preoccupation elsewhere, Green had never taken his eye off M&S, and nothing would please him more than to add another montage of congratulations to his office – this time featuring M&S. Successive dividend payments from Bhs meant that Green had been accumulating substantial cash reserves. Some of this would have gone on paying for his tycoon lifestyle. Nevertheless, Green was undoubtedly building up a significant cash war chest and it was time to find something to spend it on. He was now in the big league and later admitted that only giant takeovers were now of interest to him. 'David Barclay said to me: "Philip, only think about the quantum leap." And basically, where we are in terms of scale, there are only one or two things in the UK that are of any interest.'[2]

But there was more to it than that. With his success at Bhs and Arcadia, Green was now beginning to see himself as the natural successor to Simon Marks, Marcus Sieff and Sir Richard Greenbury, the three men who had done most to steer M&S to the top of the retail pile in the previous fifty years. All three were legendary figures. Simon Marks died in the office in 1964, aged seventy-six, fulminating to staff about substandard garments. In his latter years, despite his immense skills, he had become, as Judi Bevan wrote in her biography of M&S, 'something of a despot'.[3] Marcus Sieff was renowned for his countless mistresses but was also a much admired and respected leader. Greenbury too brought success before he fell from grace. When Vandevelde removed the portraits of the three men and all the other previous chairmen from the boardroom, it proved one of the most controversial decisions in the stormy history of M&S.

Capturing M&S – and turning it around, no mean feat – would give Green the public recognition that his earlier heroes had gained and which he so badly craved. He had also never forgiven the company's board for what he viewed as the unethical tactics they had used to thwart his first attempt on the high street chain. His comments to Holmes may have been partly in jest, but they were also a sign that Green had not really given up on his long-held ambition. For him, M&S was unfinished business. Green had also never tried to disguise his contempt for the way M&S was run. On the handful of occasions Green met Sir David Sieff, he liked to tell him what was wrong with M&S and how it should be run. Holmes and his senior colleagues were only too aware that Green seemed still to cast a towering shadow over their every move.

Although M&S had to some degree lost its way, it was still a prize catch. Despite falling market share, it had a turnover of more than £7 billion, remained a highly profitable company and was still one of the most popular stores in the country with a remarkable 10 million customers a week. M&S had its problems but they were far from terminal.

By the winter of 2003, Green had achieved a lot at Bhs and Arcadia, had flirted with Safeway and Sainsbury's, and it was now time to turn his focus elsewhere. His first attempt on M&S had been made when the company was especially vulnerable. Successive sales figures had been poor, it was without a permanent chairman, had a lame-duck chief executive and was known to be in internal disarray over tactics. In January 2004, the parallels with 2000 were striking. M&S was at another low point. Vandevelde and Holmes had failed to turn the company's lacklustre sales performance around. At first seen as an asset, Holmes's management consultancy background and obsession with management theory was fast being seen as a handicap. His perhaps fatal lack of experience of the fashion industry was beginning to show. Despite some early success, Holmes and Vandevelde had failed to dislodge the culture of complacent paternalism that continued to afflict the company. The result was unresponsive management, dithering over top personnel and womenswear, and growing disenchantment with a semi-detached chairman.

By now it had become clear that Vandevelde, once seen as the potential saviour, was bored with the constant backbiting and wanted to leave. Holmes had tried to change the way Marks & Spencer looked at the world and made his own enemies on the board in the process. His position was now far from secure. The squabbles in the M&S boardroom on the twentieth floor of its Baker Street headquarters were hardly a secret. Around the corner at his Bhs office in Marylebone, Green could barely disguise his glee. He sensed that his turn was coming again, that the prize that had eluded him in 2000 might at last be within his grasp. Secretly he started to plan a strike.

First he would have to secure the cash. He was anxious to avoid the embarrassment of 2000 when DLJ had abruptly pulled out. Now he felt able to set his sights on some of the biggest financial names in the City. At the end of January, he had lunch with two top executives at the world's leading investment bank, Goldman Sachs. He also started discussions with advisers at Merrill Lynch, the bank that had declined to take a leading role in the 2000 bid. Then Green had complained bitterly of 'old boys' clubs' and City bias. Now, four years on, he had won round more of the financial establishment and was able to recruit from the cream. The City may have remained wary of the man, but it knew he was capable of making big money.

Buying the company would require raising around £10 billion –

more than twelve times the amount he had paid for Arcadia. This time Green planned to commit up to £1 billion of his own money. The rest would have to be borrowed. What was being planned was the biggest buy-out ever attempted in Europe. If he succeeded Green would be taking over a public company, but the great prize of M&S was, he considered, worth the flak.

Throughout early spring, Green and his banking advisers worked on the financial arrangements of the plan, which somebody with a sense of humour had codenamed Project Mogul. Green had assembled an impressive group of backers: Bob Wigley at Merrill Lynch who had worked with him on the acquisition of Arcadia and on his potential bids for Woolworths and Safeway; Michael Sherwood and Richard Sharp, both senior partners at Goldman Sachs; and his old ally Peter Cummings at HBOS. Also on board were the Royal Bank of Scotland and Barclays Capital. To have all three of these banks funding one man's takeover plan was something of a first. They agreed to put up the bulk of the finance, with the lion's share coming from HBOS. Goldman Sachs and Merrill Lynch emerged as equity partners. This meant more risk but also potentially more gain if Green delivered the better earnings he promised.

Although a formidable team had been assembled, putting the money together had not been easy. According to the *Financial Times*, one of the first banks to be approached was HSBC, the largest bank in Europe, but it had refused to co-operate. Some senior bankers at both Goldman Sachs and Merrill Lynch were nervous that working with Green, a man who still came with a good deal of baggage, might adversely affect their reputations and upset their other major clients.[4] What won them round, it seems, was Green's track record of repaying his loans, often in double-quick time.

While the planning was conducted in the utmost secrecy, with a large number of City advisers involved, it is hardly surprising that rumours soon started circulating. A decade or less before, M&S had been seen as too large to be taken over but the continuing fall in its share price had opened up the possibilities. As spring arrived, a number of private-equity groups were known to be 'running the numbers' to see if they might themselves make a bid. The company's vulnerability was inevitably a hot topic in the City. Philip Green was expected to be among the first to put his head above the parapet.

The City lives off rumours, guesswork and hunch even where there is nothing concrete to go on. Those whose hunches are proved right make money, sometimes big money. On 20 March, the *Independent* claimed that Green was planning a bid for M&S and even quoted a price of up to 400p a share. Green, of course, was swift to deny it: 'This is the first time I have heard of it.' Then, on 18 April, the *Scotland on Sunday* again identified Green as a potential bidder along with the American takeover specialists Kohlberg Kravis Roberts. Takeover fever was in the air.

While tongues were wagging about a possible bid, Green continued to work on his plans. On 28 April, Green's assistant, Katie O'Brien, rang Stuart Rose's PA, Julie Phayll. Green wanted to meet Rose and a meeting was put in both diaries for two weeks later on 12 May. Rose had left Arcadia in December 2002 with no bad feelings on either side and the two had stayed in touch. Green knew that Rose was temporarily out of a job, and wanted to discuss whether he would accept a top post in any Green-controlled Marks. Green's motive was clear. He knew that Rose had long wanted one of the top jobs at M&S and, in the words of one retail insider, would 'rather have Rose on the inside pissing out than on the outside pissing in'.[5]

Rose may not have known what the meeting was about but the bid rumours continued to spread. In early May, Bob Wigley and several senior Merrill Lynch colleagues were seen leaving Green's Arcadia offices late one evening. On 7 May, five days before the scheduled meeting with Green, Rose was on his way to Folkestone to talk to Saga, the over-fifties insurance and holiday firm, about the possibility of becoming chairman when, according to Green, he received a call from the Bhs owner on his mobile phone.

Despite its private nature, less than a month later this call was to become the source of immense public speculation about its content and purpose. Less than ninety minutes after they had spoken, two investors bought two blocks of M&S shares. Some six weeks later, Rose admitted that he was one of them. He had instructed his broker, Brewin Dolphin in Manchester, to buy 100,000 shares at 276p a share at a total cost of £276,000. The other investor remains unknown.

Rose has always maintained that the timing was a coincidence, that the deal was not triggered by the call, that he had no idea what Green wanted to talk to him about. This may be so, but his curiosity must have been aroused by Green's earlier request for a meeting and subsequent phone call and, as a close M&S watcher, he would have been aware of the rumours circulating in the City. Indeed, the day before the phone call, Rose had bumped into William Lewis, the *Sunday Times* business editor, at a packed media party at Soho House. During their conversation, according to Lewis, Rose had revealed that he had suspicions that Green was 'up to something'. 'Could be M&S. Check it out,' he added. According to Lewis, Rose was fishing around amongst journalists for information, acting in many ways 'like a reporter, exchanging information with a variety of sources in order to get an accurate picture about what was going on at M&S'.[6] Rose disputes this account and says that it was Lewis who asked him about the possibility of a bid for M&S by Green.[7] Either way, Rose must have suspected that something significant was in the air.

Of course, the purchase would still have been a gamble, but a calculated one. That Rose suspected that Green was planning to go for M&S was also indicated by a conversation Rose had with Alex Brummer of the *Daily Mail* four days after he bought the shares and the day before he met Green. According to Brummer, Rose intimated that he thought Green would bid for the company.[8]

Rose was not the only member of Britain's newly enriched club to buy large numbers of M&S shares during April and early May when they were selling at around 260–280p. At this price they would have been a bargain if a bid was subsequently announced. On 15 April, the billionaire Reuben brothers, businessmen who were neighbours of Green in Monaco, had purchased 760,000 M&S call options. A day later, Green's longstanding friend and business colleague Tom Hunter bought 375,000 shares for a trust set up in his children's name.

Then, on 11 May, Michael Spencer, the head of ICAP, the world's largest money broker, bought 2 million M&S 'contracts for difference' – bets on the share price rising – at a cost of £5.5 million. Spencer, a former Oxford mathematician and a poker-playing extrovert, was one of the richest men, if not the richest, in the City. His wealth was esti-mated to be in the region of £330 million. Such contracts have become highly popular amongst hedge fund operators and sophisticated, very rich private investors. They enable the purchase of a financial interest in a company while not actually buying the shares and have the significant advantage of having much weaker disclosure rules – the purchaser's name does not have to appear on the share register, for example. In this way wealthy investors are able to acquire significant interest in companies while enjoying total secrecy.

The purchase came the day after Spencer had met Rose for a drink on the terraces of the exclusive Mayfair restaurant George. Spencer has always denied getting a tip and claims that the meeting had been about the upmarket Image restaurant business of which the two men were directors. Nevertheless, it seems that M&S shares, which had been out of favour for so long, were suddenly becoming all the rage in some small and exclusive circles.

On the same day as Spencer was acquiring his substantial financial interest in M&S, and after weeks of press and City speculation, Vandevelde finally announced his decision to step down as chairman, though he would stay until a successor was found. Vandevelde had certainly been under pressure to go or up his time. Despite his three-day-a-week commitment, many institutional shareholders felt that he had too many other business interests to be able to keep his eye on the ball at M&S, and was 'spreading himself too thinly'.

Green was not the only businessman who had courted an interest in M&S. Unknown to him and M&S, Rose had himself been exploring a possible bid for the company. He had talked briefly with the American private-equity group Blackstone in late 2003 and then had further discussions with a venture capital group. On 11 May, while Spencer was betting heavily on an imminent hike in the M&S share price, Rose was meeting with Simon Reuben to discuss the possibility of putting together a joint bid for the company. The meeting with Reuben had in fact been arranged some weeks before.

On 12 May, Rose and Green finally met for their pre-arranged tea at Green's office. Rose was first asked to sign a confidentiality agreement not to reveal the meeting to third parties and then Green outlined his plans to bid for M&S. Green wanted Rose to be part of those plans and made him a proposition that he was confident his former colleague would jump at. The details of this conversation have never been fully revealed, though it was subsequently claimed that all Green offered Rose was the position of head of food.

Meanwhile, speculation mounted about who would replace Vandevelde. The M&S board were deeply at odds with the shareholders over the replacement, the board wanting a traditional City figure while the institutional investors preferred a hands-on retailer like Rose. A 'platinum, gold and bronze' shortlist was being drawn up at headquarters. The board's preference was for Conservative MP and former chairman of Asda, Archie Norman, but he made it clear he was not interested and had already turned the job down when approached in 2000. Other names in the frame included Sir Christopher Gent, former chief executive of Vodafone, Sir Derek Higgs, the City banker who chaired a controversial government review of boardroom practices, and David Varney, the departing chairman of mobile phone operator MMO^2. They may have been City grandees, but none of them had experience of selling clothes.

The glaring omission from the list was Stuart Rose, despite his credentials as a proven retailer. Rose had never made it a secret that he was desperate for the job and had been ever since he left Arcadia. He had indeed been canvassing for it ever since it became clear that Vandevelde wanted out. As he put it, 'It is like fancying a girl, but she doesn't fancy me and goes off with someone else.' Rose's detractors argued that his track record had been confined to tarting up failing companies before selling them and pocketing a hefty pay-off. His first chief executive's job at Argos lasted merely a few months, and he was at both Booker and Arcadia for less than two years. Critics could argue that he had failed to defend both Argos and Arcadia against takeover, though in Argos's case he did secure an excellent deal for shareholders.

Despite the fact that he had never run a big company for any length of time, M&S's leading institutional shareholders were markedly keen on Rose. But there was strong opposition to him on the board. Some, ironically, saw him as too close to Philip Green. Others feared he might shake things up too much and undermine Roger Holmes in the process. Few doubted that if Rose was appointed, Holmes would be gone within weeks.

While speculation mounted about Vandevelde's successor, Green was getting closer to the moment when he would be able to launch his second takeover bid. This time, backed by some of the world's biggest banks, he was more confident of success.

Nevertheless, clouds were gathering on the horizon. One of the darkest took the form of the competition authorities. A combined M&S, Arcadia and Bhs would account for a fifth of the UK clothing market and slightly more than a quarter of women's clothes, very close to the point where the Office of Fair Trading would be obliged by law to intervene.[9] If Green saw a threat that the OFT might block the bid, forcing him perhaps to sell off part of his empire to guarantee continued competition on the high street, he chose to ignore it. He pressed ahead with his plans.

On Monday, 24 May, Green was taken in his chauffeur-driven Bentley from his Monaco double penthouse in Rocabella Apartments to the Fontvielle landing strip. There he took a hired helicopter to Nice airport where he keeps his £30 million Gulfstream G550. From Nice airport he flew to RAF Northolt, the west London airfield used by government ministers and royalty, and, increasingly, the super-rich. It had become a pretty regular Monday morning trip ever since he was given the twelve-seater jet from his wife Tina as a Christmas present a few months earlier. As usual he spent the two-and-a-half-hour journey checking through the weekly sales figures before his normal Monday meeting. The rest of the week would be anything but normal.

On Tuesday, 25 May, Holmes announced the company's eagerly awaited full-year results. M&S's market share in clothing had continued to fall while the new £15 million LifeStore in Gateshead that had opened in February had failed to meet its sales target by a mile, with its modern products proving 'too contemporary' for the targeted middle-England shoppers. Holmes's presentation was long on jargon, short on eye-catching proposals. Vandevelde, who had already announced his decision to leave the company when a replacement could be found, looked uninterested. The City was certainly not impressed with Holmes's plans to improve performance by switching suppliers to cheaper sources in the Far East, introducing new product ranges and giving the stores a new look. They had heard it all before. Shortly after Holmes's presentation, Green called Kate Rankine, a business reporter at the *Daily Telegraph*, to ask her what she thought. 'Not much,' she replied and went on to ask if it wasn't time for him to buy M&S. 'Nah,' drawled Green. 'My wife doesn't want me spending any more money.'[10]

Green certainly knew how to keep a secret. The next day, he was rung by Neill Denny, who was fishing for information about the rumours of a possible link between Rose and M&S. Green was about to launch a multi-billion pound takeover bid, the biggest move of his career. But as Denny remembers, 'Most chief executives would have avoided journalists like the plague at that point, but not Green. He took the call and gave nothing away. It shows just what a cool customer he can be when he wants to be.'[11]

The details of the ambush on M&S were still being prepared. On the evening of Holmes's announcement Green met Bob Wigley and a number of senior colleagues at Merrill Lynch to put the finishing touches to the plans. The plan cooked up with his advisers was to approach the M&S board first, probably in the course of the next week, and inform them quietly of their proposal. The last thing they wanted was for details to be leaked to the press.

Thursday, 27 May was hot, the crowds were enjoying the third day of the Chelsea flower show, corporate news was thin on the ground and the City was having its usual lethargic trading day in the run-up to a Bank Holiday weekend. Throughout the morning, rumours started about an imminent bid, but dealers did not take them seriously. The shares had opened at 290p and stayed there throughout the morning. That all changed after lunch. Just after 2.20 p.m. the share price of M&S edged upwards to 295p. Thirty minutes later, there was a spurt in trading and the shares passed 300p. By 3.30 p.m., the share price had risen by more than 6 per cent in an hour. It appeared the secret was out.

The sudden rise in the share price forced the Takeover Panel, which had been monitoring events closely, to move. They informed Green that to put a stop to the destabilising speculation he would have to declare his hand. It was earlier than Green had planned. That afternoon, at 3.45 p.m., Holmes's secretary interrupted her boss to say that Philip Green was on the line, probably the last man on earth Holmes wanted to hear from. The call was polite but to the point. 'I think we've got a surprise for you,' said Green, going on to explain that he was working on a bid and would be making a Stock Exchange announcement shortly. The call lasted barely a minute. It was the first time the two had spoken since their prickly exchange in October. Holmes was only too aware of the rumours – he had had to deal with calls from anxious suppliers for weeks – and the news would hardly have come as a surprise. Nevertheless, he was still shaken. As he put the phone down, he knew that his days at M&S were numbered.

At 4 p.m. Green made his plans public through the London Stock Exchange. In anticipation of a possible bidding war, the share price finished 19 per cent higher at 345p on the day. Those who had gambled just a few weeks before on just such a rise had done so correctly. Michael Spencer was sitting on a tidy paper profit of £1.7 million, Rose of around £80,000, the Reubens close to half a million and Hunter some £360,000. Spencer and the Reubens cashed the shares a few weeks later, turning the paper profit into a reality.

In 2000, Green had been invited to take part in a Monopoly game organised by the *Sunday Telegraph*.[12] His fellow competitors were entrepreneurs in the same mould. One was Stuart Wheeler, founder and chairman of spread betting firm IG Index and an international poker player. Another was Luke Johnson, the multi-millionaire and son of right-wing columnist Paul Johnson, who had made his money through deal-making and financial engineering. The two-hour board game ended in an emphatic victory for Green.

Now, in 2004, the Monopoly game was with real money, and was to be played at the very highest level and in the full glare of national publicity. The City loves a full-blown takeover battle. As well as the fees for the bankers, lawyers, accountants and PR advisers on the winning side, there is also the theatre. And this one looked as though it would be a titanic battle for control of Britain's best known and best loved chain in which the winners would sweep the board and the losers be swept aside. And both sides knew it. If Green were to succeed, it would be sweet revenge for what he saw as the underhand way in which the board had fought his bid four years earlier. If M&S were to fight him off for a second time, it would be a remarkable victory, possibly ending his ambitions for good. But this time the odds seemed to lie with Green.

He was not the kind of man to risk his reputation a second time unless he was convinced he could win. But, strong as his position now seemed to be, there remained a risk – Green still divided opinion and the M&S board was hardly going to welcome him with open arms.

Could they repeat the trick of 2000 and see him off? Vandevelde was, as usual, abroad on non-M&S business and it was left to Holmes to take the usual first step on news of a takeover threat – to summon the finance director and senior advisers and inform the non-executive directors. At M&S headquarters the announcement had the impact of an exploding bomb. The company's suppliers, who had been jittery for weeks, knew that they too would be caught in the explosion. With a lame-duck chairman, a vulnerable chief executive and declining fortunes, the board was hardly in a strong position to fight off such a determined challenger. As one investment banker put it, 'There is nobody within that business that is even vaguely capable of leading a defence against a man as determined as Philip Green.'[13]

Green's intervention was going to have a dramatic impact on the future of M&S, whether he won or lost. The rules of the game had changed for ever. Vandevelde and Holmes may not have been perfect and they may have made some mistakes, but they had set in train a long-term improvement strategy. Those plans would now have to be torn up. To fight off Green would mean playing more closely to his rules, gearing up for better short-term results irrespective of the effect on the long-term health of the company. Such was his power. It was a prospect that was to divide the City, M&S staff and shareholders as well as the country.

Baker Street was not the only place where the impact of Green's announcement was to be felt. The following day the Financial Services Authority, the watchdog responsible for monitoring the financial services industry, announced that it was investigating dealing in M&S shares prior to Green's declaration because of what they described as 'suspicious price movements'.

The last thing the management team wanted was Green. Most of them knew they would be out if he took over. With his preference for hands-on decision-making and his dislike of hierarchies and tiers of management, non-productive 'suits', as he typically saw them, would also be in the firing line. Green would shake M&S to its very core and the staff knew it. Unlike the existing management, Green was not a man to be persuaded by historic sensitivities. Whatever their past significance, Green would not be wedded to particular stores, locations and the traditional ways of doing things. What remained of the past would be brushed aside. He would be the last person to agonise about the 'M&S feel' – the attempt to offer a distinctive M&S product and look that had long dogged the company.

A Green takeover would mean fewer lines, fewer tiers of management, less clutter, faster turnover and speedier responses to consumer whims. Of course, M&S had already started down the road of modernisation but they had not travelled as far or as fast as Green would like to go. He certainly believed that there were significant excess costs to be stripped out of M&S – Holmes himself had admitted, for example, that the company paid a large premium in staff salaries and pensions. He claimed it needed to do so to retain the best staff consistent with what middle England expects. Green would be unlikely to be so generous.

The suppliers would also be in the firing line. M&S could be a demanding client, but the food and clothing manufacturers who had served it over the years had made a pretty lucrative living. Some outsiders felt that the relationship between head office and the main suppliers was perhaps a little too cosy, that there was still plenty of room for better deals. Green was the man who could squeeze more out of them. The particular issue of British versus overseas suppliers had long tied the hands of reforming bosses. Green had no such scruples. He knew the Asian and East European markets, and understood how to get quick turn-round, how to delay payment. He was certainly not wedded to M&S's longstanding if declining commitment to British manufacturers.

Having dithered for months about how to tackle their wavering performance, M&S now moved with electric speed. Bank Holiday weekend plans were dropped, phones buzzed, cabals formed, temperatures rose. A rare sense of urgency replaced the usual complacency. One outstanding issue, the replacement for Vandevelde, had been dragging on for weeks. And the growing dissatisfaction at the performance under Roger Holmes had not yet resulted in any move to replace him. Now both of these issues were sorted out almost overnight.

Most of the board had been at best lukewarm about the prospect of Rose joining the company and, until Green's announcement, he had been planning to spend the Bank Holiday weekend at his 40-acre farmhouse near Woodbridge in Suffolk. On Friday morning the phone rang. It was Paul Myners, one of the non-executive directors on the board, the former head of fund managers Gartmore, a Tate trustee and chairman of the Guardian Media Group. Myners, who was now pulling the strings, invited Rose to his multi-million-pound Chelsea home. The meeting had been arranged behind the backs of Vandevelde and Holmes and, for obvious reasons, could not be held at M&S headquarters.

When Rose arrived he was greeted not just by Myners but also by two other non-executive directors – former chairman Brian Baldock and former MI5 chief Dame Stella Rimington. When offered the job of chief executive rather than chairman, there was no hesitation in his own mind. As he later admitted, 'I didn't have to think about it: I'd been thinking about it for the previous ten years.'[14] Nevertheless, knowing that he now held the upper hand, he made a series of demands before he agreed to come. He insisted on bringing with him thirty-eight-year-old Charles Wilson, who had worked with him at Burton, Booker/Iceland and Arcadia. Wilson would bring with him a key advantage – while Rose left Arcadia soon after the Green takeover was completed, Wilson had stayed on for six months and knew at first hand how Green operated.

Rose also demanded major changes in the M&S advisory team. He believed that M&S's blue-chip PR advisers Brunswick had been briefing journalists off the record that he was unsuitable for the job and insisted that it was replaced by Tulchan, a smaller firm set up a few years before by a former Brunswick employee, Andrew Grant. Rose also insisted that Rothschilds, M&S's investment bankers, should be replaced by Citigroup, the American investment bank which had worked with him when he defended Argos against GUS's £1.9 billion bid. There was one final demand. Rose believed that Vandevelde had been the main barrier to him joining the company at an earlier date, had dismissed him as being only able to run 'small retailers'. Now Rose was to get his revenge – he insisted Vandevelde stand down as chairman with immediate effect.

That Friday afternoon Rose was driven down to his Suffolk home by his chauffeur, Caroline. The next day Myners rang to agree to his conditions and offer him the job. On the morning of Bank Holiday Monday, the board met formally at Baker Street. Neither Vandevelde nor Holmes was present. It was a sign of the crisis now gripping the company that the M&S senior directors caved in to all Rose's demands. And on top of this, although Rose had once joked that he would do the job for nothing, he in fact managed to negotiate a football-style £1.25 million joining fee, an £850,000 salary and the promise of the same again in bonuses together with an undisclosed number of shares.

Holmes, who had lasted little more than eighteen months, was not the first to have found M&S a difficult nut to crack. He may have guessed his job was on the line but was only told of the decision a few hours before the shake-up was announced. It was Vandevelde, summoned back from France, who was asked to deliver the news. Holmes left with a £820,000 payment, Vandevelde with some £600,000. Sacking bosses does not come cheap.

Once treated as a virtual leper, Rose was now cast as the store's potential saviour. At 5 p.m. on Bank Holiday Monday, the board announced the results of their drastic measures. Luc Vandevelde and Roger Holmes had been ousted; Paul Myners was promoted from deputy to acting chairman until a permanent replacement could be found; Stuart Rose was to become chief executive with immediate effect. The City had got its way. It was one of the bloodiest and swiftest coups in recent boardroom history and the non-executive directors who had engineered it were said to be mightily pleased with themselves. As one observer noted, M&S had made a 'seismic shift'.

Just before the announcement was made, Rose rang Green to break the news. It was not an easy conversation. When asked by the press for a response to Rose's appointment, Green playfully replied, 'I think I should send Stuart the headhunters' bill, seeing that I got him the job.' Rose was, characteristically, more diplomatic: 'If that is the case, I should send him a thank-you note.'[15] Behind the quips, however, Green could scarcely restrain his anger. As he saw it, the two men had been friends, if not bosom pals, he had offered him a key role in his own plans and now Rose had betrayed him. Even more crucial for Green was that the appointment of Rose would shift the odds significantly in favour of M&S.

Now the future of the company was to be decided by a bare-knuckle fight between two larger-than-life and deeply determined men. Unlike most industry bosses, neither was a university graduate or a management theorist. It was the second time the two had been lined up in a commercial battle, but this time it was for much higher stakes.

Rose told the *Guardian* shortly after his appointment: 'Philip is the most stimulating, entertaining, amusing and intelligent man that I have met in a long time ... But I don't want to work for him. I describe our friendship this way: we see each other for a meal, but we do it in a restaurant, not in our houses . . . He's a great guy, but one of the reasons I get on with him is that he doesn't own me ... I wouldn't work for him for five minutes.'[16]

And as Green knew only too well, Rose would put up a much tougher fight than his predecessor. Round one had gone to M&S.

Chapter 11

DIRTY TRICKS

W hen Rose arrived at Michael House in Baker Street the day following his appointment, he was M&S's fifth chief executive in the same number of years. As he was shown into his new office, he found it still full of his predecessor's belongings. Holmes had only 'stepped down' the night before and had not had time to clear the room. So sudden and unplanned was Rose's arrival that his name had not been registered on the staff computer. Visitors reported that reception did not know who he was at first. Journalists who were able to get through to ask about his strategy were bluntly but very politely told, 'I've only just found out where the lavatory is.'

Rose may have been the City's preferred choice, but he knew it was going to be a close race. His job was to convince shareholders he could build a strategy that could arrest declining sales and see Green off, and he had precious little time to put one together. Rose would not be seen much in his usual late-night London haunts for a while. The first effect of his unexpected appointment was to create a big hole in Green's plans. One City investor summed up the mood: 'This will make the chances of Philip Green getting hold of M&S a lot lower and the price he would have to pay a lot higher.'[1]

This was not just going to be a highly personal contest between two of the biggest egos in retail. It would also be a battle of City titans. M&S's line-up was a roll-call of the City old guard. Heading the list was the Eton-educated David Mayhew, the softly spoken chairman of Cazenove, the Queen's stockbroker, and one of the most respected men in the Square Mile. Then there was Simon Robey, head of Morgan Stanley in the UK and another prominent member of the old City elite. And the third key member of the team was Robert Swannell of Citigroup, also a heavyweight corporate financier of the old school.

Those backing Green were relative newcomers by comparison, but formidable opponents none the less. Bob Wigley at Merrill Lynch and Michael Sherwood and Richard Sharp at Goldman Sachs were not part of the established elite of British financiers. But if the American banks they represented lacked pedigree, having arrived in the City only in the 1980s, they were two of the biggest in the world and had huge clout.

Goldman Sachs's offices in Fleet Street had a greater concentration of multi-millionaires than any other in Britain. This was partly because of the sums received by the partners when the firm – known in the City as 'Goldmine Sachs' – floated in 2000. But it was also down to the sky-high fees the firm could earn from its specialist activities – mergers, acquisitions and corporate finance. Michael Sherwood and Richard Sharp were worth more than £125 million each. In 2004, a PA at the bank was found guilty of stealing £4.5 million from the personal bank accounts of two of her bosses without either of them noticing.

From day one, events were to move at a frenetic pace. Within hours of arriving Rose was shocked to find that the City law firm appointed by Green – Freshfields Bruckhaus Deringer – had also earlier acted for M&S when they had drawn up the contract with George Davies for the Per Una range. M&S immediately went on the attack. Their lawyers, Slaughter & May, won a high court ruling that the law firm could be in possession of confidential information that could be harmful to M&S. So, on day two, Freshfields was banned from acting for Green. This was a symbolic victory for Rose, his first scalp in the battle to fight off his friend. It was an irritating setback for Green who was forced, hurriedly, to appoint a replacement law firm – Ashurst.

Rose's arrival sparked a flurry of activity at M&S. Top managers briefed him one by one. Within days Charles Wilson, given responsibility to help with the turnaround strategy, was to be seen patrolling the Baker Street store with his trademark black notebook. At the same time the crucial task of wooing M&S's investors began in earnest. David Mayhew of Cazenove started the process of putting the case for Rose and Myners, while Rose took to calling some analysts himself, apparently the first time some had heard from an M&S chief executive in years.

Green too had to act quickly. He had been pressured into making an earlier announcement than he would have liked before a coherent plan was in place and now had to catch up. While M&S were busy juggling their top management over the weekend, Green had announced that he had secured the agreement of Lord Stevenson to join his team as the senior non-executive director at Revival Acquisitions, the company Green had created as a vehicle to mount the bid. Dennis Stevenson was chairman of both HBOS and Pearson, the giant publishing house. As HBOS were putting up the bulk of the finance, he was no doubt keen to be in a position to keep a close eye on Green. Stevenson's appointment was critical. A City heavyweight, he provided respectability for Green and reassurance for potential investors, and also took on the role to find a chairman who commanded the confidence of the City. Fifteen years earlier, he would not have been such a fan of Green's. He had played a leading role in bringing down Tony Berry at Manpower because of Berry's practice of making unauthorised loans of company money to friends and business associates. One of those helped out in this way, as we have seen, had been Philip Green.

On Thursday, 3 June – Rose's third day in the job – Green summoned his personal bodyguard, Sean, and asked him to deliver an envelope to the M&S chief executive personally. Sean, a shaven-headed former soldier and martial arts specialist, was used to being asked to play a key role in Green's business affairs. The envelope sent to Rose in this unusual way contained details of his intended offer. The formalities had begun.

When Rose and his advisers studied the contents, they were surprised. The proposal was much less straightforward and much less generous than they had expected. It involved a mix of a cash payment to buy M&S shares at a price of between 290 and 310p a share with a share element equivalent to a 25 per cent stake in the newly formed Revival Acquisitions. The plan was for Revival to be floated on the Alternative Investment Market, giving former M&S shareholders the chance to share in the turnaround Green was sure he would deliver.

But the deal was also highly conditional on Green having access to detailed commercially sensitive information in a number of areas. His prime concern was to establish that there was no black hole in the M&S staff pension fund, an important consideration for any prospective buyer. In a number of other high-level examples potential deals had foundered because of the deficits discovered in company pension funds.

Analysts calculated the offer to value the company at between £7.5 and £9 billion, the equivalent of between 340 and 390p a share. Green was making a personal commitment of £1.1 billion, and liked to give the impression that all of this was coming out of his own pocket. 'The biggest personal cheque ever signed' is how he liked to describe it. Although he didn't like them saying it, many financial analysts took the view that this was doubtful, that at least some of his own contribution would have to be borrowed, possibly using some of his other assets as collateral for the loan.

The rest of the finance was being put up by a consortium of five banks. Three of them – HBOS, the Royal Bank of Scotland and Barclays Capital – were to put up the bulk of the loan, while Goldman Sachs and Merrill Lynch were to put up equity. Goldman was to invest £800 million from its own private equity fund, a nest-egg used by Goldman staff for their personal investments. This represented one of the biggest single investments ever made by a Private Partners' Fund. It seemed they considered Green a good horse to back. It was certainly remarkable to have put together such a 'highly leveraged' deal, one in which such a high proportion came from bank loans with only a limited equity and cash cushion, and was a testament to Green's skill at driving a tough bargain with bankers as well as with suppliers. The reason the banks were willing to play ball with what one financial analyst calls 'a virtually unprecedented package' was their faith in his now proven ability to generate cash out of companies he took over.

But if Green expected the City to give his terms a ringing endorsement, he was wrong. The dominant reaction was that the proposal was too mean and too complicated. Many also thought the level of debt finance involved was abnormally high, even after the release of cash from the sale of the M&S financial services arm and from the sale of M&S property. It looked to many as if Green had gone in with the previous week's terms, making no upward adjustment for the arrival of Rose. The City in effect delivered the thumbs down.

Baker Street was delighted. Green seemed to have made a tactical error in pitching his first bid so low. It was by now pretty clear that the shareholders would not back Green for anything less than the equivalent of 400p a share and would probably want something even higher. Seven hours after receiving the proposal, M&S rejected it as derisory, claiming it significantly undervalued the company. Although it is customary in most takeover situations to reject the first offer, Rose's way of putting it – 'the City would have been gobsmacked if we had accepted this' – chimed with City opinion. Rose also made it clear that M&S had no intention of disclosing the commercial information Green was insisting on.

Green may have had a head start on M&S when he first made his intentions public ten days earlier, but events had not been kind. City bookies switched their odds in favour of Rose and away from Green. Morale was rising at M&S headquarters and sinking in the Green camp. He had been outmanoeuvred by what he and others had considered a leaden-footed board at Baker Street. He was clearly rattled by the course of events and let it show. The day his bid was handed in, he abruptly cut short an interview with *Channel 4 News* presenter Jon Snow when the interview was not going his way. Green accused Snow of being aggressive and rude and more or less threw the startled presenter out of his office.

The next morning Rose was pulling up in his BMW at the side entrance to M&S headquarters only to spot a clearly agitated Green marching towards him. It appeared to most onlookers that Green had been sitting in his chauffeur-driven Mercedes, with its blacked-out windows, waiting for Rose. Green reached the car and started to drag the M&S chief executive out by his lapels, watched by Rose's startled chauffeur, Caroline. 'I want a fucking word with you,' he shouted. 'You owe me. I got you that job. You did nothing for twenty months and then they paid you £1 million. You could have made £250 million if you came with me.' Rose was heard to reply, 'I didn't want the money – I wanted the job.'

After a series of heated and very public exchanges, and a further stream of invective from the Bhs boss, a still rattled Green rang his wife Tina in Monaco on his mobile phone and handed the phone to Rose: 'Tina wants a word with you.' Tina took up where Philip left off, haranguing Rose in almost equal measure down the phone. Rose later told M&S colleagues that she had called him 'the lowest form of life'. As the exchanges calmed down, Green said, 'Well, you can send me a case of your best wine at least. I got you the job.' Rose promised to send him one when the bid was over. 'No, send it today,' roared Green as he stormed off towards his car.

Green claimed that he had not been waiting for Rose to arrive but had been passing by on his way to his Bhs offices in nearby Marylebone Road when he had spotted Rose arriving in Baker Street in his BMW. The whole incident – about twenty minutes long – was witnessed by startled bystanders, company security guards and hordes of M&S staff hanging out of the windows of the company's head office. Green later dismissed the encounter as just a bit of fun: 'If I'd been serious, he'd have gone through the window.' He was now emerging as the closest thing retail had to a rock star, and the sort who was constantly misbehaving in public.

A few days after the incident, Green, ever the practical joker, telephoned Rose on his mobile to sing, 'If you go down to the woods today, you'd better go in disguise . . .' Rose joked that in order to avoid Green, he now 'walked around in dark glasses and a moustache'.[2] Traditional City fund managers may not have found it quite so amusing. Because of the size of the potential deal, Green had this time appointed a City PR company, Finsbury, an influential firm that could boast a large number of FTSE 100 clients. They would have known that handling Green was not going to be their easiest assignment, but it appeared to be turning into something of a nightmare. As one analyst summed up the incident, Green 'has never been able to see that the way he behaves is what gets people's backs up'.[3]

It was certainly getting him noticed. Shortly after the incident, Green was due to appear at a business conference organised by the *Sunday Times*. The opening speech was given by the Chancellor, Gordon Brown, who began by declaring himself proud to be the 'warm-up act for Philip Green'. When Green started his speech, he began by saying that the Chancellor was 'probably looking forward to the stamp duty'.

Green may have attempted to make light of the set-to with Rose, but M&S's own spin-doctors, Tulchan, were quick to turn it to their advantage. Is this the sort of man to run one of Britain's most hallowed stores? they asked. M&S advisers spread stories aimed at undermining the credibility of Green, pointing not just to his erratic behaviour, but suggesting that he was not as good a retailer as he liked to claim, that though profits had increased at Arcadia and Bhs, his record on sales and market share had been poor. Green, of course, always disputed he was little more than an effective cost-cutter. According to his PR team, desperate to stop the rot, his record showed that he also bought better, sped up the decision-making process and, despite his short fuse, built real loyalty amongst staff.

Despite Green's early setbacks, he was as determined as ever to press on. He had had a bad few days, had lost his cool in a key television interview and allowed himself to get embroiled in a public tantrum with his principal opponent. He now had to recover some of this lost ground. He spent the first weekend in June with his family in Monte Carlo. Monday morning he was back at his desk in London.

To have any chance of success Green needed first to raise more money to up his bid. This would mean either a higher commitment from himself – and £1 billion was already a record-breaking contribution from a private individual – or more from his backers. Speculation began to mount about whether Green might sell Bhs, which would give him more money to put into the deal and simultaneously eliminate the risk of a veto from the regulators worried about Green's excessive market share. Nobody was prepared to write Green off – he had proved too astute an operator for too long to be dismissed easily after a difficult few days.

But success would also depend on winning the support of the big institutional investors. Since 2000, M&S's share ownership base had been changing sharply. Amongst those that would help determine the company's fate were three large American investment companies. The most important of these was Brandes. It had been upping its stake since Green's first attempt on M&S, and was now the largest holder with 12.5 per cent of M&S shares. Other American holders included Capital Group – like Brandes California-based – which owned 4.8 per cent, and Artisan Partners with 4 per cent.

Throughout the early weeks of June, the companies' respective financial advisers stepped up their lobbying of these and other institutional investors. Green personally devoted a lot of time trying to woo Amelia Morris, Brandes's leading fund manager. The attempts were initially inconclusive, with some reports saying that Brandes, a highly traditional organisation, did not know what to make of Green.

Meanwhile, the mutual mud-slinging became increasingly personal. While M&S were spinning away against Green, his own pitch to investors relied heavily on attempts to question Rose's track record. Green's advisers started to deploy the very arguments that M&S executives had earlier used to resist hiring Rose in the first place, portraying the new chief executive as a short-term operator who had made a series of quick lucrative exits from the companies he had run. Green, in particular, liked to portray Rose as a man who had little hands-on experience of the rag-trade and the supply chain. M&S responded in kind, asking why, if this was so, Green had been so keen to hire him and accusing Green of only being interested in paying off debt as fast as he could.

A further problem for Green was that with Rose in charge, M&S were now much more likely to implement the kind of strategy that Green had in mind when he first decided to take the company on. Rose's priorities included a review of the under-performing Lifestore chains and of the stand-alone food outlets, Simply Food. He was also intent on improving the margins while attempting to make M&S clothing more competitive in price. He had also already decided that the headcount at the Baker Street headquarters, itself a symbol of the bureaucratic tendencies of the company, could be drastically pruned. On his arrival he discovered the company had two separate human resources departments, two separate departments looking at change, a bureau of standards and a department responsible for colour management.

Another key priority was to sort out the ongoing problem of the supply chain with successful products tending to run out too quickly. M&S gave only 'rough design ideas' to suppliers instead of the detailed specifications laid down by competing high street chains. Controlling the supply chain, of course, was one of Green's proven strengths. Although the decision had been taken by Holmes, Rose announced in his first week that M&S was terminating a contract with clothing manufacturer Desmond & Sons, based in Northern Ireland. M&S was Desmond's sole customer and the manufacturer, given two months' notice, was forced to call in the receiver with the loss of 300 jobs. This decision continued a steady process of switching from UK to overseas suppliers.

The issue of restoring M&S's former but largely lost reputation for offering quality at a reasonable price was a much more uphill task than sacking a few hundred staff and axing some failing new initiatives. Rose knew there was a desperate need to reposition Marks on its core customer, those aged over thirty-five, a group he once described as the 'premium middle ground'. He hinted that he was about to dump what had proved to be a misguided shift of emphasis towards youth, encouraged by M&S's younger management school graduates and marketing executives.

Rose was to reveal the much-awaited details of his plans for the store at a special meeting of institutional shareholders on 12 July, just two days before the company's crucial AGM. Both events were subsequently to have a decisive impact on the outcome of the bid.

Within days of Green signalling his intentions, M&S turned to a favoured trick in these situations and one they had used during 'round one' in 2000 – they issued a flurry of 212 notices aimed at forcing individuals and companies to disclose details of their share dealings. Most of the notices were sent to a close-knit circle of Green's friends and allies. M&S was attempting to identify the strength of Green's potential support and hoped that in the process the legally flushed out information would prove embarrassing to Green's camp. The list – a short 'who's who' of super-rich entrepreneurs and businessmen – included Tom Hunter, Bernie Ecclestone, Allan Leighton (now the chairman of Royal Mail), the Reuben brothers, Terry Green (now chief executive of Allders), Robin Saunders, top QC Lord Anthony Grabiner, the chairman of Arcadia, and several directors of Green's companies. Most of them declared they had no shares.

The notices had some of the intended effect – they flushed out the details of Tom Hunter's purchase on 16 April when he bought 375,000 shares for the trust he had set up for his children. The Reuben brothers also revealed that they had purchased call options on 760,000 shares on 15 April. But the share purchases by Rose and Spencer – made on 7 May and 11 May respectively – were not public as yet.

Meanwhile, Rose was acting to prove he would bring tough management to M&S. On 9 June, barely a week after his arrival, Vittorio Radice became the next high-level casualty of M&S's management cull. Radice, who had lasted barely fifteen months, had ruffled several feathers during his short stay, in particular for criticising the group for a lack of continental flair, and for concentrating on middle-aged, middle-class women in market towns, whom Rose knew he would have to win back to make his mark. It had been the flamboyant Radice who had pledged to turn M&S into the world's biggest sellers of G-strings. His departure meant that his initiatives, including Lifestore, were unlikely to survive.

A week later, on 16 June, in the middle of Royal Ascot week and a favourite date in the business calendar, Green rang Rose to ask for a private meeting. It was held at a Mayfair townhouse office in Upper Grosvenor Street owned by Morgan Stanley. It was attended on one side by Green and Richard Sharp, the head of private equity at Goldman Sachs, and on the other by Paul Myners and Simon Robey of Morgan Stanley. Green had insisted on a small meeting without the usual entourage of merchant bankers and advisers. Chain-smoking as usual, Green explained that he was able to up his offer, now renamed Operation Socrates, to £11.9 billion – the equivalent of 370p a share – a sum that broke UK records for a bid by a private individual for a company.

Green was prepared for a heavy grilling on his plans and was surprised when the M&S bosses withdrew after a mere forty-five minutes. Myners hastily convened a board meeting that began shortly after 5 p.m. The response was clear and unambiguous – no.

It was left to Myners to inform Green that 370p was not enough. Green was quick to retort that he had made it clear in the meeting that the offer said *not less than* 370p. 'Are you saying there is no discussion?' he went on. 'No,' answered Myners. What Green had offered was a bit more money and an even more complex version of his earlier offer, this time with a choice of all in cash or, if investors wanted, a mix of cash and equity.

The following evening a dejected Green tried to watch England play Switzerland in the first round of Euro 2004 in Portugal. But despite England's emphatic 3–0 victory, his mind was firmly elsewhere. With M&S digging in, the future fate of the two warring sides would depend heavily on three factors. First was the question of which way the American shareholders would jump. Without support from Brandes, Green would almost certainly be forced to walk away from M&S again. Then there was the strength or otherwise of Rose's recovery plans to be delivered on 12 July. Having dismissed Green's offers so unambiguously, he had to convince shareholders that he could do better. Lastly would be the reaction of the company's 360,000 small shareholders at the AGM to be held on 14 July.

The next day bankers on both sides tried unsuccessfully to get hold of Amelia Morris at Brandes. That week, the American company had unloaded a tiny proportion of its stock holdings but enough to make a substantial profit. Brandes was notoriously secretive and most observers thought that it would wait until Rose's presentation on 12 July before revealing its hand. What Green was hoping for was that Brandes would at least put pressure on M&S to open its books in the way that he had twice requested. That would enable Green and his advisers to table a more formal offer and for shareholders to make a more rational judgement of the relative merits of the two strategies on offer.

City opinion remained divided. Some investors thought the response of M&S was cavalier and sympathised with Green. Others doubted he had really changed his spots since his bust-up with the City over Amber Day when he had shown himself to be the sort of company chief who resented interference from institutional investors. Still others took the view that Green always bought on the cheap and that his offer must therefore have undervalued the company. That said, there were some in the City who would have been happy to take the Green cash and run if they thought it was a better deal than Rose could deliver.

Rose was clearly ahead on points at this stage, but that was all about to change in the most spectacular and unexpected way. And it was Rose's earlier share dealings that were to rock the boat.

When Rose joined the company he owned 135,000 shares – 100,000 of which had been bought on 7 May, apparently immediately after his phone call with Green, and the other 35,000 earlier in the year. At this stage such information was not public knowledge. But, under City regulations, new directors of a company are obliged to notify the company of details of any share interest within five business days of appointment. Quoted companies are then required to disclose details of the date of purchase, the price and amount by the end of the business day after receiving it.

Rose in fact informed Myners of his holdings during the Bank Holiday weekend discussions before he started work on 1 June. M&S was thus required to have revealed the details of Rose's stake by 2 June. They did not do so. M&S tried to defend this delay by saying, 'Frankly, it wasn't the company's top priority that week.'[4]

It wasn't until fifteen days later on 17 June that details of the Rose shares were finally released by M&S, the same day that the press hounds were busy trying to interpret the significance of Green's second rejected bid. M&S subsequently claimed that the delay was due to the slowness of the appropriate department in checking the details of Rose's share dealings, and that it was not part of a 'co-ordinated attempt at a cover-up'.[5] Maybe, but some parts of the press were not going to let up. They were certainly suspicious that this potentially controversial information was put out on a busy news day and might have been part of a deliberate attempt to avoid it being spotted.

The *Mail*, which reported M&S's statement on Rose's shareholdings on 18 June, certainly scented a potentially damaging angle on the ongoing saga and contacted Tulchan with a very specific request for details about when the shares had been acquired. According to the paper, Tulchan 'stonewalled', claiming that M&S was not required to give such details. This was wrong. The regulations are clear that disclosure should include the date, price and amount of any transactions. Tulchan's reply simply aroused further suspicion. It looked as if the company and Rose had something they would rather not disclose. When the *Mail on Sunday* carried details of the apparent evasion on 20 June, Tulchan caved in under the mounting press interest and provided the required information – Rose had bought 100,000 shares on 7 May.

The date, so close to his joining M&S, raised some eyebrows, but its explosive significance was not yet clear. On Monday, 21 June, with the date of purchase now out in the open, the *Mail*, scenting that there was more to reveal, rang Green's office to ask what contact he had had with Rose before his meeting with him on 12 May, a meeting which had earlier been revealed to the press. Green asked his assistant at Bhs head office, Katie O'Brien, to check his mobile phone records. According to the Green camp, these showed that Green spoke to Rose at 1.47 p.m. on 7 May in a call that lasted three minutes and twenty-seven seconds.

This was potential dynamite. Green passed the information to his PR advisers, Finsbury. Green's merchant bank, Goldman Sachs, then combed records of share dealings, which showed that two parcels of 100,000 shares had changed hands that day – at 2.16 p.m. and then at 3.13 p.m. – at 276p each. One of these had to be the tranche bought by Rose. This meant that Rose had bought the shares within ninety minutes of his conversation with Green, possibly within thirty minutes. (M&S have always insisted that the only source for the call was Green's team.)

The revelation – devastating to both Rose and M&S – was now leaked to the *Daily Mail*, which printed it in detail the next day. The episode proved a spectacular PR disaster for M&S and especially for Tulchan, which had compounded the backlash by the way it had chosen to handle the disclosure in the first place. Tulchan had of course originally issued the 212 notices thinking that any embarrass-ment over share dealings would rebound on Green. It turned out to be the opposite.

M&S may deny claims of a conspiracy, but at the time it certainly looked to some as if it had been trying to hide the embarrassing breach of the company code. Up to that point the 'dream team' had not put a foot wrong. Now they were looking distinctly tarnished. The failure to act according to the rulebook also rebounded on Myners, who had long been a champion of corporate transparency and better governance. The Green camp was ecstatic.

M&S attempted to recover the situation by trying to switch the spotlight onto Green's advisers, by accusing them of leaking the details and of 'a pretty serious smear campaign'. But, whether the Green camp acted unethically or not, the damage – and it was pretty serious damage – had been done. A big question mark now hung over Rose's action: did he buy the shares on a punt or as a result of a helpful tip-off? Suddenly, M&S's carefully constructed plan to contrast Rose's integrity, professionalism and squeaky-clean image with Green's more unpredictable and stormy reputation was looking distinctly thin.

Moreover, to the irritation of Rose and his employers, the affair refused to go away. First, the details of Rose's share dealing started to ring further alarm bells at the Financial Services Authority. On 25 June they announced that their initial enquiries into M&S share dealings had given way to a formal probe. Rose was shaken by the news. The announcement implied that the watchdog had found prima facie evidence of wrongdoing. At the height of their fight for survival, M&S and Rose now had to face a full-blooded investigation by the financial watchdog. For the FSA to go public in this way was quite exceptional. It meant that there was a real chance that M&S might lose Rose, now their only real line of defence against Green.

Further uncomfortable revelations were to follow. Over the weekend, the papers carried details of the £427,000 profit made by the Reuben brothers when they cashed in their shares on 11 June.

Then, while the share dealing affair was still simmering, Rose was to face further embarrassment when remarks he was alleged to have made at the Chelsea Flower Show on 24 May, three days before Green's bid, were reported by the *Sunday Telegraph*.[6] According to the paper, a senior banker working for Goldman Sachs claimed he had overheard Rose telling Rosemary Thorne, the finance director of Bradford & Bingley, about Green's pending bid and that he had been asked to chair Green's bid company. The banker reported this information to Goldman Sachs and purportedly underscored it by signing an affidavit to that effect. He knew Thorne because Bradford & Bingley had also hired Goldman Sachs to represent them in their attempts to convert to a bank. If the banker had heard correctly, Rose's remarks were a clear breach of the confidentiality agreement he had signed with Green and might have been the source of the rumours spreading around the City which led to a surge in the share price immediately before Green's formal announcement. Moreover, if substantiated, they raised doubts about a highly paid professional's capacity to keep a secret. When the paper asked Rose about his alleged remarks he responded, 'This is bollocks. That is an outright lie.'

The day after the revelations, Rose wrote to Goldman Sachs denying the allegation and demanding a retraction. He claimed that though he had spoken to Thorne, he had mentioned being offered the chairmanship of Saga not Revival. Moreover, according to Rose, Green hadn't actually offered him the job of chairman – the post on offer was to head up M&S food. Thorne also backed Rose's account saying they had just been engaged in 'social gossip'. Despite these protestations from Rose, the denial by Thorne and the veiled threats of legal action, Goldman Sachs refused to retract its allegations. No legal action was subsequently brought by Rose or M&S against Goldman Sachs.

The press revelations did not stop there. The same weekend, the *Sunday Times* revealed details of Michael Spencer's purchase of 2 million shares on 11 May and that they had followed a drink with Stuart Rose at George's the day before. Spencer was shocked because he had not told anyone, there was no public record and details had not been flushed out by the 212 notices, simply because 'contracts for difference' have weaker disclosure rules. Spencer claimed that only a 'microscopic number of people' knew about his dealings and they could not have come to light accidentally.

M&S was now becoming deeply suspicious as to how personal and damaging information had been leaking out and began to suspect that someone had employed private detectives to snoop on the company. It was not clear, for example, how the press had got details of some of Rose's phone calls or how they knew about his meeting with Michael Spencer at George's. Rose suspected that someone had accessed his MMO[2] phone records. In addition his wife, from whom he was now separated, found that her mail appeared to have been tampered with. According to M&S, Jenny Rose had received bank statements which had 'been opened and re-sealed

with Sellotape before they arrived'. Rose was also concerned that his
diary had somehow been accessed.

When Rose checked with MMO^2, he was asked for his password.
This came as a shock as he did not have one. When he explained this,
he was told that someone had set up a security system with a password
on 23 June, the previous week. It appeared that someone impersonating him had already contacted the company to assess the records. This
was likely to have been the source, or at least one of the sources, of
some of the remarkably accurate newspaper stories at the end of June.

On Wednesday, 30 June, Rose issued Green and his advisers with
notices under the Data Protection Act to force them to disclose any
personal information they were holding on him. The letters included
£10 to cover the cost of returning the information and were sent to
Goldman Sachs, Merrill Lynch and the financial investigations agency
Kroll Associates. The implication was clear. M&S believed that Green
or someone working for Green was behind the apparent corporate
espionage.

Green refused to take the notices seriously. He asked his bodyguard, Sean, to collect two prostitutes' calling cards from a phonebox
and to deliver them to Rose with a note: 'Dear Stuart, please find
enclosed the information I have on you. Here's a picture of the two
girls that had dinner with you at Harry's Bar a few weeks ago. I enclose
£10 which they told me to return to you. Philip.' It was the kind of
wind-up that Green especially enjoys but it was also a sign of how
much the relationship between the two sides had deteriorated. It also
added a touch of farce to the whole proceedings. Rose was also
believed to have received other tongue-in-cheek replies to his request.
One said: 'Here's the £10 back. Why don't you buy three M&S shares
with it.' Another said: 'Here's the £10. This might help towards your
FSA fine.'

Concerned that sensitive information was leaking from their Baker
Street offices, M&S also called in security experts to check if meeting
rooms had been surreptitiously bugged. Over the last weekend in
June, M&S's entire headquarters was swept for bugs and from then on
security guards were posted outside corporate meetings and confidential conversations were restricted to offices marked 'This Room is
Secure'.

To carry out this work, M&S had initially tried to hire the world's
two largest security agencies – Kroll Associates and Control Risks. Four

years earlier, Kroll had been employed by Donaldson, Luftkin & Jenrette (the investment bank hired by Green during his first attempt on M&S) to check out Green, their own client. In recent years, however, it had been attempting to move away from its image as a corporate detective agency engaging in shady espionage, preferring to promote itself as an international 'risk consultant'. Both firms turned down the offer claiming a conflict of interest while failing to spell out what they meant.

The implication was that the Green camp had also been trying to recruit the same firms, hence Kroll's inclusion in the list of Data Protection Act demands. Green resolutely denied that he had appointed Kroll, based in suitably anonymous premises in London's Blackfriars, or any other private security firm, to dig the dirt on M&S. In a reference to the two private Mayfair dining clubs frequented by Rose, he told the *Daily Telegraph*, 'We already know where George and Harry's Bar are without Kroll.'[7] On the other hand he appeared not to rule out the possibility that one of his City advisers might have done so. He said to the *Daily Mail*, 'I cannot vouch for the investment banks. I don't run their business.'[8] Goldman Sachs, already in the firing line over the Chelsea Flower Show affair, and renowned for its aggressive tactics in other deals, refused to comment. Green's other advisers simply issued denials. An alternative theory, of course, was that if there had been some kind of espionage, it was initiated by the press rather than someone in Green's camp.

While M&S were busy tightening their internal security, both Rose and Green were summoned to appear before the FSA at their Canary Wharf offices. Rose had hoped his appearance would have remained confidential. He had the most difficult questions to answer and was accompanied by his lawyer. He was grilled at length about why he bought shares within ninety minutes of his conversation with Green. Green was pressed on who knew about his takeover plans before they were formally announced. The FSA were attempting to find out whether Rose had had a tip-off and if so from whom, and also how Green's plans leaked out and fuelled a leap in the share price in the two hours before his statement.

All those who had made a killing out of their share dealings denied any wrongdoing. Hunter was highly irritated to have become embroiled. He claimed he had no knowledge of Green's intentions and that he had simply seized what seemed to him like a good buying opportunity because he felt the City had over-reacted to a downbeat trading statement from the company. Spencer also denied he got a tip, but asked the regulators if they would investigate how his investment became public. He did, however, admit to William Lewis of the *Sunday Times* that his purchase had been 'embarrassing'.[9] Rose continued to deny that he had been tipped off by Green in their 7 May phone conversation, Green backed his story and Rose continued to get the full support of the M&S board. This was hardly surprising – if M&S had jettisoned yet another boss, Green would have been home and dry.

Following the furious and very public clash between the two men outside the head office of M&S at the beginning of June, Green had been outmanoeuvred by Rose. But by the end of the month, the balance had swung firmly back to Green. Most of the mud that had been flying around, and there had been bucketfuls of it, had landed on Rose and M&S. Although Green's camp may have helped to fuel the flames, and some friends and associates of Green had also bought shares, it was Rose who had emerged with new doubts over his reputation. With only ten days to go to Rose's critical 12 July presentation, City sentiment had started to shift in Green's direction. As one analyst put it: 'Philip Green now looks like a paragon of virtue. Two weeks ago, he looked like a street bully. Now the whole focus has swung onto Stuart Rose smooching around London restaurants gossiping about M&S. There's no doubt his reputation has been damaged.'[10]

But although the odds were at last moving in Green's direction, he had a problem. The Takeover Panel had given him a very tight deadline of 6 August to make a formal bid. Progress had been slow in winning the support he needed and time was fast running out.

TANKS ON THE LAWN

W hile Green was fretting over the ever-tightening dead-line, Rose had been invited to attend the annual awards ceremony of the Prince of Wales's charity Business in the Community. At the prestigious event – held on 6 July at the Royal Albert Hall before an audience of 1,600 business leaders, ministers and opinion leaders – M&S was named Company of the Year 2004. It had been chosen for its 'outstanding' impact on society in sustainable food production, encouraging good labour practices among its suppliers and for its work experience programme designed to help 2,500 disadvantaged people to find employment.

The award seemed to sum up the reason why so many loyal followers didn't want Green running their company. M&S had long been recognised for taking a lead in business social responsibility and had obtained a clutch of awards for doing so. It had also been named as the Dow Jones Sustainability Index's most sustainable retailer in the world for the last two years.

Just before the ceremony, Julia Cleverdon, BITC's chief executive, used an interview with the *Financial Times* to launch a direct attack on Philip Green – who had snubbed the organisation by refusing to allow Bhs and Arcadia to become members – suggesting that a takeover by him would threaten it as a responsible retailer. 'These aren't values by which Philip Green runs the business,' she said, then added, 'I think these values will go if he takes over and takes it private.'[1] BITC is renowned for its diplomacy, and such a public rebuke was unexpected. It certainly didn't go down well with Green.

Cleverdon was forced, not least by the threat of litigation, to attempt a grovelling apology in the *Financial Times* the next day: 'In no way did I intend to imply that there was anything wrong with the personal values of Philip Green.'[2] One of the ironies was that the winner of the award hosts and pays for the following year's ceremony.

Should Green emerge the victor of the battle for M&S he would be asked to host the event in 2005.

While Rose was shaking hands with the Prince of Wales, Green was locked in detailed and lengthy telephone negotiations with Amelia Morris at Brandes. Emboldened by the slide in support for Rose across the City, Green had rung her at 6.00 p.m. British time and, with his usual bluntness, attempted to secure her support for a new 400p cash offer.

After hours of internal wrangling with the organisation's senior analysts and lawyers, Morris finally rang back at 2.30 a.m. to tell Green he had a deal. Green liked to suggest that she had been won over by his humour and charm. The truth was more prosaic. Brandes had at last been convinced that his new deal made good business sense. Securing Brandes was a major coup for Green, making it more likely that other investors would move his way. As Green finally went to sleep in his hotel bedroom in the early hours of the morning, he knew the heat had once again been turned on M&S. It had been a hard slog; Green had been ringing Morris almost daily for nearly three weeks.

The cost of the bid had been steadily rising and was now close to £12 billion. More than half of this sum was coming from HBOS, the largest commitment the bank had ever made to a single project. Green had upped his own contribution from £1.1 billion to £1.6 billion – enough to show just how serious he was.

The next morning, Green issued a formal statement through the Stock Exchange that he was making a third bid of 400p per share. Green had, at last, 'put his tanks on the lawn'. Ironically, had he tabled this bid at the beginning, the City would have been more supportive from the word go. It now looked somewhat belated. Anxious to dispel the idea that he would up the offer again if it were rejected, Green insisted that this was his 'final, final, final' proposal. 'Not a penny more,' as he put it.

Green was now offering shareholders a choice: a straight 400p or a cash-and-share alternative of 335p in cash and a 30 per cent equity stake. Under the new offer, Green would still have ended up owning a significant majority of the company, a prospect that worried a number of long-term investors and had made many existing M&S share-holders wary of backing Green. 'If you get into bed with Philip Green and you are in a minority, you are somewhat vulnerable,' one City editor commented.[3]

Shortly after he tabled the bid, Green started phoning his friends and a few favoured journalists, singing, 'We're on our way to Wembley, we're on our way to Wembley, my knees are going trembly, la, la, la, la . . .'[4] The reason for Green's jubilation was that he had also won round another top-ten investor, Schroders.

The news that Brandes and Schroders were backing Green's new bid came as a shock to M&S. Cazenove had been wooing Morris as heavily as Green. When they sought clarification, Morris e-mailed the M&S team, making it clear that their acceptance of the Green offer was conditional on a recommendation from the board. This of course was a significant qualification to what Green had earlier portrayed as an 'irrevocable' commitment. 'Elastic' might have been more accurate. That evening the M&S board, which had been on the back foot for some weeks, disbanded after three hours without making a decision. Opinion amongst analysts remained divided about whether the board would now finally be forced to hold talks with Green.

While M&S were weighing up this latest unwelcome news, Green attended a party at the entrepreneur Robert Earl's new private members casino, Fifty, a four-floor nightclub venue in London's St James's. Earl, the former Planet Hollywood owner, was another multi-millionaire friend of Green's and was throwing the party to celebrate that day's Formula One exhibition event in Regent Street, a stunt organised to promote the case for a Grand Prix in the capital. Green, despite his late-night negotiations, was cheered by the day's developments and was in good spirits as he partied into the early hours. It was noticeable, though, that he did not try his luck at the blackjack tables.

The next morning, the M&S board resumed and rejected Green for a third time. The company insisted that the bid still undervalued M&S and that Rose would emphatically demonstrate this when he unveiled his plans the following Monday. Those who had predicted that M&S would cave in had been proved wrong.

Behind the scenes, however, the M&S board knew it would be harder to fight off the third Green offer – a considerable improvement on the earlier proposals. Nevertheless, by declaring it final, Green now found himself boxed into a corner of his own making. He could not now raise his bid and had ruled out the idea of a hostile takeover. With the 6 August deadline looming, success depended on the M&S board changing its mind and at least opening negotiations.

That evening, Green, never short of a party to go to, attended the sixtieth birthday party of Lord Levy, the Labour Party's chief fund-raiser. The day before, Green had announced that Arcadia was providing £1.25 million to sponsor fifty secondary schools specialising in business and enterprise, one of the government's flagship educational policies. At the party he met and chatted to Tony Blair about the sponsorship scheme. The timing of the declaration, the day after the attack on his record on social responsibility, raised a few eyebrows, but Green insisted that the plans had been in fruition for weeks.

Meanwhile, the FSA announced that they had dropped their enquiries into the acquisition of shares by both Rose and Spencer. It subsequently cleared others who had bought shares earlier and finally closed the investigation in September having found nothing 'untoward'.

The issue with Rose was whether his share purchase had been prompted by prior knowledge that Green was about to pounce. If he had such knowledge, as a result of a direct tip-off from Green himself or from anyone else party to the plan, it would have been illegal. On the other hand, if he had made a very shrewd investment on the basis of hunch, it would not have been. Rose's defence had always been that he had regularly traded in and out of M&S shares and that Green did not tell him during the crucial phone call what their meeting was about. Even so, with the knowledge or suspicions he had at the time – an upcoming meeting with Philip Green, a forthcoming lunch with one of the billionaire Reuben brothers about a possible bid for M&S and the mounting speculation in retail and City circles – it must have felt like a one-way bet, which is what it turned out to be.

Details of such timely and profitable share dealings are rarely made public. In this case their exposure provided a rare insight into the way in which the already very rich can make themselves even richer, if not by insider dealing, then with the knowledge and intelligence that comes to them as part of a small but well-connected club. The episode certainly did not look good to outsiders who saw a system that favoured wealthy men operating in a privileged and narrow social circle.

Although Rose was cleared by the FSA, his actions left a question mark over his personal and business judgement. He may not have done anything illegal, but seeking to make a fast buck in this way was widely seen to be at best unwise and certainly naive. It was certainly a surprise that such an experienced businessman who thought that his turn to run M&S might be on the cards hadn't been more circumspect. It also meant that at the first signs of trouble at M&S, Rose in particular would have more difficulty winning the confidence of the City. As one retail analyst put it at the time, 'If there aren't any tangible signs of turnaround, the market is not going to be as patient as it might have been.'[5]

Green was, meanwhile, doing his utmost to force the M&S hand. On the Friday before Rose was due to present his vision of a new M&S, Green let it be known that he now had the backing of 22.6 per cent of the shares held by institutional investors. The 400p cash offer had, apparently, finally done the trick. Of course, these shareholders wanted the offer to be firmed up with cash on the table in the form of a formal bid, something that would only come when Green had access to the M&S pension fund accounts and other commercial information. Nevertheless, the pressure on M&S to allow Green to look at the books was growing.

That afternoon he was sufficiently confident to fly to his Monaco home for the weekend. He seemed especially unworried by what Rose would have to say the following Monday about reviving the M&S fortunes. As he put it to Kate Rankin at the *Daily Telegraph*, 'What's he going to say? That he's suddenly found an oil well under Marble Arch. That he's stopped his expenses?'[6]

While Green was sunning himself on the deck of his yacht, Rose was spending the weekend at Baker Street putting the final touches to his Monday presentation with a team from Morgan Stanley and media advisers Tulchan.

Monday, 12 July 2004 was a date that had been circled in red on City and media calendars. On that morning M&S's institutional shareholders – a notoriously demanding and fickle bunch – were to listen to Rose unveiling his survival plans for the company. The importance of the occasion could hardly be exaggerated. It was a meeting that would help seal the fate of Rose, Green and M&S itself. Rose had had barely six weeks to prepare his master plan to keep Green at bay. There had been some judicious dropping of hints along the way about what he might do, but he would need more than the usual blend of cost-cutting and the slaying of M&S sacred cows to meet the expectations that had been building.

The meeting was set for 10 a.m. at Cabot Hall, a giant corporate conference and entertainment centre in Canary Wharf. The towering office development had been constructed during the Thatcher years in the heart of the decaying Docklands. Although most of the financial services industry continues to be based in the old square mile in the City of London, the Wharf is a monument to the kind of more cut-throat global capitalism that emerged from the 1980s, one that M&S had for years been reluctant to embrace with full conviction.

For most of its life M&S had been run as a paternalistic and patriotic company, a policy that had won it award after award. Simon Marks, son of the founder of M&S, for example, may have become 'tyrannical' towards the end of his remarkable career, but he had run the company according to a very clear social principle, that the company had a responsibility to put something back into the community and a responsibility to their 65,000 staff. This is why the company had been generous to employees and had a policy of backing British suppliers throughout most of its history. That alone has had a dramatic impact on the British clothing manufacturing industry. Without M&S support, it would have disappeared much more quickly. The question of a 'British label' has long been a sensitive one at M&S and the store has always been more reluctant than its competitors to abandon British suppliers towards whom it has felt a good deal of loyalty. In the past, buying British had paid off, appealing to the patriotism of its customers. Now it was a model that was proving more and more difficult to sustain in an increasingly competitive and fast-paced retail market.

The question now was whether M&S could stick to its founding principles and still take first place in the modern market economy. Some critics had long argued that at the very least staff rewards would have to be tied more closely to performance, that suppliers would have to be chosen on the basis of price and quality rather than on their geographical location, and that the bureaucratic culture that had become such a feature in Baker Street would have to be swept away. Green was certainly in no doubt what needed to be done, and nor was Rose. M&S had already started the process of modernisation. Five years before, for example, 80 per cent of M&S clothes carried a 'made in Britain' label. Now it was closer to 20 per cent.

The key question on the minds of those gathering to hear Rose was how far he would be prepared to go in making the changes that the

City, not bound by sentimentality, had been demanding for years. Rose was facing one of the biggest challenges of his career. The stakes could not be higher. Rose knew that there would be no place for him at M&S if Green's bid were to succeed.

Rose arrived early. Despite the obvious pressure, he had been buoyed up by his clearance by the FSA and was at least outwardly remarkably calm. He was convinced that he and his team, many of them hastily assembled, had come up with a blueprint that would convince the sceptics. One point had to be driven home: with him in charge and a new strategy in place, M&S was potentially worth more, indeed noticeably more, than the 400p a share being offered by Green.

Rose was also only too aware of how the battle for M&S had been affected by a dramatic change in the way British companies were owned. Even in the late 1990s, M&S shareholders had been dominated by traditional UK-based institutional investors representing pension funds or managing large savings accounts, groups that tended to take a long-term view of the company's performance. But subsequent years had seen the arrival of a set of more volatile investors. Some of these new-style investors were super-rich private individuals only interested in making short-term profits by speculating on the share price. But most of them were financial institutions with a very different outlook from the old pension company investors.

Even before Green declared his hand on 27 May, close to 30 per cent of M&S shares were held by American institutions, the largest being Brandes. Most of the holdings by Brandes had been bought at a price of between 260 and 280p. Since Green's declaration of intent there had been a huge turnover in M&S shares: close to three out of four of the company's 2.2 billion shares had changed hands.

Those buying in were mostly speculative institutional investors looking for a quick killing, many of them consisting of hedge funds – the ultimate short-term investments. Many of these investors were American, betting on cashing in on the difference between the buying price and the 400p per share offer if Green were to turn his phantom offer into a formal bid. One of New York's speculative traders, a thirty-something, fast-talking guy called Harry, had put a good deal of his own hot money into the company that week and declared that 'Rabid dogs now own Marks & Spencer.'[7] This was capitalism 2004 style, characterised by the flow of global 'loose' money looking for a potentially lucrative home, money that could determine the future of many British companies.

It was those investors only interested in making a quick buck that were mostly lining up behind Green. They typically had little or no interest in the good of the company or in Rose's plans for long-term improvement, and Rose realised there was little he could do to win them over. He was banking on there being enough of the old-style, long-term investors to allow him to hold off the Green challenge.

The great concern of these investors was that the Green package would threaten the future viability of the company by landing it with a huge level of debt. It is an oft-repeated criticism, one levelled, for example, by Manchester United fans against Malcolm Glazer's dramatic takeover of the club in May 2005. Under the Green scheme, simply paying the interest on the loans he would need to take out would have swallowed up much of the company's cashflow. But the additional debt would also lower the company's credit rating, a measure of its credit-worthiness, making it more difficult and more expensive for it to borrow in the future.

With the aid of his banking advisers, Rose had found a clever way to exploit this risk. For weeks, Green had been trying, unsuccessfully, to get the firm's pension fund trustees – supposedly an independent group – to open up the books for him to see. But they had repeatedly refused. Green saw this as deliberate obstruction. But the reason, according to Sir David Sieff, one of the trustees, was that 'our job was to protect pensioner interests, and neither to hinder nor promote a bid. And in any case, Green hadn't, at that stage, actually made a bid so why would Green be any more entitled to see the figures than anybody else?'[8]

This decision not to mount a formal bid had proved a problem for Green from the beginning and was the excuse used not just by the pension trustees but also by the M&S board to refuse to co-operate with his other demands for crucial information. Over the weekend, the chairman of the trustees, David Norgrove, a mild-mannered former M&S director, replied to a question put to him by the M&S board: if M&S's credit-worthiness were to deteriorate, what impact would it have on the funding of the pension scheme?

The question may have looked innocuous but it was anything but. Norgrove's reply was that the company would be forced to put in more cash – of between £350 million and £785 million – to top up the scheme. It was a bombshell response to which Rose must have known the answer before he asked it, and it made it much more difficult for Green to claim that his numbers added up. It was the first bit of good news for Rose in two weeks of battering. To Green and his advisers it looked like more careful stage-management by M&S. Green, who had always questioned the so-called independence of the trustees, a group he liked to portray as being 'in hiding', saw this as a confirmation of his suspicions.

By 9.45 a.m. the Cabot Hall conference room was full, a sea of dark suits representing most if not all of the most powerful institutions in the City and Wall Street. Few City presentations had been more eagerly awaited. Rose, an experienced and polished public performer, was used to addressing such meetings and only too aware of the financial muscle assembled before him. The audience, buzzing with anticipation, was equally experienced at judging these situations, weighing every nuance of presentation, assessing every soundbite. As Rose entered the room, the gathering fell silent.

One thing was clear – few members of his audience were wearing M&S suits. Nor was Rose. For him, this would have been a concession too far. While Paul Myners, the new, temporary chairman had been happy to don a £199 M&S Italian suit, Rose was still to be persuaded that loyalty meant dressing down. On the day he was wearing a £2,115 suit by top Savile Row designer Richard James, the tailor also favoured by Paul McCartney, Tom Cruise and Hugh Grant. When pressed, Rose revealed, however, that he was wearing M&S underwear.

As he started to lay out his plans, he could sense the audience's thoughts – he knew they would be looking for some surprises, enough to convince them he could deliver perhaps another 20 per cent improvement in the share price on top of Green's 400p. He knew too that they would be summing him up. How was he coping with the pressure? Was he the man to save M&S? Would their money be safer with Green?

Some of Rose's thinking had already been trailed or even implemented. As he unveiled some of the detail, much of it was what the audience had been primed to expect. There was to be a further round of cost-cutting to bring savings of £320 million within two years by a further squeeze on suppliers, cutting markdown costs and axing 650 jobs. The company's food and clothing suppliers had already been warned that the price M&S was willing to pay was being cut. This was, of course, straight out of Green's book. The under-performing and expensive LifeStore homewares chain was, as predicted, to be axed. Rose was blunt; the chain, re-christened 'DeathStore' within M&S, had been 'a disaster'.

There were some carefully selected surprises – without them Rose would have been scalped. The company was buying the successful Per Una label for £125 million but was dropping the less successful Per Una Due brand. The mainstream brand had made a £17 million profit the previous year and creator and owner George Davies himself had agreed to stay on as chief executive for at least two years. The decision to buy Davies out of the contract made by his predecessors was a clever deal and one that the City had not anticipated. It also meant that Davies was richer to the tune of £125 million.

Most eagerly awaited was the promise, already widely trailed, of a £2.3 billion handout, the equivalent of £1 a share, to shareholders through a buyback to take place in September. This was being funded partly by the sale of the financial services arm, M&S Money, to the high-street bank HSBC for £762 million. The City had expected the sale of the savings business, but the deal also included a clever and surprise formula to allow M&S to hold onto some of the potential upside of the business through a profit-sharing joint venture with the bank. As the package was unveiled, it was clear just how influential Green's intervention and the arrival of the newer speculative investors had been – it was these events that had effectively forced the company to include the cash return and the sale of its financial services arm, moves that the board under Holmes had earlier resisted.

But it was not only good news that was on offer. The company's latest trading figures were again poor. Sales had continued to slide. Rose was scathing about past performance, lambasting the company structure and by implication his immediate predecessors. There had been, he said, a 'lack of leadership'. He could hardly have been more direct. Under Vandevelde and Holmes the company had become 'too complex, too inward-looking, the stores too cluttered'.

The strategy could perhaps be best summed up in Rose's own phrase 'back to basics', a risky slogan. His audience, young as many of them were, would mostly have remembered that, ten years earlier, the then Conservative Prime Minister, John Major, had made a similar call to return the country to a previous morality, and lived to regret it.

Rose was in essence offering a change in emphasis and a simpler operation. There would be fewer goods. By promising to cut 1,000 lines from clothes and 500 from food, the stores would become less cluttered. The recent flirtation with the youth market was to be dropped in favour of its traditional and core customers aged between thirty-five and fifty-five. As Rose put it, M&S had neglected ladies' nightgowns, forgotten about men's pyjamas, made knickers that were 'too high in the leg'. It had hedged its bets in clothing lines by making six or seven different versions of each product – ending up with huge markdowns to clear unsold stock.

Rose was a master of just this kind of occasion. It was a polished presentation, smooth, unruffled, schoolmasterly perhaps, but would it prove enough to convince the City? At the end of his speech, the institutional investors left in animated huddles. It was too early to gauge the reaction. Had he lost any support? Had he done enough to turn the doubters?

One effect of the presentation was that the respective offers were now clearer. Going with Green would bring investors 400p a share. Rose was offering a guaranteed dollop of jam today – through the share buyback – and the promise of the rest of the jar tomorrow. The tomorrow bit was of course uncertain and depended in part on Rose's promise of savings from new deals with suppliers, better stock control and fewer sales markdowns.

The first reactions were less than flattering. The lunchtime edition of the London *Evening Standard* dismissed Rose's offerings as too heavily weighted towards the giveaway cashback – 'all bribe', as the paper's City columnist, Anthony Hilton, put it somewhat icily. He went on: 'If I were M&S's recently fired chief executive Roger Holmes, I might feel aggrieved at this point. He too could have sold assets to return cash if he had thought it was in the long-term interests of shareholders. Instead, he thought – mistakenly, it would appear – they wanted him to focus on building a business for the future. Silly boy.'[9]

Also under scrutiny was the lack of a strategy for sales. Rose had given a lot of emphasis to the cost savings and the cash offer, which would mean less to invest in the business, but little to how to produce the sort of clothes customers wanted to buy. The dismal trading figures revealed by Rose seemed to underpin the problem only too clearly.

That afternoon, Green gave his own scathing response in a conference call to investors. It was a predictable barrage of criticism. He derided the further savings to be squeezed out of suppliers and on markdown as little more than guesswork and was brutal on the lack of detail on how to win back lost customers. He was dismissive about the deal to buy Per Una. M&S, he said, had provided free shop space and free shop fits to build the brand and now had to pay for it: 'I have not seen any retail magic in this, nor any surprises. It is déjà vu. They have been here before.'

Few had expected Green to praise the plans, of course. But his history was correct. When he had made his first attempt on M&S in December 1999, the board had borrowed to give shareholders back a comparable sum, and the company had embarked on a series of similar cost-savings measures all with little long-term gain. When Holmes took over he made the same noises on costs, supply and product. The problem was that over the past four years, bureaucracy and political infighting had combined to prevent M&S executing their recovery plans effectively. Keeping core customers happy and improving the supply chain while trimming unnecessary costs hardly added up to a revolutionary strategy. Leveraging the balance sheet to hand cash back to shareholders is little more than a short-term ploy – raiding the family silver – that carries longer-term costs by stripping potential investment out of the company.

Of course, it was easy to dismiss Rose's plans as full of flannel but Green was still inwardly relieved – he could see nothing in the strategy to make him anticipate defeat. The war of attrition between the two men continued as Green went on to repeat his earlier spurning of Rose's track record: 'I bought Arcadia from Rose in October 2002. How come we managed to double profits in ten months? We have actually done it – why didn't he do it?'

Back in their City offices, the analysts were working feverishly at their spreadsheets, and further outbursts by Green carried little weight with those doing the sums. Both Green and Rose knew it was in these calculations that the future of M&S would now be decided. The early signs were more mixed than Rose would have hoped. Some were undoubtedly impressed. One retail analyst described Rose's plans as 'a killer blow' and the sales of financial services and a cashback to shareholders as a 'brilliant bit of financial engineering'. Several others also had upbeat assessments. Others were more wary in their notes to clients. One said he was impressed with the review's thoroughness but added, 'This may still not be enough.' Another said: 'We think this statement increases Green's chances of winning.' One expert added just £20 million to his final year profits forecast, much less than the prediction implicit in Rose's estimates.[10]

These were hardly the ringing endorsements that Rose had been hoping for. Nevertheless, not all was black for the M&S board. By the end of the day, the share price had slipped 4p to finish at 364p. This suggested that whatever some investors and analysts were publicly saying, the market believed that Green's bid was less likely to succeed. Indeed, if the City had been unimpressed with Rose's offer, they would have bid the share price up, edging it closer to Green's offer of 400p.

With everything still to play for and time running out for individual fund managers to make up their minds, the lobbying moved up a gear. That afternoon, while Green tried to convince some investors, Goldman Sachs and Merrill Lynch were on the phones to still uncommitted US shareholders. One US fund manager was phoned while sunbathing in Spain. Another described Goldman as sounding 'desperate'.

Nevertheless, the intensive lobbying was starting to work. Behind the scenes, more companies were asking M&S to open their books. The only manager that day openly to back the recovery plan outlined by Rose was Standard Life, then M&S's third biggest UK investor with a holding of 2.1 per cent. Many fund managers remained undecided, though Green claimed the following day that those backing him had risen in the last few days to 27 per cent.

Rose had hoped that his presentation would clinch the matter. But it had not. The outcome of the six-week-long battle remained as uncertain as ever and the vote at the company's AGM, to be held in two days, would now be critical.

On Tuesday, the day after the presentation and the day before the crucial AGM, it emerged that Deutsche Bank had bought 88 million shares in the past few days and, as a result, had emerged as the second largest holder with 8.3 per cent of holdings. This was widely interpreted as a sign that Deutsche would back Green. On the same day, Richard Sharp of Goldman, buoyed by their growing support, phoned David Mayhew, chairman of Cazenove, to propose talks. The approach was, unsurprisingly, rebuffed.

Chapter   1 3

THE DAY OF RECKONING

W hen Rose arrived at M&S, it was expected that most institutional shareholders would have declared their hand before the annual meeting of the company. The small shareholders who came along would then be presented with a *fait accompli*. It had not turned out like that. The AGM, to be held on Wednesday, 14 July, was now to be the second day of reckoning in one week.

On the eve of the annual meeting Paul Myners stayed up late preparing for his presentation. It would be the largest group he had ever addressed and he knew it had to be right. Myners was not as practised a public performer as Rose and had taken special coaching from Susanna Voyle, a former retail correspondent of the *Financial Times* who now ran her own communications company. While Myners was being put through his paces, Green was meeting William Lewis of the *Sunday Times* and Jeff Randall at the Dorchester Hotel's oriental restaurant for dinner. The journalists were hoping Green would update them on his latest thinking. The luxurious restaurant, with silk wall hangings and antique artefacts, is a popular haunt for rich businessmen, journalists and politicians.

Green and Randall were, of course, long-standing friends. Randall was only too aware that senior executives in the news department at the BBC were nervous about his close relationship with the entrepreneur for fear it might have been seen as prejudicial to his coverage of business stories in which Green was a principal player. Randall was obliged by the BBC to report objectively on Green and his rivals, and had to be scrupulously careful to avoid taking sides.

Randall and Lewis were waiting at the table when Green walked in, as usual with a mobile phone glued to his ear. As he got to the table, there was a shout from across the subtly lit restaurant: 'So now we know: Philip Green and Jeff Randall, a-ha!' The whole restaurant turned to see who it was. Green turned to Randall and said, 'It's that fat c**t Lord Soames.' Nicholas Soames, the then shadow defence secretary and a grandson of Winston Churchill, was dining with his brother, Jeremy, and one other companion. He continued, 'So that's why the BBC coverage is like it is – nice cosy chats. Ho ho ho! We'll be able to see your coverage now, won't we? Their kind keep it all together, as ever.'

Both Randall and Green took this to be a direct reference to the two of them being Jewish. Randall, furious that his integrity had been impugned, immediately phoned Maurice Saatchi, the advertising supremo who was also chairman of the Conservative Party. Saatchi eventually rang back about 11 p.m. The next morning, the day of the AGM, Soames called Randall and is said to have apologised for the incident, also strongly denying he had intended to make a racist slur and insisting that his remarks had been misinterpreted. Others had an alternative reading of the spat, that when Soames said 'their kind', what he really meant was 'wide boys'.

Those who had been eagerly awaiting the AGM on Wednesday woke up to a wet and blustery July day. It did not appear to act as a deterrent. The venue for the meeting – the Royal Festival Hall on the south bank of the Thames – seemed especially apposite. It had been the centrepiece of the Festival of Britain of 1951, a patriotic attempt to celebrate all that was good about Britain in an age of austerity. Like M&S it had become a national institution symbolising the past more than the future.

By 9 a.m. shareholders started to arrive, forming an orderly and very British queue outside the entrance, fending off the rain as best they could with umbrellas and cagoules. By 11 a.m. the cavernous auditorium, which held over 2,500 people, was full, even though, outside, hundreds of people were still queuing and the rain still falling.

Inside the hall the interim company chairman, Paul Myners, walked to the rostrum to announce that the start of 'the momentous meeting' would have to be delayed. As if to reassure them, he promised, 'It is going to be a cracker.' No one looked remotely as though they wanted to leave. M&S and Festival Hall staff were left frantically trying to organise overspill arrangements, with CCTV screens and two-way sound to accommodate those still arriving. Experienced observers reported that it was the largest turnout ever seen for an AGM of a publicly quoted company.

The company's individual shareholders knew only too well that this was a decisive day for the company. And these were no ordinary shareholders. They were as close as it gets to middle England on the march – a middle-aged, middle-class, rank-and-file battalion, polite, patient and single-minded, with not a placard, mini-skirt or pair of trainers in sight.

M&S probably has more individual shareholders than any other company – some 360,000 of them. In 2004 they commanded as many as a fifth of all shares. This compares with 2 per cent at Vodafone and some 6 per cent at Tesco. M&S bosses, of course, thought they knew their shareholders and were quietly confident that they would get the endorsement that they needed. But even they had totally under-estimated the turnout on the day and were conscious that the end result might not be as predictable as they hoped.

Certainly, some small shareholders had, at least initially, welcomed Green's intervention and the stir-up it brought. Moreover, shareholder power was a growing force in Britain. Recent months had seen a raft of rebellions at company AGMs, rebellions led by both institutional and individual shareholders. The protests had started at GlaxoSmithKline in May 2003 when a majority of shareholders voted against a highly controversial pay deal awarded to the company's French-born and American-based chief executive, Jean-Paul Garnier. Never before had shareholders voted so decisively against company policies. It was a strong signal that company boards could no longer have it all their own way and that an era of tougher accountability had been born. Over the next year, the rebellions came thick and fast. Protests were mounted at a whole raft of FTSE 100 companies – BAE Systems, WPP, BSkyB, Sainsbury's. The M&S board could not be sure that they could avoid the same fate.

The meeting eventually started more than half an hour late. As Myners rose to open the meeting, a hush descended over the packed and expectant auditorium. He began by informing the audience that while waiting for the meeting to begin, he had met Mrs Powell from Carlisle. She had bought her shares in 1932. 'Under the terms of the Takeover Code,' he said, 'I'm not allowed to . . . give Mr Green what she said to give him.' To the evident relief of the organisers, the audience burst into spontaneous applause. This was merely the opening salvo in what had been carefully planned by Tulchan as a charm offensive on shareholders. It could not have started better.

Myners was frank. The business had not performed as well as it should have, market share was being lost, mistakes had been made. The shareholders, of course, didn't need to be told; that was why they were there. But they listened quietly and intently none the less.

Then came the same forty-five-minute presentation from Stuart Rose that he had given to the institutional shareholders two days before. This was long by AGM standards, but there were few signs of boredom. He began by gleefully informing his audience that he was appropriately dressed for the occasion – in a 'revolutionary washable Aertex travel suit – from Marks & Spencer, of course'. He might have got away with Savile Row at Cabot Hall but not here.

Rose, in his half-moon glasses and looking like a public-school headmaster, is not a showman like Green, but this was another cool and confident performance. The audience lapped it up. They laughed in the right places and applauded on cue. It was not quite a standing ovation but the speech was warmly received. This was all by way of prelude to the real business – the questions and the vote. The M&S board had certainly expected some tricky questions but it was no coincidence that the opening contribution came from a retired M&S press officer who could hardly be more friendly: 'Welcome back, Stuart. I'd prefer an M&S through Rose-tinted spectacles to one growing Green around the gills.'

However, a few questions were more pointed, like the one from a Mr Flunder: 'Year in year out we get a new management team but nothing really happens. Does anyone think the shares would have gone up and the £2.3 billion found for a share buyback if there hadn't been a takeover bid? Of course there wouldn't. All the new teams do is sack staff. Wouldn't it be a good idea to keep the dedicated staff and sack the board?'

Another challenged the payback as only offering 'short-term gains'. Someone else did not want 'to screw the suppliers'. One amusingly spoke of how he had picked up one garment, a pair of shorts, to find it tagged with no less than four labels. One gave the price, and the other three all said the same thing – that they were shrink resistant.

There was applause when one shareholder called for the return to the St Michael's label, which had been dumped in 2000. This was after all an audience who, by and large, could still remember such things. Several questioners began by proudly announcing that they were dressed from head to foot in M&S clothes. One sales assistant got a round of applause for her plea to the board to 'listen to your staff, we listen to your customers every day'.

But though there was sniping, it was nothing compared with the strength of anti-Green feeling. M&S has been described as the BBC of retail, part of the fabric of middle Britain, catering for a largely conservative group in tastes and standards, people who in general don't like upheaval and unnecessary change. Those attending the AGM were overwhelmingly representative of the M&S core customer, which had certainly been neglected by the store in recent times.

Only two shareholders were brave enough to say that the chain would be better run by Green. One, a Mr Leonard Bash, demanded: 'Take his offer, it is the best offer, it's the finest offer since sliced bread.' He was roundly booed. Paul Myners thanked him for his contribution, commenting: 'Bash by name and bash by nature.' The audience enjoyed that.

To most of these loyal, well-informed but far from uncritical footsoldiers, Green was the worst kind of predator, threatening all they believed in. Although many of them probably shopped at least occasionally at Bhs and Arcadia as well as at their beloved M&S, they were instinctively hostile to the man they felt would move the company in directions they would not like. Green had created an image for himself that did not play well with these middle-Englanders. They had read the stories of his fiftieth birthday party and of his fracas with Rose, and did not much like the impression they had gained of a tasteless and aggressive man with too much money to spend. Encouragingly for Myners and Rose, the small investors were not especially interested in who would make them the most money; they were more concerned with the company's long-term future than what they saw as a quick fix.

But there was still the possibility of an upset, of an anti-vote for the resolutions endorsing the new board. Even a modest rebellion would have made it more difficult for the company to resist Green. But the vote soon dispelled any doubts. The resolutions backing the new chairman and chief executive were passed with huge majorities of over 98 per cent. The votes, electronically recorded, counted and displayed within seconds, showed 'East European majorities' as a relieved and delighted-looking Mr Myners put it. He added, 'Mr Bash, there is your answer.' That brought the biggest smiles of the morning.

It was indeed a powerful vote of confidence in the board and their strategy, and something of a killer blow for Green. As the meeting ended and the shareholders started to disperse, they were rewarded for their attendance, and their votes, with lunch packs containing a luxury roll, a packet of gourmet hand-cooked crisps and a bottle of chilled pinot grigio, M&S finest, all packed in special cool carrier bags. By this time the rain had stopped, the sun had come out and London's South Bank complex was full of shareholders munching away and absorbing the lessons of the morning. As one observed, probably truthfully, 'Mr Green would never have given us a free lunch.'

This was far from a typical blue-chip company annual meeting. It was more like a rally than an AGM. Yes, there were some tough and well-informed questions to keep the board on their toes. But the silent majority had spoken volumes. They liked their store, its history and traditions, and did not want it turned into just another lookalike high street chain. Green may have been capturing the support of the hard-nosed, volatile institutional shareholders – many of whom had, somewhat pointedly, not bothered to turn up to the AGM – but he had singularly failed to dent the hearts and minds of the army of individual M&S loyalists.

Now Rose had won the popular support from individual share-holders, Green was left with seriously narrowing options. He had still not been allowed to look at the pension fund books. He could put together a bid by the August deadline but, without the advantage of having seen the books, this would have been a high-risk strategy. Green had always made it clear that however much he wanted M&S, he was not going to overpay for it. Paying too much would prevent him generating sufficient cashflow to pay off the debt and make money without threatening the future of the store. As Green had already described his 400p offer as 'final', under the City Takeover Code he could not increase it unless a rival bidder emerged. He would not in any case have wanted to pay any more. He could still launch a hostile bid, but had rather ruled that out by announcing he would only pursue the takeover with the co-operation of the board. In any case, Goldman Sachs with its own £800 million stake was also unlikely to back a hostile bid.

While the shareholders were still pouring out of the Royal Festival Hall, Paul Myners knew that the balance had swung heavily their way. Grateful for the way she had helped him with his own performance, he sent Susanna Voyle a text message of thanks: 'Love ya baby.' Shortly after that his mobile phone rang. It was Philip Green, who had been speedily informed of the AGM's backing for the board. It was 1.30 p.m., less than twenty minutes after the chairman had called an end to the meeting. Green was boiling. His call came out of the blue and, as Rose and Myners had come to expect, it was direct. According to Myners, 'There were a lot of expletives . . . He said what was I effing going to do now. He said, "I have got 34 per cent of your effing shareholders in my pocket."'[1]

Green then told Myners firmly that with his growing support, it was time to stop playing games and open a dialogue. This may have been an attempt to up the stakes but the problem for Green was that he was not really in a position to put pressure on M&S. Although the institutional shareholders had continued to move his way, he had needed significantly more than a third of them to get the board to move.[2] Now he had even failed to achieve a divided vote amongst private investors. It was thus somewhat premature to try to put the screws on Myners, and the M&S chairman knew it.

A fuming and almost defeated Green spent the afternoon at Goldman Sachs pacing up and down and smoking furiously, waiting for Myners to ring with a response to his demand. Calls were put in to M&S advisers at Citigroup and Morgan Stanley, but their mobile phones were turned off. By 3.30 p.m. the waiting team had heard nothing. Mike Sherwood, European head at Goldman Sachs, called David Mayhew, his opposite number at Cazenove. Mayhew was fishing in Scotland and explained that no decision had yet been taken. Green, of course, is hardly renowned for his patience and when an hour later he and his advisers had still heard nothing from Myners, he could sense his sought-after prize slipping from his grasp for a second time. At 4.30 p.m. Sherwood called Cazenove again, hoping that Myners would at least agree to talk.

An hour later, with the silence continuing, an increasingly explosive Green called Mayhew himself and shouted at him down the phone, demanding an answer that very evening. Mayhew explained that M&S was holding a board meeting at 6.00 p.m. Myners was apparently at another board meeting, unrelated to M&S, and Green was asked, politely, if he could wait a little longer. Not that he had any choice. Green was, however, given a promise that there would be no announcement until he had been informed of the outcome. While they waited for the news, Green and his advisers adjourned to his Bhs office.

The M&S board had three items on the agenda: to welcome two new non-executive members following the resignations of Dame Stella Rimington and Brian Baldock; to get shareholder feedback from Cazenove; and to discuss Green's latest move. At 7 p.m. Green rang Mayhew, who again urged him to wait. Another hour then passed with no calls from Myners or his team. At 8 p.m. Green discovered that M&S had been briefing journalists that the board had not changed its position on access, information that had not been passed to Green or his side. In fact, the board never even formally discussed the third item. For Green this was the last straw. He had built up his hopes only to see them shattered and the M&S board had not even bothered to pass on the news.

At 8.30 p.m. an exasperated Green issued a statement to the Stock Exchange announcing his decision to withdraw. He had had enough of the board 'constantly messing us about' as he later put it. It was as dramatic as it was unexpected.

According to Rose, the M&S team took the news with no sense of triumph: 'There was no whooping or glee. No one got the champagne out. I think everyone was just knackered.'[3]

Shortly after his announcement Green rang his thirteen-year-old daughter Chloë to say he had pulled out of the bid. She was delighted. Chloë had been horrified earlier in the year when she was told of the proposed bid. Green recalled how 'she had burst into floods of tears, telling me I'd promised her I wouldn't buy anything else and that I would spend more time at home'.[4] Brandon, his twelve-year-old son, on the other hand, had been keen for him to go for it. From the beginning, it seems, Philip not only faced a divided City but a divided family as well. Green always talks proudly of his children: Chloë loves to dance and is sharp on clothes – 'She knows a good garment when she sees one' – while Brandon is a keen poker player. Green would like both to go into the family business; he has said, 'I would be terribly disappointed if they didn't.'[5] Chloë has even occasionally worked for the day in Bhs in Oxford Street, although Green has said: 'Don't pay her.'[6] He has always been conscious of his split life and has made a rule to spend Friday evening at home in Monaco whenever possible, a commitment his private jet has made it much easier to keep to.

After pulling out, an irascible Green made a series of scathing attacks on Rose, Myners and the rest of the M&S board. He was a bitter man and showed it. As he explained to the *Sunday Telegraph*: 'We were sitting there with 34 per cent, and the only public support he [Rose] had received was 2 per cent. If it was boxing, the ref would have stopped the fight.'[7] He was openly furious that he had only secured one face-to-face meeting and that the board had refused to open the books. He singled out Myners for much of the blame: 'Who does this guy think he is? He gets £50,000 a year. He doesn't own the company.'[8] Shortly afterwards he accused Myners of being an 'anti-Semitic left-winger' to Jason Nisse at the *Independent on Sunday*.[9]

The evening he pulled the plug Green gave an emotional interview to Jeff Randall on BBC's *Newsnight*. He was bristling with anger and claimed to have been treated with contempt by the M&S board: 'I've got some of the world's leading banks with me and it's contemptible never to have a meeting with somebody who has produced 12 billion.' But he ended the interview with a warning of 'a very clear judgement day in every street in the country'. They were not the words of a man prepared to let the matter rest.

Given that Green actually had until 6 August before he would have been required to withdraw, the City was mostly taken aback by his sudden decision. Even though the odds had moved heavily against Green, nobody had expected him to pull out quite so abruptly, including M&S. It was typical of his impulsive nature, but to many it looked precipitous, especially as the momentum amongst the institutional holders appeared to be moving his way.

One active M&S institutional investor said he was 'surprised' by the development, especially given claims that some previously undecided investors, such as Deutsche Bank, were likely to back Green. Although Deutsche had refused to say openly who they were backing, it was widely assumed that their dramatic acquisition of 88 million shares the Friday before the AGM was a sign of support for Green. By withdrawing his bid before the deadline ran out he had left such institutions high and dry. His defence – that he had no choice and had always made it clear that he did not want to win at any price – cut little ice in some quarters.

The wider reactions in the City were mixed. Green had spent years trying to win support there and loved to gloat about how he had lined up some of the most prestigious City names. Even though they knew the risks, most of these backers would now be licking their wounds. Green of course faced hefty fees, but his financial backers had lost the deal, the bonanza pay-off and the massive bonuses they had been playing for. Brandes and the institutional shareholders who had bought early enough to have started to unload shares from the middle of June at a tidy profit could have few complaints. Others may have felt like jilted brides but they had been gambling heavily with their choice of partner. By jumping in just a few days before Green pulled out, Deutsche Bank would have lost millions and would not have forgiven him in a hurry. Many of those who had bet heavily on his success, including the hedge fund managers in the ten days up to the AGM, were forced to sell at a substantial loss. By Friday the M&S share price was down around 12p closing at 348p as speculators unloaded their shares. Whether those who had had their fingers burnt would be prepared to back Green in any future deals of a similar scale remained open to doubt.

In the end, Green had been outmanoeuvred by M&S. The critical factor was the swift appointment of Rose, an astute move by Myners who had more or less single-handedly organised the coup. Green was especially angry about the way the supposedly independent pension fund trustees refused to co-operate, only to leak highly sensitive and damaging information at a crucial time, an act that he blamed on Myners. As he put it at the time, 'I'm getting very annoyed. They're messing me around. Paul Myners is supposed to be working for the government on pension issues. He's thinking he's going to get a knighthood; he'll get a nightcap instead.'[10] This was not the only heavy-handed jibe at Myners. On the same day, he ranted, 'Do me a favour, give your chairman a proper fucking kick in the head.'[11]

He also liked to argue that he had been the victim of his own achievements: 'Nobody wants to sell us anything. We are being unfairly handicapped because of our past successes.' Peter Cummings at HBOS, the main funder of the bid, agreed: 'His success is his Achilles heel. When he tries to buy a business now, people are saying they should not sell because he will be buying on the cheap.'[12] The problem for Green, of course, was that this was partly true. It may have been with the benefit of hindsight, but Green had obtained Sears, Bhs and Arcadia on the cheap, and thus at the expense of shareholders in those companies, and he wasn't going to be allowed to pull that trick again.

Another problem for Green was his choice of tactics. He never made a formal bid, although without access to the books, it would have been risky to do so. As one City watcher describes it, 'He merely invited the board to give in and hand the company over.'[13] With no real money on the table, M&S was able to continue to present Green's plans as phantom. They may have been in difficulties but were nowhere near the state that Sears or Bhs had been in. He dangled the 400p, but it is likely that Green had no intention of paying as much as this, which M&S suspected. Once invited in, Green would undoubtedly have seized the opportunity to chisel away at the price. The M&S board also knew that once Green had been allowed in, he would have become difficult to reject.

At the end of the battle for M&S, *Retail Week* carried an article by Robert Clark, a highly regarded retail consultant. In the article Clark suggested that if Green had bought M&S at £4 a share, he would in fact have got it on the cheap.[14] Green complained to the magazine at the time that the article was wrong. In October 2004, three months later, he was invited to a party to celebrate the relaunch of the weekly. At the party, Clark was chatting to some colleagues when he spotted a determined-looking Green heading in his direction. 'That article you wrote – it's a load of bollocks. You don't understand anything,' he said. Clark defended his article, while Green continued to complain. Eventually Green went off in a huff, only to return twenty minutes later to carry on his tirade, much to the amusement of those in the group, some of whom could not hide their fits of giggles.

Neill Denny, former editor of *Retail Week*, describes the incident as classic Green: 'He reads what people write because he cares what is being said about him. He still remembers what was written months before even in quite a small magazine. That he should want to tackle the journalist to put what he saw as the record straight even on a trivial point is typical of his obsessive nature. You can't see a Terry Leahy bothering.'[15]

It was certainly true that Myners liked to portray Green as attempting to 'steal the company', but Green had also contributed to his own failure. Green's first bid, with hindsight, was too miserly and played into M&S's hands. It may have been made to look feebler than it was by the sharp rise in the share price but Green should have taken that into account.

It was also Green who turned it into a personal battle. He may have been rattled by the way he felt Rose had betrayed him and that Myners and Rose had quickly gained the upper hand, but turning his fury into an avalanche of public invective against Rose and Myners hardly helped his cause. The Baker Street brawl and Green's public displays of petulance allowed M&S to portray him as mercurial and brash, not the sort of man to run M&S. It was certainly not the way to win round the private shareholders. From the beginning, Green had made it clear that the takeover depended on a recommendation from the board. He knew that the private shareholders would not have pledged their shares to him without a nod from the M&S directors.

His allies and friends may have been able to dismiss Green's outbursts as the idiosyncratic behaviour and bizarre sense of humour of a brilliant businessman, the harmless result of his need for attention-seeking. That may be so, but behaving and talking like a dodgy second-hand car dealer, even if it's meant in fun, does not go down well with some sections of the financial establishment. His unusual tactics had also, apparently, failed to convince the public. In a survey for the trade magazine *Retail Week*, 16 per cent said M&S should be taken over by Green while 62 per cent said Rose should be given a chance.[16] His previous victories at Sears, Bhs and Arcadia had been conducted less publicly and much more calmly. This time, as his final attacks on Myners seemed to indicate, he appeared to be a man incapable of losing gracefully. Green had also grown increasingly frustrated with his own advisers. A can-do man who abhors meetings and likes to take instant decisions, he found the formalities of a takeover bid stifling.

With Green and Rose on opposing sides it was always going to be a virility test between the two but it turned out to be more than this. The second battle for control of M&S became the highest profile takeover battle in recent memory. It was a story that dominated the news and gripped City brokers, business journalists and the public alike.

It also left some crucial questions unanswered. What did Green and Rose talk about on the phone on 7 May if it was not M&S, as both men claim? How did the details of Michael Spencer's share dealings come out? Exactly who was snooping around Stuart Rose's mobile phone records? If private investigators had been used, who hired them? If Green had finally made a real bid, just how much would he have offered when he saw the books?

Green may have been the main loser but the City also did itself no favours. The inner workings of Britain's business and financial world were revealed as details of embarrassing and sometimes questionable boardroom behaviour, and tactics were exposed on an almost daily basis. In the process the City's reputation for fair and open play was undoubtedly damaged. There was the lingering smell of insider dealing despite the protagonists having been cleared; there were the high-profile smears, the deliberate leaking of private and damaging information, the allegations of bugged offices and other forms of industrial espionage against M&S.

M&S may have won the day, but their defence had cost them upwards of £40 million in bills to lawyers, bankers and public relations officials, and their reputation for integrity and fair dealing was hardly enhanced. The limitations of the powerful Goldman Sachs – which had put a lot of its own money into the deal – were also exposed.

Green was left licking his wounds for a second time. The exhausted entrepreneur, who had had little proper sleep for weeks, had promised that if M&S refused to respond to his offer he was 'off to the beach'. But before he carried out his promise, he had one more thing to add: 'Actually the deal nearly didn't come off for an entirely different reason. I'm very superstitious, and I've used a special Bvlgari pen to sign every deal I've done over the past twelve years, but during the M&S negotiations I lost it. My wife rang everywhere in the world that I'd been, trying to find it. Luckily it turned up behind a desk. I wouldn't have signed anything without it.'[17]

On Friday, thirty-six hours after he had pulled the plug, Rose's loyal chauffeur, Caroline, was spotted delivering a case of 1997 Chateau Cheval Blanc wine direct from Rose's extensive personal cellar to the Bhs headquarters on Marylebone Road. At up to £3,000 a case, Cheval Blanc is one of the most expensive of French wines. It is the least perhaps that Rose could have done. Without Green's intervention, he would not have got his dream job, M&S would probably have fallen and Rose might well have ended up as chairman of Saga.

BREATHING DOWN THEIR NECKS

The day after Green withdrew his bid for M&S was also the day that several advertising agencies had been summoned to present their marketing proposals for Bhs and Dorothy Perkins. It was not the best of days for a Green-style grilling. As each made their pitch in turn they were confronted with a man not only hopelessly distracted, but, unsurprisingly, in the darkest of moods. One agency had the disconcerting experience of having to make its case while Green was in a room next door bellowing at one of his unfortunate staff, 'I didn't ask you to fucking do it, I told you to fucking do it!'[1]

Green may have been the one forced to pull out, but he is also the sort of man who likes to have the last word. At the same time as he announced his decision to quit, he issued a stark warning: 'M&S are going to have us breathing down their necks in every street, in every shopping centre in the UK . . . We will see who is the best retailer.' This was a typical display of Green defiance, but what did it mean? His rivals were going to have to wait to find out.

On Friday afternoon Green flew to Sardinia to join his family for a six-week break, the kind of consolation only open to the very rich. A few days later a calmer Green rang Rose from his yacht, which was docked in Athens, to thank him for the case of wine. Rose asked him if he was staying for the Olympics, which were due to start the following week. Green replied, 'You must be joking. I've just run a marathon and I'm bloody knackered.'[2] Rose later confided, 'And then he called me a c**t, which is probably a good sign.'[3]

He spent the summer cruising in the Mediterranean, recharging his batteries. But what would he get up to when he returned? The seven-week battle for M&S had taken its toll, but on past form, it would not keep him quiet for long. When he returned in early September, deeply tanned but a little fuller – he had reportedly put on six pounds during his holiday – the speculation returned. Would he mount a price war against M&S and other rivals? Would he start to stalk other stores – Sainsbury's, perhaps, or even Boots, both experiencing trading difficulties? Would he make a third attempt to seize the trophy asset he has always sought?

The immediate issue was the seriousness of Green's threat to turn up the heat in the high street. The months running up to Christmas – 'the golden quarter' – are the most critical in the retail calendar and, for some stores, can account for up to three-quarters of annual sales. Green still felt slighted by the way things had turned out and no doubt would have liked to have gone for the kill. But though his threat to take M&S on may have sounded tough, the reality was that Green was in no position to launch an all-out war against M&S or any of his chief rivals.

In the first place, although there was a growing overlap with Green's empire, M&S catered for a largely different market. Secondly, a price war in particular would have proved damaging to his own business, cutting margins and possibly profits. The last thing he wanted to risk was a threat to his revenue stream. Much more likely than a price war was a marketing and style war, an advertising blitz on customers and an attempt to prove that Bhs and Arcadia offered better value. Green may have enjoyed sniping at M&S with promises to give them a hard time in the run-up to Christmas 2004, but he knew that he had his work cut out. His real priority was not to plot guerrilla campaigns against his competitors but to concentrate on pepping up his own businesses. During the autumn and winter months, that is what he concentrated on.

The first signs of Green's much-awaited plans came in the week after his return, proof that he had been far from idle during his six-week escape. Even during his holidays, a day rarely goes by when he is not on the phone to his senior managers. Within days, Dorothy Perkins announced a £4 million promotional campaign to be run by creative advertising agency Grey London, which had scooped the business following the pitches in July.

He also planned a £3 million Bhs campaign in the run-up to Christmas. It was the store's first television advertising in a decade. The ads, created by HHCL/Red Cell, introduced the line 'Feel Bhs'. Previously Green had shunned the use of advertising as ineffective, but with competitors putting more effort into promoting their brands, he had little choice but to do the same.

The promotional blitz was not confined to advertising. In mid-September, Green summoned 250 Bhs managers and staff to a conference centre in the former Billingsgate fish market. The event – a cross between a fashion show, a school prize-giving and a rally and somewhat reminiscent of the mass conventions held by big American corporations – began with a warm-up act provided by Paul Ross, the television presenter. 'Imagine Philip Green has just walked on to the stage wearing a Bhs leopardskin thong,' he quipped.

Wary at first, most staff at Bhs had grown to like their new boss – 'PG', as they mostly called him. When the tanned Green took the stage, flanked by giant TV screens, he was greeted with a standing ovation. Tina sat proudly watching from her front row seat. Green began his speech with a reminder of how he had been written off in 2000 when he bought Bhs: 'Everyone said I was crazy. Everyone said I was mad. The brand was broken, they told me.' During the event, the company's best-performing store manager – Mario Azzoni from Uxbridge – was awarded a black Mini Cooper. It was vintage Green, ever the show-man, parading his success for all to see and loving every minute of it.

After the awards, the speeches and the pep-talk, Green unveiled his plans for Bhs. In the next few months he would invest £20 million refurbishing the top fifty stores by giving them 'the Oxford Street treatment'. Up to that point, Green had largely skimped on invest-ment. He had revamped some twenty-five to thirty stores but in general they were in need of improvement, especially in the provinces. He had been planning to expand rather than consolidate his empire and the refurbishment of Bhs had not been a priority. Now he had failed in that plan and had to improve his competitiveness, his priorities had shifted – he had little choice but to up the rate of refur-bishment after years of under-investment.

Central to the new strategy was the upping of sales. Specifically, he was aiming to increase the volume of sales per square foot by a quarter to £250. 'That is the challenge. That is where we have to get to. Then we will be motoring,' he told his attentive and slightly doting audience. To help boost sales, new clothing lines were unveiled. Green was also moving Bhs upmarket, though the word he used was 'upscale'. To do so he had hired new design teams in both men's and women's clothes. The new lines were to be introduced after Christmas.

In October, Green made more high-profile announcements, this time about profits. First came Bhs. For the year ending in March 2004, operating profits had risen around 4.5 per cent, taking them to nearly £104 million.[4] Green also awarded himself another tasty dividend – this time for £40 million. This came on top of the £367 million dividend he had already paid himself in the two previous years. Tom Hunter, who owned 5 per cent of the chain, received £2 million. The boost to profits, modest in comparison with the first two years, had come from a small rise in gross margins resulting from further operating efficiencies and improvements in the supply chain. But critically, underlying sales were flat. To those who had been following events closely, the announcement was a confirmation of what some had suspected, that after the rapid progress of the first two years, maybe Bhs was beginning to run out of steam. Although Green tried to devote 40 per cent of his time to Bhs, he also admitted that during his hunt for M&S he had taken his eye off the ball and could not afford to do so again: 'Obviously when you're engaged twenty hours a day doing something else, even I've gotta have four hours sleep.'[5]

Those City analysts who claimed that Bhs profit figures might have reached a peak were simply dismissed by Green: 'people like them can't add up' is one of his favourite forms of dismissal. In 2002, he had taken legal action against the *Independent on Sunday* and one of its journalists, Jason Nisse, for an article (published on 22 December) claiming that sales at Dorothy Perkins and across Arcadia were falling when they were actually rising at the time. The paper had also written that Arcadia was facing financial difficulties. The paper later issued a retraction and apology.[6]

On 20 October, Green dined with his closest banking advisers at Les Ambassadeurs, one of his favourite Mayfair restaurants. Among the guests were Peter Cummings of HBOS, Michael Sherwood of Goldman Sachs and Bob Wigley of Merrill Lynch. The dinner was to celebrate Arcadia's latest results, which showed that over the previous year, pre-tax profits had leapt by some 30 per cent to reach £246 million.[7] In Stuart Rose's last year, Arcadia achieved £116 million. 'Stunning' is how one analyst described the new figures.

The next day Green jumped on stage again, this time in front of his Arcadia team. To the sounds of 'Ain't No Mountain High Enough', Green told his top staff at the champagne breakfast that they had made retail history. Not only were profits soaring but the rest of the £808 million loan from HBOS to buy the store two years earlier had now been paid off. This was again ahead of time – the 'quickest payback ever' as Green put it. And there were other goodies to announce. As M&S was pulling out of Europe he was intent on going in. Six large-scale Topshop outlets, all 'flagship stores', were to be opened in major European cities. And he was writing himself a cheque for £460 million – certainly one of the biggest individual dividends ever paid in Britain. Green had now awarded himself a total of £500 million in a single year from the two companies in which he had originally staked less than £100 million of his own money.

Green also handed a cheque for £40 million to Peter Cummings. HBOS still held an 8 per cent stake in the company. Unsurprisingly Cummings was full of gratitude on behalf of his bank. Nevertheless, given bankers' normal reticence, what Cummings said in his thank you speech was extraordinary: 'As a shareholder, stakeholder and banker, we can only thank you from the bottom of our hearts for your effort in delivering a first-class set of results. It is outstanding.' Cummings went on to single out Green as one of the 'most conservative and prudent finance managers I have met'. He also praised Green for his decision to pull out of M&S: 'To walk away at four pounds was the right thing to do, and that is called integrity. Your leader has that by the barrel-load.'

The staging of the event – a champagne breakfast for staff and specially invited bankers and journalists – was typical of Green. He was parading his success to a mix of fawning staff, powerful bankers and business journalists. But there was another motive. As Alan Sugar had pointedly argued two years earlier, Green, a private entrepreneur, was under no obligation to announce his results in such detail and with so much of a fanfare. The fact that he did so was partly a matter of ego. But the timing was also deliberate. The event was held the day before M&S shareholders were due to meet to approve the £2.3 billion cashback deal that had been part of the company's bid defence.

Green was using the opportunity not just to demonstrate what a successful boss he had been and to take a dig at Rose, but also to rub it in to M&S shareholders. This, he was smugly pointing out, is what you could have had.

Despite the praise and the money, Green was still smarting over M&S. He was desperate to prove that his stores could outperform the competition and especially M&S. Green likes to claim that his anger is nothing to worry about, that it is short-lived and soon forgotten, that he never bears a grudge for long. His wife told the *Daily Mail*: 'He's got a big lion's roar, but it's over in three minutes. It's gone.'[8] This did not seem to be the case with Rose. Two months on Green was still nursing a bruised ego and rarely missed an opportunity to snipe at M&S and its chief executive.

The Arcadia results were certainly impressive – profits up, debt cleared, a launch into Europe, a further swelling of the family coffers. So, how had Green pulled it off? Some of the improved cashflow since he had acquired the company had been achieved through clever 'financial engineering', including, as we saw in chapter nine, the re-mortgaging of part of the property portfolio and the rescheduling of profits for its storecard. After acquisition, Green had secured more than £220 million from a mortgage on the flagship Oxford Street branch of Topshop and other stores. Such secured borrowing is cheaper than the original loan finance and the cash was used to repay a sizeable chunk of the loan. Green could in fact have borrowed more in this way but chose not to because he did not want to carry too much debt.

Much of the rest of the improved cashflow had arisen largely through greater operational economies for which Green could take much of the credit. A master of detail, he knew which levers to pull to boost efficiency and had pulled them in every area of the business – buying and shipping merchandise, warehousing, stock control, managing discounts and negotiating leases. Green had stripped out overheads and pruned the management hierarchy. Arcadia, like Bhs, was now a lean operation. According to Richard Hyman of Verdict, 'What makes Green unique is that he can carry out a whole range of key functions simultaneously – he is a brilliant negotiator, brilliant at finance, good on property, on sourcing, and good on the operational side. This is how he was able to de-layer the top teams when he took over. He can run a billion-pound business with the same size of hierarchy and management that you would find in a business a sixth of the size.'[9]

The changes had produced a strong rise in profit margins from 13.9 to 17.9 per cent. Every sale was more profitable than at M&S, which had achieved only a 10.4 per cent margin, and even Next, which stood at a little over 14 per cent. Hyman believes that 'Green is not only ahead of his competitors on costs, he will maintain that edge.'[10]

Green's ability to improve efficiency in this way was recognised in the 2005 'wealth creation league tables' published by the Department of Trade and Industry. These showed that Arcadia emerged as the most efficient wealth-creating business in UK retail, beating competitors such as Next and M&S, and had proved more successful than other companies at getting 'value-added' out of their resources.[11] Most of the wealth gain, of course, had accrued to Green himself.

Nevertheless, behind the razzmatazz, there were doubts about whether the Green empire was quite as strong as his bullish public pronouncements suggested. There were certainly question marks about the real strength of the finances. In particular, the remarkable dividend at Arcadia was not funded directly out of cashflow and profits. Indeed, the payment was close to double pre-tax profits. Green was indeed quite open that it was being paid by taking out another bank loan for £500 million. In essence he was paying off one loan and taking out another.

There is nothing untoward about paying for the dividend in this way and the lenders were perfectly happy with the arrangement. They wouldn't have lent the money if they were not. Green called it 'prudent'. But although it was not exceptional in a private firm, it did raise question marks about just how sustainable the financial strategy was, especially given that Arcadia, according to its accounts, had limited reserves. Ian Griffiths in the *Guardian*, not one of Green's favourite journalists, described the pay-out as 'not actually a dividend but, rather, a clever financing ploy' and the process used to generate it as 'mind-boggling'.[12] In essence, he was financing the dividend by borrowing from anticipated future profits. Some experts maintained that Green was using Bhs and Arcadia as cash cows – running the companies for short-term gain as a way of making money to finance his next deal. This does not necessarily mean that his approach was damaging to the long-term health of the companies, but only time will tell if this is the case.

There was also the nature of his retail empire. Green's portfolio is diverse enough to cover most of the market. But some stores are much stronger than others. Miss Selfridge has established itself as a fashion brand for a slightly younger core shopper than Topshop but has struggled with its identity and contributes a tiny proportion of Arcadia's overall profit. Dorothy Perkins is the largest of the Arcadia brands, is highly profitable and gets a good press. Topman is rated, if not popular with Green personally. He was once asked if he wears Topman, but just shook his head and patted his tummy.[13] Tina buys most of his clothes and it would appear that his own stores are not high on her shopping list.

Topshop, which has set out to exploit the increasingly fashion-conscious youth market, is the jewel in the Arcadia crown. The chain was launched in the 1980s by Sir Ralph Halpern as part of the Burton group. It was then hardly known for its style. As Louise Foster, former fashion journalist at *Drapers*, recalls, 'When I was at school in the mid-nineties, Topshop was known as "Topshit" – we wouldn't go near it, it was seen as embarrassing.'[14] Viewed as a 'lame duck' for most of the nineties, it was from the end of that decade that it started to become a hot store, known for its cutting-edge fashion. Its rise to dominance in the fashion stakes really began under John Hoerner, the 'godfather of the Arcadia reinvention' as one retail expert put it, and the baton was then picked up by Stuart Rose when he took over the group.[15] In the last few years, it has developed an unrivalled ability to copy catwalk looks and attract new fashion designers and celebrity name shoppers, including Kate Moss, Sadie Frost and Radio One DJ Edith Bowman.

It is a store that is certainly loved by fashion watchers. As Erica Davies, fashion editor of the *Sun*, proclaimed in 2004, 'Maybe it's because I'm a fashion whore, but I can't get enough of Topshop's Oxford Circus branch for their fabulous frocks, shoes and cute tops that work seamlessly into my wardrobe. Either that, or perhaps my almost daily checks have something to do with the fact that I get *serious* discount there.'[16] The 40 per cent discount cards granted to fashion editors may help with the praise but it is mostly genuine – fashion journalists are often to be seen in Topshop clothes.

Topshop's renaissance over the last five years has been helped by clever marketing. The store swallows up the lion's share of Arcadia's overall marketing budget and PR, which does not always go down well with the other brand directors. In 2003, while the marketing team at Burton had to make do with just one member of Blue fronting the autumn campaign because Arcadia's top brass would not pay for the rest of the boy band, Jane Shepherdson reportedly refused to cut back. One story has it that she was once hauled in by one of Philip's top henchmen demanding, 'Do you fucking realise that we spend more on fucking photography than fucking *Vogue*? Can't you do it fucking cheaper?' The steely and fiercely independent Shepherdson replied 'No' and marched out.[17]

Green, not exactly renowned for throwing money around, lets

Shepherdson get away with her promotional budgets because Topshop has driven Arcadia's profit growth. Green may not like her getting too much publicity, but she is the only one of his brand directors to be given a lot of free rein. In early 2004, M&S had attempted to poach her to head up womenswear, but she stayed with Green. While he insists on being involved in choosing clothes through range reviews for most of the eight Arcadia brands as well as Bhs, he steers clear of Topshop. In fact, he hasn't seen any Topshop ranges since he started and admits: 'It's not my forte, that product. I may have a view, but I haven't got the expertise to know what's on trend.'[18] As one retail watcher puts it, 'Green couldn't really fiddle with Topshop too much because of its cult status.' For a relatively small store, Topshop punches well above its weight and Green knows it. He respects Shepherdson's judgement. As one senior insider put it, 'Philip will pay whatever he needs to keep her. If Philip hasn't got Jane, he hasn't got Topshop.'[19]

Just how important Topshop/Topman is to Green is illustrated by the high rating it gets in what the trade calls the 'brand power' stakes. Brand strategy expert Brand Finance has compiled a league table of winning and losing British stores ranked by 'the strength of their brand relative to their sector competitors'. Each of thirty retailers is given a 'brand power' rating based on how it scores in ten categories pitted against its sector.[20] Stores are rated from AAA at the top to C at the bottom. Topshop/Topman comes eighth in the list with a score of BBB+ (average plus), below Next but higher than M&S. Dorothy Perkins, by contrast, comes in at twenty-third with a relatively poor rating of BB (under-performing). The measurement 'determines whether a company can attract and win customers better than its competitors'.[21]

Topshop is the exception in Green's empire, however. None of his other shop brands can be seen as innovators or landmark stores. Wal-Mart, Tesco, Ikea, Virgin and even Next have, arguably, set trends and changed the way we think about shopping.

Green's Achilles heel has been sales. As he told the *Sunday Times* a year after he had taken over Bhs, 'The margins might be better but you can't bank margins. You need to actually sell the stuff first.'[22] The profit growth across his companies has been achieved mainly through a mix of financial engineering and higher margins rather than a boost in sales. Green has good relationships with suppliers, is amongst the pack leaders on sourcing and can move faster than many of his rivals, especially the larger and more bureaucratic M&S. Making the supply chain and business more efficient produced strong initial results, but such major improvements in margins are, as retail consultancy Verdict warns, 'one-off, sustainable but unrepeatable'.[23] The cost savings are sustainable, but further gains in operating margins will be much harder to come by.

Most larger suppliers – such as Yorkshire-based BMB, which supplies much of Green's menswear – are generally happy with the way he does business. They like the fact, for example, that once he's done a deal, he sticks by it, a Green principle that goes back to his early days. But they would not want to be pushed any further. Some claim they can't make money supplying Bhs alone and keep afloat by leveraging Green's volumes to achieve better margins on other customers' orders.[24] He has probably reached the limit of potential savings from this route. Squeezing suppliers further would risk rebounding on Green by affecting the quality of the product. To stay in business they would be forced to 'take it out on the garment' by cutting corners and using cheaper materials.

Boosting sales, however, is likely to prove an even bigger challenge than rooting out waste and raising efficiency. Indeed, sales at Bhs and Arcadia under-performed in the crucial womenswear market in 2003–4 and both suffered a slight fall in their market share as a result. If Bhs had been able to overtake M&S in womenswear, as Green would have liked, M&S would have become more vulnerable to his bid. But M&S enjoyed 13.5 per cent of the womenswear market in 2003–4 while Bhs and Arcadia combined had 13.1 per cent.[25]

Green achieved some early gains in sales at both Bhs and Arcadia but he was unable to sustain the rise. He always insisted that his priority had been efficiency and profit margins – 'getting our house in order' – and no retailer, however able, can pursue too many goals at once. But his mixed record on sales across his empire has led some to wonder just how good he really is at spotting trends and firing public interest, perhaps the ultimate test of a magic touch. Some suggest that Green is a 'one-trick pony' who, in the jargon of the retail trade, 'can engineer businesses to have a healthy bottom line but not to muster top-line growth'.[26] Green is always swift to dismiss such 'paranoia with sales', but retail companies have to evolve to survive. Sainsbury's and M&S are both examples of companies that didn't learn this lesson until it was too late.

To date, Green has concentrated on short-term goals, including paying off debt and giving generous dividends rather than investing for the future, 'harvesting rather than building his brands' as one expert describes it.[27] Green would argue that this has been the right strategy – 'you first build an efficient machine' – but the test is how he will develop his empire from now on. Robert Clark says, 'The jury is still out on Green. He has not yet had to evolve his formats, his store environments and his overall offer – he has simply made Bhs in particular, but also Arcadia, much more efficient. The test now is whether he can evolve to the next stage.'[28]

Green acknowledges the room for improvement. 'Are we the best? No. Are we the worst? No. But we're better than average.'[29] For the moment. If Green fails to improve or even maintain his relative position, he will risk a stagnant and even falling market share and eventually lower profits. Green showed that he is worried by this by setting a target to raise Bhs sales by a quarter. In 2003–4 sales per square foot stood at £200, which is relatively low for the sector. M&S, for example, achieved £570 (a figure boosted by food sales), Primark £430, Woolworths £257, TK Maxx £245 and Debenhams £241.[30] Primark in particular shows what can be achieved.

Raising Bhs sales to Green's ambitious target of £250 would double profits but can it be achieved? One of Bhs's main strengths has been that its prices have traditionally been significantly lower than in M&S, but from the moment he started, Stuart Rose set out to cut prices and close the gap. Green may have improved the store's image, but it still lacks grab appeal. As one retail analyst put it, 'It was said during his bid for M&S that [Green] would bring theatre and magic to M&S but where is the theatre and magic in Bhs stores?'[31] Janet Street-Porter, the former editor of the *Independent on Sunday* and not one to mince her words, was even more blunt: 'With all the will in the world, I hardly think tourists from Abu Dhabi to Athens are flocking to Oxford Street to spend thirty minutes in Bhs. Its wares are worthy but totally forgettable.'[32]

In addition, many of the stores are less inviting than some of the competition, especially outside of London, and the refurbishment budget may not be enough to bring sufficient transformation. As Verdict puts it: 'Too many of the stores look tired and uninviting and value retailers are producing lower priced products in much more appealing environments.'[33] Green, in general, is not believed to rate the importance of the 'store look'. 'His strength is in cost-control rather than format and is somewhat behind the times on the latter,' one expert has commented.[34] Other competitors have certainly been willing to go further to create more of an overall shopping experience. Neill Denny says, 'Put Green in a high end fashion shop and he'd have a fit; he hates it, all that white space, granite and art features. He can't bear that, he likes his shops to be well merchandised, well stocked, to look the part, not turned into an art gallery.'[35]

One retail professional even sees him as 'cheapening the whole retail process . . . You can take the savings on fixtures and fittings, the cuts in staffing levels, the shaving of margins too far. He saves on carpets, he's crammed all the shelves to get more stock in, it all looks a bit downmarket.'[36] Green's argument is that the customer neither notices, nor cares. This may be true of some but not all.

Bhs competes with both middle-market players like Next, Debenhams and M&S and value players such as Matalan and Primark. Green's plan to move Bhs slightly upmarket was a recognition of the tough competition from the value-end of the market. But attempting to upscale Bhs inevitably carries the risk of alienating the store's existing customer base. It was a lesson that M&S had to learn the hard way when the store decided to chase the youth market under Vittorio Radice, a move, ironically, that the board's older guard warned against at the time.

Some of the most successful retailers of recent years have been Primark, George at Asda, Tesco, TK Maxx, H&M, New Look and Next. Although some of these are still small players, all have gained market share through a clever mix of value-for-money, design, throwaway fashion and improved store environments. Next, for example, has been closing the gap on M&S remarkably quickly, and has virtually stolen the formalwear and smart workwear market from them. In 1998, Next had a quarter of M&S's market share in womenswear. By 2003, it was just under a half.[37] Today the cachet is no longer wearing expensive but the cheapest smart. Asda in particular has made a name for selling cheap chic, perfect for both the budget shopper and the savvy customer who likes to get style for their money. In the process the value stores have been squeezing mainstream retailers like M&S, Bhs and Arcadia.

Consumers are more and more demanding and expect quality and style as well as value. The discount retailers that have attacked on low price have been forcing the mainstream stores to lower their prices, too. Primark has been opening larger stores in more prominent locations and has, like George at Asda, been chipping away at Bhs's core customer base.

Green likes to dismiss the out-of-town supermarkets like Asda and Tesco: 'Don't talk to me about them. They sell clothes by weight, they're not fashion retailers.' Maybe, but they've also been steadily eating away at the market share of their rivals. In August 2004, figures produced by the retail research agency Taylor Nelson Sofre showed that George at Asda overtook M&S for the first time when measured by the actual number of items sold. The figures also showed that Tesco had been growing strongly and that Bhs had lost market share in both volume and value during the twelve weeks to mid-July, though some of Green's shops, including Dorothy Perkins and Topman, grew or held firm. The figures, based on secret sales surveys, were dismissed as 'rubbish' by Green while others in the rag-trade thought they were an aberration, but they still sent a shiver down the spines of some in the industry. Asda offers in many ways a similar core product to Bhs but at lower prices – its jeans sell for £4 – and now has several stand-alone George high street stores. George at Asda appears to be giving customers what they want, and many of them will be ones who would have gone to Bhs in the past. As one insider puts it, 'In a world of disposable fashion, you are going to be tempted by three tops for the price you pay for one at Wallis.'[38]

The strength of the competition from these relatively new entrants was illustrated by an analysis of the back-to-school market for *Drapers* magazine in August 2004. This showed that nine items of standard schoolwear cost £15.40 at George, £19.50 at Matalan and £20.00 at Tesco compared with £34.00 at Bhs and £50.00 at M&S, though M&S was offering better quality and durability. The value retailers were thus pitching their prices at 40 to 50 per cent below the middle-market operators.[39] More recently Green has started to recognise the force of the opposition but still insists that it's not right to compete on price alone.

To increase sales, Green knows that although he has a head start over many of his rivals on delivery and fast fashion he also has to compete on price, value for money, product design and customer service. In the latter, Arcadia and Bhs are well down the league table. 'Conversion rates' in clothing – the rate at which customers who enter a store end up buying something – have been rising but much of Green's empire performs poorly. His stores attract plenty of loyal visitors but they appear to be fickle and much less likely to buy than amongst his principal rivals. In 2004, for example, M&S enjoyed a conversion rate of 45.5 per cent.[40] In contrast, Bhs ended up bottom of the class with 19.8 per cent, way below the sector average of 31.7 per cent. His high fashion stores – Topshop and Dorothy Perkins – came in at 24.4 per cent and 24.5 per cent respectively. All three stores were beaten by George/Asda, Matalan, Primark, Next, New Look, Littlewoods and Debenhams. Only Evans, the specialist store catering for larger women, came close to M&S with 44 per cent.

Life in the high street for the more established names has been getting increasingly competitive. According to Richard Hyman, retail is now facing its 'biggest crossroads of the last twenty-five years. It is now operating at full capacity, at a level of maturity and saturation not seen before. With much fiercer competition, most retailers will find it much more difficult to grow than in the past.'[41] Green has the advantage over his rivals of his better profit margins, but the gap may narrow if not close. A fast efficient supply chain, foreign sourcing and direct relations with manufacturers are now necessities. Retailers will sink without them and most of his rivals are having to up their game. Primark, still a small player but one of the fastest-growing retailers, already has a successful policy of buying direct from manufacturers and cutting out the wholesaler. M&S is playing catch-up by improving its own supply chain. Green may have helped to lead the way in improvements in sourcing and speed of delivery but others are now copying him.

In addition, the harsh truth for Green and some of his rivals is that market trends, notably the rise of out-of-town retailing, are moving against more mainstream stores and are likely to continue to do so. Mixed-good retailers or variety stores (the trade name for chains like M&S and Bhs) have also been under-performing the retail average, losing out to the more focused specialists on the one hand and the grocery superstores on the other. Some observers argue that as the social and retail landscape has changed, big variety high street chains like Bhs are an outmoded concept, relevant to the past but less so to the future. C&A pulled out of Britain, Littlewoods is a dog's dinner, Allders went bust and M&S is on a slippery slope.

In a forecast made in 2004, Verdict predicted that by 2008, shifting shopping patterns would have eroded the mainstream's market share – including Bhs and Arcadia – by a further 4.1 percentage points, a total loss over the decade of nearly nine points.[42] The erosion of past brand loyalties led to what Stuart Rose once called the 'toppling of the icons' in the 1980s, and something similar could happen in the future. Green is not known for his complacency, but life in the retail market has and will become increasingly tough for even the shrewdest of operators.

The danger for Green is that though Bhs is much better than it was, it may have hit a plateau. Green acknowledges the risks, at least in private. During the battle for M&S Eric Musgrave, a senior editor at *Drapers*, was talking to Green on the phone and suggested that the Bhs type of high-street-based multiple may have had its day. Green accepted that he might be right, but he was at the time seeking to get some positive press coverage during his bid. A few months later, Musgrave put the same point to him in a press event on his own territory. Green replied, 'Eric, stick to journalism, stick to your soppy magazine. Leave retail to me.'

Chapter 15

LET THE STRESS BEGIN

I n Green's rococo office at Bhs headquarters there is a kitsch sign
that greets visitors: 'Good morning . . . let the stress begin.'
That's a permanent fixture. Less permanent is the usual
scattering of Bhs products that he likes to keep around the
office. In December 2004, an outsize teddy bear sporting a crown sat
in the corner. More significant was a bulky set of papers on his glass-
topped desk – M&S's interim results for the previous three months.

Green may have been focused on how to boost sales across his
stores, but M&S was never far from his mind. Winning it has become
his lifetime ambition. Nothing would please him more than to be
remembered as the fourth in the dynasty of his M&S heroes – Simon
Marks, Marcus Sieff and Richard Greenbury. As Neill Denny has
commented: 'When Green dies, they will find M&S engraved on his
heart.'[1]

Whether his dream would ever come true now depended heavily
on Rose. The new chief executive was only too aware that Green – who
had dismissed his plans as 'half-baked' – would be watching his every
move and would love him to fail. The personal and commercial war
between the two was far from over. Seeing off Green in the summer
had been the easy bit. Rose now had to do what his five immediate
predecessors had failed to do – make M&S work. If he failed to deliver,
he – like them – would be out of a job and Green would almost
certainly be back.

While Green was concentrating on his own companies, Rose
continued with his shake-up. By Christmas 2004, every former
executive director had been axed or had quit and the executive board
had been halved from six to three people thus putting Rose firmly in
charge of all buying and merchandising activity. Rose set out detailed
plans for reducing the number of clothing and food items. He started
to copy some of Green's business methods, some of which would have

been unacceptable to Vandevelde, Holmes and their predecessors. M&S mortgaged some of its property and started getting tough with suppliers by altering their trading terms and on occasions cancelling orders. The new chief executive also started to reduce M&S's dependency on UK-based agents.

But the company's trading performance continued to weaken. In a sign of just how dire trading figures had become, M&S held two pre-Christmas promotions in which all goods were offered at a 20 per cent discount. It was a first for the beleaguered store. Rose, usually remarkably cheerful, was beginning to show the pressure and in one interview let his irritation with the sniping show: 'I don't like to see my company being bashed up unfairly. I don't like to read constantly that this is the embattled Marks & Spencer . . . a struggling company. We made £700 million profit last year, more than any company in UK clothing retail. Twice what Philip Green made in his two companies. It's not struggling. It's a car which has got an engine which is not running super-tuned.'[2]

Some of Green's plans were aimed at making life difficult for M&S. The Dorothy Perkins and the 'Feel Bhs' campaigns were timed to compete head-on with M&S's own advertising campaign, 'Your M&S', throughout the winter months. In general, however, they were not seen as a great success and probably had little impact. Green had always taken a lukewarm view of advertising and was not prepared to put significant funds into it. He once described spending on advertising as 'knick-knacks' and a senior advertising executive said the campaign was 'in danger of urinating into the wind by spending too little; the ads are pretty forgettable and particularly bland-branded'.[3] Another thought the ads were 'ordinary, rather like some of his stores'.[4]

Although Green had hinted at a price war, it was in fact Rose who took the lead on prices with a series of promised price cuts across M&S ranges. He had quickly come to the conclusion that of the four key criteria of success he was constantly stressing – 'quality, value, service and innovation' – value was the most important for increasingly sophisticated and informed customers. M&S may once have been seen as a bastion of value but now they were considered to be expensive. M&S prices were relatively high partly because they had always overpaid for clothing. Some experts claimed that because M&S did not monitor its factories closely, it was paying between 5 and 10 per cent too much for its clothes. As one retail expert put it, 'Even Matalan has a team of twelve people who just go round the factories checking the labour content and that they are not taking too much profit on the contract.'[5] Determined to tackle this head on, matching the prices of his rivals became a key part of Rose's turnaround strategy. Of course, this was not good news for suppliers who would have had to bear the brunt of the new discipline. While the price cuts were targeted mainly at Next, which had been eroding M&S's market share, they would also hit Bhs and some of the Arcadia stores.

In the event, the price cuts did not appear to be quite as significant as Rose had implied. A study for Deutsche Bank showed that 'Despite claims that M&S has cut its prices . . . clothing prices relative to its competitors are worse in spring 2005 than in spring 2004.'[6] The reason was that rivals such as Next had also made reductions. The tougher market conditions were forcing a deflationary climate across retail.[7]

The bidding war had, in many ways, helped to define both Green and Rose. Some watchers were very diplomatic. When Sir Richard Greenbury, the former head of M&S and one of Green's heroes, now effectively retired from business, was asked whether he would have preferred Green or Rose, he replied, 'Green is a capable man, but Stuart Rose is a very capable man, too.'[8]

The brutality of the contest had changed the standings of the two men. Rose had gone in with a reputation in some quarters as a chancer. He emerged somewhat tarnished over his share dealing but as perhaps the cannier of the two. On the other hand, Green's standing as Britain's leading dealmaker had undoubtedly been dented.

Former friends and now bitter commercial rivals, the two men had stopped chatting in the way they used to. This did not stop them bumping into each other. In mid-November, they had both been invited to a party held by Verdict to celebrate the consultancy's twentieth birthday. One report has it that Rose was intending to leave before Green arrived but the two bumped into each other outside. 'Who's in there?' growled Green. 'The retail glitterati,' replied Rose. 'You'd better go in and brighten things up.' Which Green proceeded to do.

The first to be cornered was David Norgrove, chairman of M&S's pension fund trustees, who Green believed had been instrumental in obstructing his request to be given access to the financial state of the pension fund. Green let fly. 'Your behaviour was disgraceful,' he bellowed.

He later chatted to Sir Richard Greenbury, and told him of how he had bumped into David Mayhew, chairman of Cazenove, at a function the night before and teased him about how his firm had charged M&S '£39 million for not having a meeting. So how much would you charge to actually have one?'

Retail is a small world and he later collared Maurice Helfgott – who had 'stepped down' as M&S's director of men and childrenswear the previous Tuesday – and grilled him on the board's behaviour during the bid.[9] Four months on, Green had apparently still not got the failed attempt out of his system. Richard Hyman, who was hosting the party and who had introduced Green to Norgrove – the two had not met before – recalls the encounters: 'Yes, he did tick them off, but what you have to remember about Philip is that in contrast to the stiffness of corporate Britain, he is a very passionate, driven and energised owner-driver, so when he tried to buy M&S, he invested enormous amounts of time and emotion and he felt, wrongly or rightly, very badly done by. When he gets the opportunity to voice those feelings, he takes it. He wasn't going around on a charger haranguing people, he was enjoying himself, he was having fun, speaking his mind and making people feel uncomfortable and doing so with a lot of humour. It was very entertaining.'[10]

In mid-December, Green and Rose again ended up at the same party, this time at the News International Christmas bash, held in the Royal Opera House at Covent Garden. Green was at one end of the room with his wife and spotted Rose at the other. He marched over, briskly shook his hand and then moved on. One reporter allegedly overheard Green say, 'Life's too short.'[11] Photos of the handshake appeared in several newspapers the next day. Others were sure it was only a show for the press photographers who were present.

Between the rounds of Christmas parties, Green also managed to fit in some gambling. And his luck was in big time. He was reported to have won £2 million in one night at Les Ambassadeurs in Mayfair and at least another £1 million on other nights. The casino, just off Park Lane, is renowned as a haunt of the very rich and is Green's favourite London casino. Green is, of course, known for his love of gaming, and bets up to £10,000 a time. On this occasion it was roulette rather than blackjack that brought him his winnings. According to friends, Green likes to back a mixture of even-money bets – red/black, odd/even, high/low and on individual numbers at odds of 35–1. A handful of other super-rich gamblers was also said to have won similar amounts over the winter. Since the odds always favour the casino, such large wins against the house are rare and meant that London Clubs International, owner of the casino, was forced to issue a profits warning in April 2005.

For Christmas itself Green spent three weeks in Barbados, some of it chatting to Michael Winner on the private beach of the upmarket Sandy Lane Hotel. The gathering of the wealthy there had become an annual ritual.

While Green was taking his break, Rose spent his Christmas minding M&S. Six months into the job, prospects were not looking too good. M&S had a poor Christmas with plummeting sales. Quoted companies are obliged to make public poor trading figures that might affect the share price, so in January 2005, Rose issued a warning to the City that annual profits would be lower than originally forecast, and even lower than the level achieved by Roger Holmes before he was axed. Of course, M&S was not alone in having a dismal Christmas. High street stores suffering sales declines included Woolworths, House of Fraser and even Next. It was, according to some analysts, the worst high street Christmas performance for more than a decade.

It was now clear that the retail and financial climate in 2005 would be a good deal colder than it had been in 2004. Faced with higher interest rates, uncertainty over house prices and an unsustainable level of personal debt, consumers were finally being forced to tighten their belts. 'High noon in the high street' was how some analysts were describing the worsening mood. In mid-April Rose was forced to reveal more bad news – that sales had declined for the sixth quarter in a row. In May, the company revealed that its annual profit figures were down by 19 per cent and its share of the UK clothing market had fallen by half a percentage point. Some analysts argue that M&S's problems were not just down to the tougher trading conditions. Richard Hyman, for example, believes that M&S is facing a more fundamental problem, 'that its core customers are now a year older than when Rose took over. The chain has an ageing profile and is failing to replace at the bottom what it is losing at the top.'[12]

Poor sales were bad enough, but Rose had other headaches. By April another bitter boardroom rift had opened up at the ailing chain over the future of Paul Myners, the group's chairman and the man who had orchestrated the coup which brought Rose into the company. Now Kevin Lomax, the senior non-executive director on the board, wanted to get rid of Myners, who had originally agreed to stay on as a stop-gap measure for a year to give Lomax time to find a successor. Although Lomax had failed to find anyone, he was insisting that the chairman and chief executive had become too close and that Myners, who by now had acquired a number of directorships in other companies, was not giving enough attention to M&S. The row continued for weeks, and was only resolved when Myners agreed that he would step down as chairman a year later, at the AGM in July 2006, when he would be replaced by Lord Burns, the former permanent secretary at the Treasury brought in by Mrs Thatcher. Although it looked like a face-saving solution, it would have done little to lift the hostility that had built up in the boardroom. It was yet another of M&S's ongoing and vituperative internal splits that had marred the store for a decade and one that Rose could undoubtedly have done without. Shortly after that came another blow when Charles Wilson, his number two at M&S, left to become chief executive at the cash-and-carry business Booker.

Despite the poor figures at M&S, it was too early to judge Rose. It would be at least a year, probably longer, before he could make a real difference. Rose always insisted that he could only really be judged on his performance over the whole of 2005–6. Nevertheless, the clock was ticking on his efforts to deliver on costs, efficiency and sales. The problem for Rose was that even the pension-fund managers who take a longer view of performance had, in recent times, become an increasingly impatient bunch.

Watching from the sidelines, Green may quietly have been rather relieved to have someone else at M&S taking the stick rather than him. He too would have struggled to make a difference in such a tricky retail climate, one of the most difficult since the recession of the early 1990s. His return from his Christmas break coincided with the public announcement of M&S's grim trading figures. Unusually for Green, he declined to comment: 'I've only just landed, I haven't even looked at the figures.' He is, of course, not usually known for his tact or reticence.

His refusal to gloat – at least publicly – may have been less to do with M&S's difficulties than his own. Unlike Rose, Green was not obliged to issue details of his own performance. It was, as one Green-watcher observes, 'super-significant that Green had not resorted to crowing about his chief rival's problems, something he would have been expected to have revelled in. His own performance may have been nothing to write home about.'[13] There is certainly no reason to believe that Green would have been immune from the darkening clouds hanging over the high street and if Bhs had done a roaring trade, the public would have heard about it. Indeed, Green went on the record to admit: 'Is it tough? Yes, it is. Is it competitive? Yes, it is.' He accepted that the middle ground was proving difficult, but also claimed 'it was rubbish that we [Bhs] are not doing well'.[14] Moreover, some of his financial changes, such as selling off some fixed assets and borrowing to pay the dividend, would have had the effect of leveraging his businesses, increasing their cost base and thus making them more vulnerable in a retail downturn.

Meanwhile, Green and Rose, despite the continuing stand-off, found it difficult to avoid each other. In February the new M&S boss was in a ski resort in the Alps when his mobile phone rang. It was Green.

'Stuart, where are you?' he asked.

'I'm on holiday for a couple of days,' replied Rose.

'I know, but where?'

'In France.'

'I know that, but where?'

'Courchevel, if you must know.'

'I know that, look behind you.'

And there, a few feet away was Green.[15] The owner of Bhs was probably the last person Rose would have wanted to bump into on a weekend break away from the retail hothouse. On the other hand, Green, in particular, liked to play games with the press and it is possible that the accounts of their continued feuding were somewhat exaggerated. A month later Rose was speaking at a business conference. During the questioning after his talk, he revealed that he had just sent Green a present for his fifty-third birthday – a bottle from his rare wine collection.

Despite the deepening retail gloom, Green continued his constant look for bargains and added slowly to his empire. When Terry Green's Allders department store chain went bankrupt in March 2005, he bought ten of their outlets from the liquidators to open as stand-alone

Bhs homeware stores. This came on top of plans to open five Bhs
stores in the Czech Republic in the next few years, the first of which
was to be opened in Prague. In April he bought the loss-making UK
arm of Etam from its French parent and added it to his Arcadia empire
in another characteristically rapid Green deal. Etam had been losing
market share to rivals like New Look and Green's own Dorothy Perkins
and Topshop. Green sold some of the stores and converted others into
his own brands in smaller towns where he had no presence. These
developments showed that Green was prepared to up the level of
investment in his businesses.

In the second weekend in May Green hosted another lavish party, this
time a £4 million three-day celebration to mark Brandon's bar
mitzvah, the Jewish coming of age. Stonemasons and craftsmen had
been flown out to the venue – on a private peninsula overlooking the
Mediterranean between Nice and Monaco – to build a temporary
synagogue big enough to seat 300 people. At the traditional ceremony
Brandon sang, unaccompanied and in Hebrew, a fifteen-minute
chant that he had spent the previous year learning by heart. Tina was
not alone in being left in tears. It is perhaps indicative of Green's
somewhat traditional views on religion that he had not arranged a
similar event for his daughter when she became thirteen.

The guests, put up at the favourite celebrity haunt and £1,000-a-
night Grand-Hotel du Cap-Ferrat, included Richard Desmond, Allan
Leighton, Tom Hunter, Bob Wigley, Richard Caring, Lord Levy and a
number of showbiz names. Music was more to teenage tastes with
Beyonce and Destiny's Child hired to perform. On this occasion,
despite their chance meeting in Courchevel, there was no invite for
Stuart Rose.

Rose had plenty else on his mind. He knew Green had not lost
interest in M&S and would certainly rather be remembered as the man
who turned round M&S than the one who made a fortune asset-
stripping failing companies. The question of whether Green would bid
again was rarely far from the minds of analysts, retailers and M&S
executives alike. In mid-January 2005, the six-month ban on him
making another bid was lifted and there was, somewhat predictably, a
flurry of press speculation about his likely intentions. Early February
even brought a small surge in M&S's share price in anticipation of a
bid. Green's shadow over M&S was such that even if he made a joke

about his interest, which he did from time to time, speculation would mount and the share price would respond.

But what exactly would a Green takeover have meant for M&S? On this, opinion is heavily divided. He would certainly have shaken the store to its roots. If Green had seized M&S in the embattled summer of 2004, he would, according to one prominent retail watcher, have 'gone through it like a dose of salts. Despite some modernising, M&S remained overly hierarchical, had sloppy management, was over-staffed and was bad at buying.'[16] Green knew it and so did most of the management.

He likes to claim that his bid for M&S did everybody a favour. Indeed it has almost become the conventional wisdom that without Green's intervention, M&S would have failed to take the difficult decisions that were critical to its survival. But not everyone agrees. One City retail insider claims his bid was 'a distinctly damaging episode in the development of the retail industry'. In his view, M&S was forced into premature decisions that will destroy the distinctive-ness of the store, threaten its long-term future and, as a result, do lasting damage to retail as a whole.[17]

Few doubted that M&S needed surgery. But there remain genuine concerns about the impact of a Green regime on Britain's most hallowed store. Has he proved he has the retailing skills to turn round M&S? He would make it more efficient, but would he have customers returning and buying in droves? Would the enormous mountain of debt needed to buy M&S create new and intractable financial problems that would add to risks about its future? Would M&S's more cuddly style of capitalism – the one that wins awards for social responsibility – survive under Green? Moreover, should Green triumph, what impact would his control of around a quarter of Britain's clothing sales have on competition, the supply chain and ultimately customers? Had he succeeded, Green would have ended up with responsibility for the jobs and livelihoods of over 100,000 people.

One of the key issues that surrounds a possible Green takeover of M&S is whether it would remain in public hands and whether he would take the obligations of running a public company seriously. As a public company, Green would have to be more restrained than he has been at Bhs and Arcadia. Rose, for example, needs to ensure that M&S will be there in a decade from now and has to take a long view of the company's future.

Green is not just one of Britain's most successful entrepreneurs. He has also been at the forefront of a very significant trend in British business – a surge in the rate at which publicly owned companies have been taken private. Private equity has been becoming increasingly powerful, now accounting for a growing share of the private sector workforce. It is changing the face of the way British business operates.

Private equity firms and publicly listed companies are a world apart. The private firm offers a very different, extreme form of capitalism. As well as Bhs, Arcadia, Selfridges, Debenhams, New Look, Harvey Nichols, Heal's and Hamleys, other well-known names that have been taken private include William Hill, the AA, Halfords and Kwik-Fit. Most of these are run not by public figures like Green but by faceless accountants and financiers who are only too happy to keep in the background.

The trend, which is not confined to retail, has been driven by the mathematics of acquisition and falling share prices since 2000. If share prices fall below the underlying value of a company they can become prey to predators who know they can make money by snapping them up and going private. This has been Green's style. He was hardly the first to spot the potential of buying up companies in trouble. But he has been one of the most successful, grabbing them mostly on the cheap, pumping them full of debt, stripping them down, refinancing them and making a pretty tidy profit in the process.

The significantly lower interest rates of recent times have also made public-to-private deals much cheaper to finance. Private buyers finance their purchase through borrowing rather than issuing shares and a typical buy-out will require two-thirds or more of the purchase price funded through debt.

For entrepreneurs, the real incentive is the lure of big money that can flow from going private. Green has made a fortune because the bulk of the 'value-added' from his efficiency drive and refinancing has accrued to him. This is how many modern-day billionaires have been financing their tycoon lifestyles. It is no coincidence that many of those at the very top of today's wealth league – including Richard Branson, John Caudwell (who founded Phones4U), Richard Desmond, Bernie Ecclestone and Stelios Haji-Ioannou, founder of Easyjet – have built their fortunes running private companies. The rise of the private equity company is one of the key factors behind the remarkable rise of a new group of super-rich in the last decade, a set enjoying levels of wealth not seen in Britain for more than half a century.

This surge in personal wealth has been driving the growing wealth gap between the rich and the poor in the last decade and a half. Twenty years ago, Britain was one of the most equal societies in the developed world. Recent international estimates suggest that while the United States tops the rich nation inequality league, Britain is now the second most polarised.

Today's entrepreneurs mostly prefer the private route, claiming that living in the goldfish bowl of a PLC diverts too much management energy into non-wealth-making activities. There are certainly big differences in the obligations required of public and private companies. Green has never made a secret of his preference for the private option. He does not have to look over his shoulder to see what shareholders and the City think; he does not have to worry about the obsession with changes in the share price; he has no need to give constant press briefings. Instead he can control the way he handles the press, ensuring that the information flow suits his side of the case. Private companies do not have to account to shareholders, are required to publish only very limited accounts and do not have to comply with regulations on corporate governance such as taking non-executive directors onto their board.

While these obligations are there for a reason – to prevent incompetent, reckless and even fraudulent or exploitative business practice – some managers running public companies have begun to compare their lot with those of private entrepreneurs and have become frustrated with what they see as the growing and time-consuming burdens on public companies. In fact, modern chief executives earn considerably more than their predecessors, and getting to the top of the boardroom of a FTSE 100 company guarantees multi-millionaire status, although many complain about the huge rows that often accompany their salaries and pay-offs, which they are obliged to disclose.

There are, however, real questions about the wider economic and social merits of the rush to private equity. Private companies are free to pursue their business objectives as they see fit and this can result in the unbalanced pursuit of short-term goals including the maximisation of the cashflow – necessary to pay off debt – sometimes to the detriment of longer term, more sustainable goals. The first call on the cashflow of a private company is the repayment of debt, which can often be hefty. Private companies in general feel less responsibility to a company's history, values and staff. It is much easier to sell assets and make large-scale redundancies than in a public company.

The real measure of success is whether profitability can be maintained. Some private companies have not performed as well as Bhs and Arcadia. Just how risky to entrepreneurs, staff and customers alike private ownership can be is starkly illustrated by the collapse of Allders. Philip's former employee Terry Green, a man determined to emulate his former boss and make his own personal fortune, came badly unstuck when he took over the chain in 2003 only for it to go bust in early 2005. Green and hundreds of staff lost their jobs, and there was serious uncertainty about the future of the staff's pension rights. Although the chain was not in good shape when he took it over, he appeared to misjudge its problems, trying to do too much too quickly in the view of many observers. The failed attempt to make himself rich turned into a disaster not just for him but for thousands of others as well.

In Philip Green's case, it is early days to judge whether he is building a sustainable high street empire or running the companies for short-term gain in order to maximise his own wealth or, as some suspect, his cash base for his next deal. Only a few more years of business will demonstrate that.

The private equity revolution has certainly had a profound impact on the high street. On Green's bid for M&S Peter Cummings commented, 'The size of the bid means that the City's sound barrier has been broken. It demonstrated the new power of private capital. We know all about private equity, but private capital in this country has never been as big as it is now.'[18] In a 2004 survey by *Retail Week* of retail bosses and private equity investors, 90 per cent believed that such deals would continue at the same rate as in the last three years.[19] The economic climate has changed since then and the downturn in high street sales will have heightened the risks and will have made going private less attractive, at least for a while, but the trend is unlikely to go into reverse.

If it does continue apace, undeterred by the high-street gloom, a future Green bid for M&S could take place in different circumstances, ones in which the private option is an even more dominant force. Of course, as one of Britain's largest and most symbolic retailers, M&S going private would have a devastating impact on the whole retail sector. Because of this, Green promised at the time of his second bid that he would keep M&S public, but there were no guarantees. The deal on the table would have involved him owning the bulk of the company anyway, with shareholders handing over a huge slice of the business and ending up with only a minority stake. Green's experience of running a public company at Amber Day had, after all, left him frustrated and reluctant ever to run a public company again.

With his private companies he is the master of his own destiny, free to run them as he wishes – for short-term gain or long-run performance. Had he taken over M&S, he would probably have soon got frustrated with having to account for his plans to institutional shareholders and non-executive directors, and been tempted down the full private road again.

Green remains very emotional about M&S, but having been embarrassed twice, he is unlikely to make a third attempt on M&S unless he knows he can win. It is possible that he has given up, resigning himself to the fact that it will never happen. He has, after all, suffered one heart attack. On the other hand, if the circumstances were right he might well be tempted again. Despite the annoyance about his sudden exit in some parts of the City, he would have no difficulty putting together the finance and the right kind of team.

Whether and when he strikes again will depend ultimately on what sort of a fist Rose makes of running M&S and in particular what happens to the share price. From the moment he took over, Rose was confident that the price would eventually rise above the symbolic 400p level, but by July 2005, a year after he had taken control, he had failed to achieve better than 374p. Nevertheless, the price would probably need to fall well below this level before Green was likely to strike again. Not only would this be easier to finance, it would be a sign that Rose had failed to make a difference quickly enough. It would also be much more likely that this time he could rely, at least in part, on shareholder disquiet to back him.

C h a p t e r   1 6

JUDGEMENT DAY

I n 2005, Green made his debut in *Who's Who*. There was no mention of his education and he cited no recreations. This is because, barring big stake blackjack, the occasional game of tennis, table tennis with his kids and poker with his son, he has no hobbies. Business is his pleasure. He lives and breathes his companies. The entry makes this only too clear – there is little else apart from a long list of his acquisitions that culminated in his purchase of Bhs and Arcadia.

Business has been Green's life. This is how he measures his success. And remarkable it has been. No one else in British history has made money at his speed. According to the *Sunday Times* Rich List for 2005, Green's fortune had risen again to £4.85 billion in that year, mainly because of another upward valuation in Bhs and Arcadia.[1]

Green is fond of arguing that his wealth could all disappear tomorrow. Assets are only worth something if someone wants to buy them, a bitter truth that was driven home in the stock market crash at the turn of the millennium, when hundreds of new internet entrepreneurs worth millions on paper found their businesses to be worthless almost overnight. Green's main assets – Bhs and Arcadia, with a joint estimated market value in 2004 of some £3.7 billion[2] – are unlikely to collapse in the way of many of the dotcom companies, however. Whether he could sell them for this sort of sum is unknown, though a string of poor trading figures would certainly cut their value.

Of course, not all of his wealth is tied up in his businesses. When Green claims, as he does, that he is only worth 'what he has in his pocket', his pockets are pretty deep by most people's standards. Green is a money-making machine. In the three years to 2004, he paid himself dividends from Bhs and Arcadia of some £860 million. He will, of course, have spent some of this. A tycoon lifestyle doesn't come cheap.

Green likes to give the impression that he is careful with money, and not particularly materialistic. He may spend millions on his parties but he buys his T-shirts from Bhs and once said that he insisted his wife returned a £500 shirt she had bought him because it was too expensive. He claims that his children wear Bhs as well as designer clothes. He once told the *Mirror*: 'I would like to bet my credit card is probably one of the least-used credit cards of any executive of any company. I am not a money-waster . . . We don't go out flaunting the pound.'[3] Exactly how much cash he really has, and how much of it he will put into his next retail adventure, which few doubt will be long in coming, is impossible to know. When asked what he plans to do with such a war chest his usual reply is dismissive – 'I haven't thought about it.' But though no one really expects him to volunteer his plans, thinking about it he certainly is, there can be no doubt of that. After the £460 million payment from Arcadia, Tina replied, 'It's inheritance for our family, for our children and our children's children.' As it stands at the moment, Chloë and Brendan – and her children from her first marriage, Stasha and Brett – have a lot to inherit.

As he has made his money, Green has moved swiftly from an obscure small trader to become a public and somewhat controversial figure. He loves the limelight, and is never happier than when he is centre-stage at a charity function or business event, lecturing high-powered and well-heeled audiences on entrepreneurship, or jumping into helicopters, usually accompanied by bodyguard Sean, to be taken off to open a new store. He is certainly newsworthy and not just in the financial and business pages. During the prolonged battle for M&S, his picture was in the papers almost every day. He is often spotted and sometimes cornered by customers in his stores. Such a profile is rare amongst entrepreneurs and business leaders, especially those running private companies. He may not be as well known as Richard Branson, but in the visibility stakes he is closing the gap. He seeks publicity and thrives on it – provided it is positive.

Money and fame have opened lots of doors, and Green can now count on a pretty formidable network of friends and admirers. Moreover, if his earlier friends had not been carefully chosen, today's are much more select. While he continues to strike antipathy and ill-feeling in some quarters, he also commands widespread loyalty. Marco Pierre White, the restaurateur, is a friend and a fan: 'I like his loyalty, I like his support. I like his generosity. He's black and white.

You know where you stand with him. He tells you the way it is, not the way you want it to be. The difference with Philip is that he plays with his own money, not a PLC's money. He puts his balls on the table every time and that's what you've got to admire about him.'[4] And despite the rupture with the Weisfelds over tactics at Amber Day, Gerald still talks admiringly of him: 'You can't take anything away from the man. The guy's amazing – a magician. Whenever you've written him off he comes up smelling of roses.'[5]

He is part of a diverse social circle that includes Terry Venables, Sir Alex Ferguson, Michael Winner and Bruce Willis. He is a close friend of the restaurateur Robert Earl. He is in regular contact with the Grand Prix set and, of course, the jet-set Riviera crowd. He has helped to bankroll the takeover of at least one football club. He wrote a cheque for £30 million to Bill Kenwright, the theatre impresario, when he bought Everton in December 1999. When asked why he replied, 'Because I liked him.'[6] Although he is reticent to talk about it, he helped overcome the stalemate between Manchester United and Leeds over the transfer of Rio Ferdinand between the clubs. It was a matter of words in the right ear.

Without the business networks he has developed, he would never have been able to put through deals on the scale he has. As well as Robin Saunders, Bob Wigley and Peter Cummings, the business colleagues he has collected en route include the Barclay twins, Tom Hunter, Allan Leighton, Michael Sherwood of Goldman Sachs and Chris Coles of Barclay Capital. It is a pretty formidable circle and all have been involved in bankrolling or supporting his activities. Most have a great belief in Green. Leighton describes him as 'the most focused person I've ever met and the best merchant in the world'.[7]

Green still likes to be seen as the outsider, a man who has broken business taboos, who has succeeded despite his lack of favour in top financial circles. But although he may have begun his business career as an outsider, that description no longer applies. He has fought his way up the pole and joined the ranks of the insiders, becoming a man with considerable influence and powerful friends in the right places. He would never have been able to stomach being part of the traditional business establishment that ran British industry for most of the post-war era, did deals on the golf course and socialised at blue-blood clubs like White's. But he is now firmly part of a new and powerful business establishment which carries huge sway in City, business and political circles. Although some remain wary of him and would no doubt prefer to do business elsewhere – 'with those they can play golf with, who come from the right side of the tracks' as one insider sees it – now he can make them money, much of the City is only too happy to court him. Not so long ago most wouldn't have given him the time of day.

The party invites Green receives reveal just how far he has come. In May 2004, he was amongst a very high-profile group invited to a lavish party at Asprey, the Bond Street jeweller, to celebrate a refit costing £50 million. The whole street was closed off and carpeted in purple. Bellboys in purple pillbox hats lined the route. Guests included the Duchess of York, Sir Elton John, the actress Keira Knightley and the Duke of Marlborough, a mix of new and old society. Tina was wearing Graf diamonds reportedly worth millions. It was a party that culminated in dinner for 250 at Annabel's. Green's invite was no doubt helped by the fact that Asprey made the special £250,000 gold and diamond Monopoly set chosen by Tina as his fiftieth birthday present.

Green has had a turbulent relationship with journalists, and acknowledges that he has a low opinion of them: 'My view of journalists is pretty poor. Three-quarters of them aren't trained.'[8] By this he means that they don't understand business or finance, and that irritates him. He describes much of what they write as 'a pile of bullshit'. Despite his mistrust, Green has come to understand the power of the press and has been careful to court journalists throughout his career, a practice that has divided opinion within press circles and dates from his running of Amber Day in the late 1980s where he quickly learnt the benefits of self-promotion. His openness and direct dealing with them is rare in top business circles. Most sizeable retailers will employ at least one corporate PR company. Green hardly ever uses them, preferring to handle press queries himself.

He has a carefully nurtured group of favoured reporters that he likes to call up on a regular basis. Sometimes he teases them, ticking them off if they have the effrontery to ask him a pointed question. One of his favourite words with journalists is 'behave' and occasionally he rings them to give them a severe piece of his mind, a practice that few are now fazed by. Many if not most of the stories that find their way into the newspapers originate from him. That way he can control the content. He offers reporters colourful copy and good stories; in this way they come to rely on him as a source. No doubt he hopes that this will make them wary about what they say about him in case the copy dries up. Although he is often seen as naive in the way he deals with journalists by giving them the opportunity to print his more outrageous outbursts, in other ways he has shown a good deal of media savvy.

He also likes to invite journalists to his stores. Sometimes this can backfire. At the peak of the second bid for M&S, as part of his campaign to persuade institutional shareholders in M&S of his suitability, he invited three reporters from the *Financial Times* to spend a day with him and some of his executives. One of the first things the journalists spotted was his imperious treatment of his own staff. During the meeting, he handed Ian Grabiner – chief operating officer of Arcadia and a leading figure on the high street – the ashtray to empty.[9]

Such visits can also reveal Green's gentler side, his personal touch with staff and customers. During the same visit, he agreed to take a call at 6.40 a.m. when he heard that the husband of his Hong Kong office manager had been taken ill, to express his sympathies and give her some moral support. He sometimes replies personally to customer complaints and once called a woman who had complained about the quality of three bridesmaids' dresses bought from Bhs. He personally arranged for a photographer to retake the wedding photos.

Green has certainly acquired a solid network of supporters and backers as he has built his empire, and is widely admired by colleagues, staff and rivals for his achievements. Many remain in awe of him. But he continues to evoke strong reaction. Not everyone has done well out of Green's eruption onto the British retail scene. You can take your pick from the long list of ex-directors of M&S. Then there are those who have lived to regret selling their businesses on the cheap, as well as those who have felt the threat of a Green takeover. Many of those who have been in the firing line, such as the owners of Moss Bros in the late 1980s, resent his oft-used tactic of rubbishing his opponents or 'shaking the tree', as one retail observer puts it. His brashness is also a factor. Indeed, rather than attempt to shake off that image, he has continued to cultivate it.

Some of the resentment may be more visceral. Many of the more old school retailers dislike the way the pushy outsider has displaced them in the power rankings. The big retailers certainly have their share of classic alpha males who would give their right arm to be as successful as Green. As Neill Denny puts it, 'Green is the biggest beast in the jungle and one reason they don't like him is that some of them are somewhat in awe of him, envious if you like, though they can't admit that because to do so would be perceived as a fatal sign of weakness.'[10]

The retail world is also full of people who are still nervous about the impact of his predatory activity. In just a few years Green has, arguably, become the Rupert Murdoch of the high street. The top management at the British Retail Consortium, for example, was nervous that if Green bought M&S and pulled the company out as he had done with Bhs and Arcadia, the organisation would effectively be stranded and might not have survived. There is barely a chief executive in retail who does not feel that Green may be eyeing them up, a potent enough threat to keep the calmest of managers on their toes.

How does Green rank in the pantheon of British entrepreneurs, in the century-long line of high-profile British retailers? That list would include: Simon Marks from Marks & Spencer; successive members of the Sainsbury family; Sir Isaac Wolfson who built Great Universal Stores into Britain's largest mail order clothing business; Sir Jack Cohen who founded Tesco; Sir Charles Clore who first took over Sears and then built it into a huge retail consortium; and the Moores family who founded the Littlewoods chain before selling it to the Barclay brothers in 2002.

Green likes to be seen as a great retailer, a man with a magic touch who has turned around some of Britain's most well-known stores. But, as we've seen, Green has had a chequered business history. Many of his early enterprises ended with a trail of debt. There were question marks about the way he ran Amber Day. Then, in his early to mid-forties, he finally made serious money almost entirely out of deal-making, asset-stripping and property management. He bought and sold a series of failing companies over a period of several years, turning himself into a multi-millionaire in the process.

His rise to prominence within retail perhaps dates from 1995 when he helped broker the Olympus Sports deal. Most of his early fortune came from the purchase and dismantling of the giant Sears conglomerate, the act which earned him the reputation as 'Conan the Barbarian'. Until he bought Bhs and Arcadia his main retail success was probably rebuilding MK One out of the ashes of Mark One, though this was, as one analyst puts it, 'small beer'.

Since 2000, however, he has steadily built a new reputation as the man who, as Sir David Sieff puts it, 'has woken up' the high street.[11] He has taken both Bhs and Arcadia by the scruff of the neck and greatly improved the performance of both. Of the two, it is Bhs that has been most transformed. M&S, forced into drastic measures, will certainly never be the same again because of his intervention.

In 2003, *Retail Week* conducted a reader's poll to find the most admired retailer of the previous fifteen years. The title went to Sir Terry Leahy, the man who had elevated Tesco to world-class commercial success. Leahy received the award because in a handful of years he had turned Tesco into the number one supermarket in Britain and the world's sixth biggest retailer, behind such giants as Wal-Mart in the USA and Carrefour in France. The runner-up was George Davies, the man who first launched Next and then master-minded the highly successful George and Per Una ranges. Davies has probably done more than anyone to keep M&S afloat in the last few years. Green and Davies's strengths are to some extent complementary. Davies is the creative one and has brought customers to Next, George and Per Una, but he can't run a business in the way that Green does. Green, on the other hand, hasn't created a single brand. That's probably why he came in third in the poll behind Davies.

Whether Green is a great retailer, able to stand alongside Simon Marks, Charles Clore or members of the Sainsbury and Moores families is a question that is too early to answer. To become a top entrepreneur requires a range of exceptional personal skills. Like all successful entrepreneurs, Green has at his core a single-minded will to win. Impossible is not part of his vocabulary. Although he has had his fair share of knocks, he has always bounced back. He is restless, determined and energetic. He sees the world through the prism of retail. Even when on holiday he likes to check out the local fashion shops in search of 'winners' and when he finds one will ring back to Britain to instruct his brand managers to place an order. Again, in common with many successful tycoons from Charles Clore to James Goldsmith, he is driven by a cavalier need to break the rules.

Winning requires taking risks, sometimes big ones, and taking risks does not always work, as the numerous stories of failed entrepreneurs show. But in Green's case many of his gambles have come off, partly because he learnt from the experience of early failure that risks must be calculated ones. He approaches deal-making in the same way he approaches casinos. He generally prefers blackjack to roulette because blackjack gives him slightly greater control over the outcome. In the end he creates his own luck.

Green likes to portray his purchase of Bhs and Arcadia as high-risk deals which nobody else was prepared to take on, but the risk was always limited by the large property empire he acquired along with the retail outlets. Without that he would not have obtained the backing of such major banks. As he admits himself, he never jumps until he has done his homework: 'Talk to anyone who works with me. I do detailed studies. I don't guess. They'll tell you I'm well researched.'[12] So we need to take with a pinch of salt Green's claims that he bought Bhs and Arcadia 'blind'. Moreover, his own stakes have always been limited. If Bhs or Arcadia had gone bust, Green might have been humiliated, but much of the financial loss – at least before he paid off the debt – would have been borne by the banks. As Richard Hyman says: 'He may be aggressive and brash on the surface, but he is also very measured and considered beneath that. Far from being impetuous, he is quite cautious.'[13]

Despite his formidable skills, Green is a particular type of business-man. He trades in existing companies. He is in essence a 'turnaround entrepreneur', one who 'amasses wealth by buying, reshaping and selling ongoing businesses . . . and who prefers systems and detail to the big picture, [whose] talents lie in cutting back unwieldy ventures instead of growing them'.[14] Those businesses he created from scratch in his twenties and early thirties went nowhere. He is not a founding entrepreneur in the mould of the great nineteenth-century indus-trialists, such as William Lever and George Cadbury, or their modern-day equivalents – Richard Branson, Stelios Haji-Ioannou and James Dyson – all men who have created new companies out of nothing. He is not a creator of products nor is he known for his ideas. He has not built market share but bought into it. But Green is open about not wanting to start from scratch: 'Wouldn't know how. Not my skill. Too hard. Too difficult. It's easier to rebuild than build . . . building from scratch one by one is just very hard work.'[15] Like many of those who sit at the top of today's wealth league, his skills lie in deal-making and improving processes; ultimately, it is the creators of new businesses who have the greater claim to entrepreneurial greatness, even if they may have made less money doing so.

John Plender of the *Financial Times* has described him as the 'foremost exponent of red-in-tooth-and-claw capitalism in the country. It commands awe. If not respect.'[16] Green is certainly ruthless in the way he runs a business. He will push as far as it is possible to do so. He is not just hard on suppliers, something he likes to deny, but is always determined to wring the best possible deal from whomever he is conducting business with, from bankers to the management of the companies he has bought. That's why he likes to be at the heart of the negotiations rather than leave it to his professional advisers.

One of Green's heroes is Charles Clore, the man who pioneered the hostile takeover bid in the 1950s. He also admires the successful and feared corporate-raider Lord Hanson, darling of Mrs Thatcher in the 1980s. The middle years of Green's career can be seen as an attempt to mimic men such as these. He has certainly been inspired by them, even dining with Lord Hanson before he died in 2004. Once spotted by a group of bankers at Santini restaurant in London's Belgravia with Hanson and Hanson's son, Robert, speculation mounted that Green and Hanson might be forging a joint deal. He has much in common with these earlier corporate-raiders. Like them, he trades in current assets, made his early money through asset-stripping and has a remarkable knack of spotting the opportunistic purchase, securing in the process a redistribution of wealth from existing management and shareholders to himself. He too is a buccaneer, a man inspired by disaffection with traditional business methods.

Green, like these deal-making pioneers, is also a master of aggressive financial engineering, a technique he has been able to carry further by taking his firms private. One financial commentator has said that 'his ability to extract cash is probably unprecedented' and that the last person to be as good at managing finances was Charles Clore.[17] But although he is, at least in part, a modern-day asset-stripper, he has latterly chosen to continue to run the companies he has acquired. This typically involves raising substantial short-term finance to buy ailing private companies from existing managers and shareholders, who are often only too happy to sell. This debt is mostly borrowed over short periods of up to five years and thus has to be repaid quickly, often through another dose of financial manipulation. This will include, for example, some mortgaging and leaseback of existing property. In both Bhs and Arcadia, Green was able to pay off the debt much more quickly than originally planned. How much of Green's turnaround success is down to financial engineering and how much to clever retailing is a matter of some debate amongst retail experts. The truth is it is a mix of both.

There are also some major differences that distinguish Green from the earlier business generation. First, Green is a much more hands-on manager, at least since taking over Bhs. For example, in contrast to Lord White, James Hanson's partner, who would boast that he had never stepped onto the shop floor of any of the companies he had bought, Green likes to roll up his sleeves. Few dispute he is a master of his trade, certainly one of the best rag-traders in Britain. Sir David Sieff described him as a 'quality merchant with a real feel for the high street. He knows what's selling, what customers want, when to buy, how much to pay and what everybody else is paying for it. You either have it or you don't.'[18]

Another difference is Green's preference for taking firms private rather than catering for their financial needs through the issuing of shares. Though rules on corporate governance were much more lax in their day, men such as Clore and Hanson still had shareholders to answer to. Going private is also the key to the much greater wealth Green has accumulated compared to his predecessors. It is this combination – private ownership together with his skill at bringing 'value-added' – that is the main source of his vast fortune.

Green has also made his fortune in a period of remarkably benign economic and political conditions. He has benefited from a period of cheap finance that has allowed him to borrow huge sums at historically low interest rates. The years following the millennium brought a remarkable retail boom that was financed by unprecedented levels of personal consumer debt. A much sterner test of his skills will be how he manages in the much more brutal retail market that emerged in the spring of 2005. Bucking that trend would be the clearest answer to his critics and would undoubtedly extend his list of admirers.

Certainly, what Green has yet to demonstrate is that he has another skill, perhaps the most crucial of all – the ability to increase sales. Robert Clark describes him as a 'consummate operator, very sharp. What he has not brought so far is evolutionary retailing flair, largely because he hasn't had to. He has yet to substantially boost sales at Bhs or Arcadia.'[19] Second-guessing his customers, knowing what they will want, is perhaps the most difficult of all the retail talents, as a succession of retail bosses, including a number of chief executives at M&S, have found to their cost. Green has yet to show that he could do better.

Many people peering behind the fast-talking, flamboyant and confident façade of Philip Green also detect a much more deep-seated insecurity, a need to achieve and to be seen to do so. He craves public recognition, and seems to need constant reassurance and affirmation. The graphologist who studied Green's handwriting in February 2003 for *The Times* found not just 'a headstrong and original thinker', but a sensitive man who needed 'a key public place in life'.[20]

Green is never happier than when his success is being recognised by flattering press coverage, prestigious business awards, or meeting the Queen or the Prime Minister. In 2004, he was interviewed by *Forbes*, the prestigious American business magazine that draws up an annual list of the richest people in America and around the world. It was the first time that Green had made it to the list. (He entered at number eighty-four. A year later, in the 2005 list, he had risen to sixty-eighth.[21])

Green's apparent attention-seeking helps to explain one of the curious contradictions of his private companies. As we have seen, one of the reasons that Green prefers to remain private is that the disclosure obligations are limited. Yet, as a private company, he could choose to give much less information away about his stores than he has chosen to. Most super-rich entrepreneurs are much more coy about their business affairs, including Richard Branson and Richard Desmond. Green's public tub-thumping AGMs and the trumpeting of his profit figures and margins are partly a matter of stage-management but they can also be seen as a form of public boasting, a prop to his own delicate ego.

If making money is one indicator of business success, there is another test. For generations many entrepreneurs have accepted that great wealth also brings social responsibility to staff and wider society. Some of the great industrialists of the nineteenth century, from Joseph Rowntree to William Lever, were great philanthropists. Simon Marks, son of the founder of M&S, was not merely a great retailer with passion, flair and attention to detail, but was also a visionary and social philosopher who developed generous and extensive welfare benefits for staff and believed in protecting his suppliers.

Green likes to see himself as a generous man, not just to friends – his parties attest to that – and staff but also to charity. In December 2003, he made a donation of some £4 million to help fund care homes provided by Jewish Care, a large health and social care charity. He is a regular at high-profile charity auctions where he usually leads the bidding and likes nothing more than to force prices up often to the point 'where it becomes embarrassing' according to one observer. At the 2004 Annual Retail Trust Charity Ball, Green and Tom Hunter between them spent £270,000 on a £20,000 MG. Hunter first bought it for £120,000 and then redonated it for Green to bid a further £150,000.

He has attended functions in aid of a whole host of charities, and is often the single most generous giver at such events. At the Breast Cancer Care 2004 Fashion Show Green ended up buying seven of the thirteen lots put up for sale. They included a shirt signed by rugby international Lawrence Dallaglio, which cost him £2,500, a test flight in a Russian Mig-21 fighter and a shirt autographed by double Olympic gold medallist Kelly Holmes. A year before, Green had paid £500,000 for another England rugby shirt signed by the entire squad at an auction organised by the children's charity the Rainbow Trust. Sotheby's, which organised the sale, claimed that it was a record bid for sporting memorabilia sold by the auctioneers.

Sometimes Green is able to combine his generosity with his predilection for pranks. In February 2005, he attended a dinner thrown by the Retail Trust at the Grosvenor House Hotel where he bid £50,000 in the auction to have Ruby Wax – who compèred the evening – work as a shop assistant for half a day. It was not quite as straight-forward as it seemed. He was paying for her to work not in Bhs but in M&S, he explained to the assembled elite of the retail trade. Judging by the look on their faces, it was a joke that did not go down well with either Wax herself or the M&S executives.

Although his donations are large in absolute terms, to Green they are little more than pocket money. And judged by the standards of some of the super-rich, he is not especially generous. His friend and colleague Tom Hunter, for example, has committed £100 million of his personal fortune to his own charitable foundation. Some have even criticised Green for giving so little away. In the aftermath of the tsunami disaster that hit South-East Asia on Boxing Day, 2004, killing

300,000 people, Green was one of the first off the mark with a donation, announcing that he was giving £100,000 in cash and £1 million in clothes. As some sceptics pointed out, this came a month after he had paid himself a dividend of £460 million.

In March 2005, Green again won the prestigious Retail Personality of the Year Award hosted by *Retail Week*. It was his third win in four years, an unprecedented achievement, and a recognition from his peers of his impact during 2004, not just in improving his own empire but on M&S, too. In 2004, he also received the CBI's award for 'the entrepreneur's entrepreneur', an award the CBI nicknames the 'patron saint of business'.

Despite his clutch of awards, however, none has been for ethical sourcing, sustainable development, care for the environment or corporate social responsibility. On these issues, 'Saint Philip' is unlikely to make the shortlist, unlike B&Q, the Body Shop, the Co-op and Sainsbury's. Following Julia Cleverdon's attack on Green before the annual BITC awards, the environmental campaigner Jonathon Porritt wrote a letter to the *Financial Times* asking: 'Where is the evidence of his personal leadership on these issues in Bhs or Arcadia? What evidence is there that he really understands that critical nexus . . . between brand, trust and performance on social responsibility – hard-edged, world-beating performance on issues that consumers really care about, as well as world-beating performance on financial returns?'[22]

Green would argue that his companies are putting something back through charity sponsorship and investing in education. In the winter of 2004, he announced that as well as putting money into secondary schools specialising in enterprise, he was sponsoring a government initiative to establish an entrepreneurial retail academy, with the government and Green each putting in £10 million. The academy, for sixteen- to eighteen-year-olds, is aimed at the training of non-academic young people to work in the retail trade. Based in Gresse Street in London's fashion district just north of Oxford Street, it opened in September 2005. His own school experience taught him that much of the formal academic education at school was of no help whatsoever in turning out people who would 'make things happen'. He doesn't want people who are academically trained. As one insider put it, 'It would drive him up the wall to employ lots of arts graduates. He wants people who left school at sixteen, like him, raw material he can mould, and that's what the academy will provide.'[23]

It might be asked why the rich give at all. Are they driven by guilt, by religion, to avoid taxation? Is it to impress? Or is it really about altruism? The nineteenth-century American banker J.P. Morgan once said that a man always has two reasons for the things he does: a good reason and the real reason. Some of the very rich choose to be very discreet about how much they give away. Green is in the conspicuous rather than the low-profile camp. Although he specified that his donation to Jewish Care was not to be publicised, he mostly prefers to conduct his giving at very public functions where he can mingle with the famous from designers and business leaders to celebrities and top politicians. As Sir David Sieff says, 'Some business leaders who are a great success do things quietly, but Philip is not quiet by nature.'[24]

At the breast cancer charity dinner, he sat at the same table as Cherie Blair and Carol Vorderman, a photo opportunity he wasn't going to let pass. Many charity dinners are sponsored by his Bhs and Arcadia group. Not only is this good publicity for Green and his stores, it enables him to be seen and rub shoulders with the glitterati. Green likes to get celebrities into his stores even if they usually shop elsewhere. When Tara Palmer-Tomkinson came to the opening of a new Dorothy Perkins store in Oxford Street in 2003, for example, she apparently arrived with two Selfridges bags.[25]

His generosity has also put him on first-name terms with leading politicians. He has met Tony Blair twice, once in a private one-to-one meeting at Downing Street in March 2004 and once at Chequers a year later in March 2005. Maybe he was being checked out for the honours lists.

Social responsibility is not just a matter of putting something back via charity. Green and his family, like an increasing number of Britain's new super-rich, choose to live abroad in Monaco. This is partly a matter of lifestyle, but it also brings huge tax advantages. While his wife Tina is a Monaco resident, Green retains British residency and thus has to pay British income and capital taxes. This is because the tax rules make it clear that you are liable to UK taxes if you are in the country for ninety or more days a year. Green – the ultimate hands-on proprietor – could not run his companies if he spent less than ninety days a year in Britain.

But, with the aid of highly paid tax accountants and lawyers, Green has set up his companies, which are registered offshore in Jersey, in such a way that his dividends accrue not to him but to his wife. It is no wonder that Green sometimes likes to joke of Tina that 'he cannot afford' to divorce her. Arcadia is in effect owned by her rather than Philip. So while his companies pay corporation taxes, it was Tina who received the £460 million Arcadia dividend paid at the end of 2004, which would have been tax-free. Without such an arrangement – which is perfectly legal – Green would have had to pay tax at 25 per cent on the dividend payment. The Exchequer is short of tax revenue of the order of some £115 million as a result. This is despite the fact that the dividend arose from business activity conducted in Britain, using, for example, staff mostly educated and trained in the British educational system.

Green argues that his companies invest in Britain and has always denied that placing his companies in Tina's name is about tax-planning, though it is difficult to see what other purpose it could serve. He once jokingly referred to the payments to Tina as 'housekeeping money'. Yet it is Philip who works long hours to improve Bhs's and Arcadia's profitability, and rings in every day when on holiday. He is the brains and the inspiration. Tina on occasions helps out a little behind the scenes – planning the design of her husband's office, and paying the occasional joint midnight visit to check the stores out, for example – but she has no public role in the operation of the Green companies currently registered in her name, and indeed, visits London mainly for the occasional charity function or business party.

Green, of course, is not alone in exploiting Britain's generous tax rules. The great majority of the super-rich arrange their business affairs in such a way to minimise their tax payments. Indeed, modern entrepreneurship and tax avoidance more or less go hand in hand. Richard Branson, Mohamed al Fayed, Lakshmi Mittal and Hans Rausing are amongst the mega-rich who exploit tax loopholes to enhance their personal fortunes. While such arrangements are perfectly legal, whether they are equitable is another matter. Britain, in effect, treats the rich as a special case for tax purposes. Increasingly, the super-rich are choosing to become free-riders, opting out of the social contract to which ordinary citizens sign up. They are paying little for the essential public goods like health, education, security and the rule of law without which societies could not function.

The effect of avoidance, legal as it is, is that the tax burden is often inversely related to the ability to pay, with multi-millionaires paying a lower proportion of their income in tax than the low-paid. Prem Sikka, Professor of Accountancy at the University of Essex and a leading tax expert, has described it as a form of 'reverse socialism'.[26]

Green still loves to promote an image of himself – that he is self-made, that he was hard done by over M&S, that he has the Midas touch, that he doesn't care what others think, that he is not as bossy and quick-tempered as his detractors like to claim. The truth is more muddied on all counts. He hardly sprang from nowhere. He came from a prosperous if not rich background, went to a very respectable public school, even if he was never academically driven enough to make a go of it. His failure at M&S was at least in part of his own making. His short fuse is now internationally acknowledged. The interview with *Forbes* magazine which took place in London began, 'Philip Green is in a tizzy. Glaring at rows of crisply pressed crew-neck tops and neatly folded pastel sweaters, Green lets the store manager have it: "It's a mess, John. It's horrible. Absolutely awful." '[27]

Green will always divide opinion. In some ways, he has calmed down over the years. He keeps safer company and makes wiser decisions, such as the one to pull out of M&S. But though he may have become more prudent in business, he remains at heart rebellious and unpredictable. There is no evidence that he is temperamentally more stable, that he has lost his abrasive, bossy and opinionated manner. He continues to fly off the handle, seems to remain bitter over the way Rose and M&S handled his takeover attempt, and still likes to let rip at journalists who, in his words, 'have lost the plot', that is, those who don't follow the script – his script.

His reckless, injudicious side, of course, may well be inseparable from the skills that have turned him into a winner. Like other successful public figures – including Richard Desmond and Alex Ferguson, also renowned for their short fuses – his petulance continues to get him into trouble.

John Jay, the former business editor of the *Sunday Times*, once wrote: 'My award for vulgarity and rudeness goes to Philip Green.' Having written the offending article about Tina's share purchases in M&S that led to a successful libel case against the paper, he had of course had his own run-ins with Green.[28] David Starkey, the historian and broadcaster with a reputation as one of Britain's rudest men himself, likes to lecture business people on the characteristics of great leaders, and once told a group that they are typically 'foulmouthed, vulgar, incapable of restraint and completely humourless'. According to Starkey, one of Green's senior directors came up to him afterwards and said, 'So you know my boss, then?' Starkey added his own description of Green: 'Has there been anything like him in history? One gets the impression of a queasy Roman emperor: the foul mouth, the vulgar excesses, the flowing toga. One might suggest he is a Nero if one didn't want to get sued.' It could have been worse – Starkey likened Lord Hanson to Genghis Khan.[29]

Some have compared Green, unfavourably, to his old sparring partner Alan Sugar, the fiftieth richest person in Britain, former Spurs owner and the host of BBC2's successful reality television programme *The Apprentice*, in which fourteen wannabe entrepreneurs competed, in the spring of 2005, for a £100,000 a year job. Sugar was openly aggressive, critical and dismissive as he went about selecting the winner, but one who knows Green describes Sugar as 'a pussy-cat in comparison. Imagine Sugar at twice the strength and you're getting close to Green.'[30]

In fact, Green was the BBC's preferred choice to front the show. Before Sugar was in the frame, Green was approached at least twice in the spring of 2004, first by the BBC and then by Talkback, the independent television company which made the show. Green made it clear, politely, that 'he wasn't interested'. Green may like to grab the limelight, but even he has his limits. What the young apprentices would have made of Green or he of them we will now never know.

Green bristles at negative descriptions. But although he is thin-skinned, he would no doubt rather this than be ignored. The back-biting means that he is now a man to be reckoned with. Many great entrepreneurs, including Simon Marks, hung around too long. At least some of the early buccaneers, the men Green admires most, found their businesses fading because their success went to their heads and they became oblivious to their weaknesses. The risks of this happening are even greater in private companies where the board is handpicked and there are no backstops in the form of non-executive directors or independent chairmen to offer sound advice. The one saving grace is that Green himself is aware of the danger of allowing ambition to take him one step too far.

Like so many entrepreneurs, Green has a limited attention span and bores easily. It is this restlessness that means even success doesn't make him satisfied. Even now, at the age of fifty-three and the fifth richest man in Britain, Green appears to need to keep proving himself. He seems to have no interest in following in the footsteps of other tycoons by buying up a premiership football club or investing in controversial art. He could upstage Roman Abramovich and buy Tottenham Hotspur or Arsenal. He could, as others have done, use his money to buy political influence and earn a peerage. He would certainly shake up the House of Lords, but his interests seem to lie in business alone.

For him a trophy asset would mean owning M&S, not a premiership football club. Neill Denny has likened him to Ian Wright and Thierry Henry, both footballers obsessed with beating their club's goal-scoring records. Only when he has achieved the equivalent and taken the M&S citadel will he think about relaxing.[31] He laughs at any suggestions that he might ease off, go into early semi-retirement and concentrate instead on spending the rest of his fortune. His mother is, after all, still running her business at the age of eighty-six.

For Green, there are still citadels to storm. Buying Bhs and Arcadia and climbing up the wealth league has provided him with profile and status, but he has not yet left his mark on society in the way that other entrepreneurs have done. Whether he will eventually make that final 'quantum leap' remains to be seen.

NOTES

CHAPTER 1: THIS IS YOUR LIFE

1 *Independent*, 19 March 2002.
2 *Daily Mail*, 15 March 2002.
3 *Daily Mail*, 18 March 2002.
4 *Daily Record*, 16 March 2002.
5 The figure of £5 million has been widely published and never challenged. It is an estimate.
6 Agence France-Presse, Cyprus, 14 August 2002.
7 www.banana-split.com
8 Reuters, 16 February 2003.
9 The names of people attending have been gathered from numerous newspaper reports and from a number of eyewitnesses at the events.
10 Interview with eyewitness, February 2005.
11 Many press reports, supplemented by interview with eyewitness, February 2005.
12 *Daily Mirror*, 19 March 2002.
13 Interview with eyewitness, February 2005.
14 Interview with Vera and Gerald Weisfeld, February 2005.
15 Interview with eyewitness, February 2005.
16 *Daily Express*, 31 May 2003.
17 Interview with eyewitness, February 2005.
18 Interview with eyewitness, February 2005.
19 *Sunday Telegraph*, 1 September 2002.
20 Ibid.
21 Information from a friend of the person in question, who reported this confession of embarrassment.
22 *Sunday Telegraph*, 1 September 2002.
23 *Daily Express*, 31 May 2003.
24 *Mail on Sunday*, 17 March 2002.
25 *Independent*, 18 March 2002.

CHAPTER 2: A COCKY LITTLE BOY

1 *The Times*, 24 October 2004.
2 Ibid.
3 Ibid.
4 Langley Road Investments Ltd, Filed Accounts, Companies House, 1962–85.
5 *Guardian*, 23 October 2004.
6 *Daily Mail*, 20 July 2004.
7 Bloombergs, 16 June 2004.
8 www.geocities.com/chaimsimons/carmelcollege.html
9 Interview with Toni Rauch, June, 2005.
10 Ibid.
11 Interview with contemporary A at Carmel, February 2005.
12 Interview with contemporary B at Carmel, February 2005.
13 Conversation with contemporary C at Carmel, February 2005.
14 Interview with contemporary B at Carmel, February 2005.
15 Conversation with Anthony Barr-Taylor, April 2005.
16 *Evening Standard*, 26 September 2003; Bloombergs, 16 June 2004.
17 *Sunday Times*, 1 September 2002.
18 An event remembered by both contemporary A and contemporary B.
19 Interview with Mrs Evans, June 2005.
20 *Guardian*, 23 October 2002.
21 Interview with contemporary A at Carmel, February 2005.
22 *Guardian*, 24 October 2004.
23 Ibid.
24 Ibid.
25 Anthony Sampson, *The Midas Touch* (Hodder & Stoughton, 1989), p. 24.
26 See David Hall, *In the Company of Heroes* (Kogan Page, 1999), pp. 7–8.
27 *The Times*, 30 May 2004.
28 *Sunday Telegraph*, 24 January 1999.
29 Interview with Vera Weisfeld, February 2005.
30 Interview with Gerald Weisfeld, February 2005.
31 Interview with Vera Weisfeld, February 2005.
32 Ibid.
33 Ibid.
34 *Guardian*, 24 October 2004.
35 Tarbrook Ltd, Filed Accounts and Documents, 1976–83, Companies House.
36 Ibid.
37 *The Times*, 22 February 2003.
38 Interview with Vera Weisfeld, February 2005.
39 Interview with Eric Musgrave, April 2005.
40 *Drapers Record*, 11 April 1981.
41 Ibid.

42   The next year Joan Collins was to get her part as Alexis in *Dynasty*.
43   Joan Collins Jean Company Ltd, Filed documents, 1981–2, Companies House.
44   Ibid.
45   Tarbrook Ltd, Filed Accounts and Documents, 1976–83, Companies House.

CHAPTER 3: THE DEL BOY YEARS

1   *Guardian*, 24 October 2004.
2   Ibid.
3   Ibid.
4   Interview with retail insider, June 2005.
5   *Fashion Weekly*, 8 May 1981.
6   *The Times*, 10 October 1981.
7   Helmut Newton, *Autobiographie* (C. Bertelsmann, 2005).
8   *Evening Standard*, 19 May 1981.
9   Ibid.
10   Wearstyle Ltd, Filed Company Accounts 1982–3, Companies House.
11   Interview with London jeans trader of the period, June 1995.
12   Interview with George Maldé, May 2005.
13   Ibid.
14   *Guardian*, 24 October 2004; interview with George Maldé, May 2005.
15   *Menswear*, 1 August 1995.
16   *MAB News*, September 1985.
17   Interview with one-time journalist of *MAB News*. Pond-e-Rosa was also meant to be a crude pun on 'Pound in the Red'.
18   Lucasport Ltd, Filed Accounts, 1985–6, Companies House.
19   Interview with George Maldé, May 2005; *Guardian*, 24 October 2004.
20   *Guardian*, 24 October 2004.
21   Interview with George Maldé, May 2005; *Guardian*, 24 October 2004. Maldé maintains that the sum to be paid to Casey was £1 million.
22   *Guardian*, 24 October 2004.
23   Interview with Nitin Shah, May 2005.
24   *Menswear*, 11 May 1989.
25   Ibid.
26   Ibid.
27   *Guardian*, 24 October 2004.
28   Interview with George Maldé, May 2005.
29   *Sunday Telegraph*, 21 April 1991.
30   *Daily Mail*, 3 June 2005.
31   Irving Scholar, *Behind Closed Doors* (Andre Deutsch, 1992), p. 273.

CHAPTER 4: NOT A MAN OF HALF MEASURES

1   Interview with George Maldé, April 2005; interview with Alan Richards, formerly Company Secretary Lee Cooper Group, May 2005.

2   Interviews with Barry Gibson, former MD, Lee Cooper Retail, and Alan Richards, April 2005.

3   *Menswear*, 11 May 1989.

4   Amber Day Holdings PLC, Filed Rrecords, 1988–9, Companies House; interviews with George Maldé, April and June 2005.

5   DTI, *Blue Arrow plc*, Hilary Heilbron and Michael Boonan, HMSO, 1991.

6   Amber Day Holdings PLC, Filed Accounts for 1988–89, Companies House.

7   *Menswear*, 11 May 1989.

8   Amber Day Holdings PLC, letter to shareholders recommending rights issue, June 1991, Companies House.

9   *Evening Standard*, 23 November 2004.

10 *Independent on Sunday*, 27 September 1992.

11 Interview with Gerald Weisfeld, December 2004.

12 *Financial Times*, 16 April 1991.

13 *Daily Mail*, 3 June 2005.

14 Interview with Gerald Weisfeld, June 2005.

15 Interview with Gerald Weisfeld, January 2005.

16 Interview with Vera Weisfeld, January 2005.

17 *Financial Times*, 11 July 1992.

18 Interview with Jim McCann, March 2005.

19 Amber Day Holdings PLC, letter to shareholders recommending rights issue, June 1991, Companies House.

20 Ibid.

21 *Independent*, 16 April 1991.

22 *Independent*, 15 July 1991 and 27 September 1992.

23 *Daily Mail*, 31 January 1992.

24 *Mail on Sunday*, 9 February 1992.

25 Simon Cawkwell, *Profit of the Plunge* (Rushmere Wynn, 1996), pp. 107–8.

26 *Independent*, 19 July 1992.

27 Interview with City insider.

28 DTI, *Blue Arrow plc*, Hilary Heilbron and Michael Boonan, HMSO, 1991.

29 *Independent on Sunday*, 27 September 1992; *Evening Standard*, 26 September 2003.

30 DTI, *Blue Arrow*, Hilary Heilbron and Michael Boonan, HMSO, 1991.

31 *Private Eye*, 22 May 1992.

32 *Sunday Times*, 14 June 1992.

33 Ibid.

34 *Private Eye*, 22 May 1992.

35   *Daily Mail*, 4 June 1992.
36   *Sunday Times*, 27 September 1992.

CHAPTER 5: 'LEAVE IT TO ME'

1   *Guardian*, 25 November 1992.
2   *Sunday Times*, 25 April 1993.
3   *Sunday Times*, 30 May 1993.
4   Ibid.
5   *Retail Week*, 4 June 1993.
6   *Sunday Telegraph*, 24 January 1999.
7   *Retail Week*, 4 January 1995.
8   *Menswear*, 21 October 1995.
9   *Retail Week*, 28 July 1995.
10   Ibid.
11   Ibid.
12   *Daily Post*, 23 January 2002.
13   *Retail Week*, 6 September 1996.
14   *Retail Week*, 31 January 1999.
15   *Retail Week*, 28 July 1995.
16   Ibid.
17   Ibid.
18   Interview with Vera Weisfeld, February 2005; email from Tom Hunter, June 2005.
19   *Retail Week*, 15 July 1994.
20   Email from Tom Hunter, June 2005.
21   *Scotland on Sunday*, 2 July 2000; *Daily Telegraph*, 18 December 2004.
22   *Daily Telegraph*, 18 December 2004.
23   Ibid.
24   *Retail Week*, 12 January 1996.

CHAPTER 6: CONAN THE BARBARIAN

1   Charles Gordon, *The Two Tycoons* (Hamish Hamilton, 1984), p. 42.
2   *Daily Mail*, 3 June 2005.
3   *The Times*, 24 October 2004.
4   *Daily Mail*, 3 June 2005.
5   *Retail Week*, 12 January 1996.
6   Ibid.
7   *Financial Times*, 4 March 1996.
8   *Retail Week*, 31 May 1996.
9   *Retail Week*, 7 June 1996.
10   *Mail on Sunday*, 23 March 2003.
11   *The Times*, 24 December 1997.
12   *The Times*, 16 December 1997.

13   *Sunday Telegraph*, 5 March 1998.
14   *Daily Mail*, 3 June 2005.
15   *WWD* magazine, 18 November 2002.
16   *Birmingham Post*, 14 October 1998.
17   *Sunday Telegraph*, 17 January 1999.
18   *Birmingham Post*, 22 January 1999.
19   *Sunday Telegraph*, 24 January 1999.
20   *Retail Week*, 29 January 1999.
21   *Retail Week*, 19 February 1999.
22   *Retail Week*, 25 June 1999.
23   *Independent*, 15 December 1998.

CHAPTER 7: PROJECT MUSHROOM

1   Interview with Sir David Sieff, March 2005.
2   Judi Bevan, *The Rise and Fall of Marks & Spencer* (Profile Books, 2002), p. 222.
3   *Mail on Sunday*, 23 March 2003.
4   *Financial Times*, 7 February 2000.
5   *Financial Times*, 12 February 2000.
6   *Independent on Sunday*, 6 February 2000.
7   *Sunday Times*, 6 February 2000.
8   Bevan, p. 220.
9   Ibid.
10   Bevan, p. 221.
11   *Sunday Times*, 13 February 2000.
12   *Independent*, 11 February 2000.
13   *Daily Telegraph*, 12 February 2000.
14   *Mail on Sunday*, 23 March 2003.
15   *Mail on Sunday*, 11 July 2004.
16   *Financial Times*, 12 February 2000.
17   Letter from Slaughter & May to Titmuss Sainer, 8 February 2000.
18   *Observer*, 13 February 2000.
19   Legal action was also initiated against the *Observer*.
20   The *Observer* published a correction and apology for the article dated 6 February 2000, on 8 July 2001.

CHAPTER 8: THE STEAL OF THE CENTURY

1   Interview with Neill Denny, April 2005.
2   *Retail Week*, 11 June 2004.
3   *Financial Times*, 16 December 2002.
4   *The Times*, 28 March 2004.
5   *Daily Mail*, 30 August 2002.
6   *Guardian*, 8 October 2002.

7   Interview with retail expert, April 2005.

8   *Guardian*, 8 October 2002.

9   Interview with retail insider.

10 All quotes from the *Sunday Telegraph*, 20 January 2002.

11 *Sunday Times*, 27 May 2001.

12 Rich List 2005, *Sunday Times*, April 2005.

13 Interview with retail expert, April 2005.

14 Interview with Neill Denny, April 2005.

15 Rich List 2002, *Sunday Times*, April 2002.

16 *Evening Standard*, 13 June 2002.

17 *Observer*, 9 March 2003.

18 Interview with Robert Clark, April 2005.

19 Interview with retail expert, April 2005.

20 *Evening Standard*, 11 February 2005.

21 *Daily Mail*, 14 February 2004.

22 Interview with Neill Denny, April 2005.

23 *Daily Telegraph*, 7 November 2000.

24 BHS Ltd Company Accounts, 2002, Companies House.

25 *Drapers*, 9 March 2002.

26 *Sunday Times*, 14 July 2002.

27 BHS Ltd Company Accounts, year ended March 2003, Companies House.

28 Interview with Paul Murphy, June 2005.

29 *Guardian*, 4 March 2003.

30 *Observer*, 9 March 2003.

31 *Sunday Tribune*, 9 March 2003.

32 *Observer*, 20 December 1998.

33 *Observer*, 9 March 2003.

34 *Sunday Times*, 27 May 2001.

35 Interview with financial journalist, May 2005.

36 *Daily Express*, 23 October 2004.

37 *Financial Times*, 26 June 2004.

38 *Independent*, 30 August 2002.

39 Interview with retail journalist, April 2005.

40 *Sunday Times*, 24 October 2004.

41 *Sunday Times*, 26 May 2002.

42 *Sunday Times*, 27 May 2001.

CHAPTER 9: THE GIANT AND THE ANT

1   *Sunday Times*, 1 September 2002.

2   *Retail Week*, 6 September 2002.

3   *Retail Week*, 13 October 2002.

4   *Sunday Times*, 16 June 2002.

5   *Observer*, 9 March 2003.

6   Interview with Neill Denny, April 2005.
7   *The Times*, 30 August 2002.
8   *Guardian*, 24 August 2002.
9   *Retail Week*, 4 June 2004.
10 *Observer*, 25 August 2002.
11 Ibid.
12 Ibid.
13 *Sunday Times*, 8 September 2002.
14 *Daily Telegraph*, 6 September 2002.
15 *Sunday Telegraph*, 8 September 2002.
16 *Mail on Sunday*, 15 May 2005.
17 *Sunday Telegraph*, 13 October 2002.
18 *Financial Times*, 7 September 2002.
19 *Sunday Times*, 19 October 2003.
20 From unpublished interview with Frances Russell by fashion journalist, November 2004.
21 *Evening Standard*, 25 February 2005.
22 Interview with Louise Foster, May 2005.
23 'Like-for-like sales' refer to sales figures adjusted to allow for changes in floor space which enable more accurate comparisons between stores.
24 *Guardian*, 5 June 2004.
25 Interview with Robert Clark, April 2005.
26 *Guardian*, 24 October 2003 and 18 June 2004.
27 Interview with Richard Hyman, June 2005.
28 Rich List, 2003 and 2004, *Sunday Times*, April 2003 and April 2004.
29 Judi Bevan, *Trolley Wars* (Profile Books, London, 2005), p. 186.
30 Interview with Sir David Sieff, March 2005.
31 *Financial Times*, 5 November 2002 and 3 November 2003.
32 Interview with Neill Denny, April 2005.
33 Arcadia accounts, 2004, Companies House.
34 *Sunday Telegraph*, 30 May 2004.
35 Taken from interview with Philip Green by Louise Foster, *Drapers*, November 2004.
36 Interview with Neill Denny, April 2005.
37 *Drapers*, 29 November 2003.
38 Interview with Louise Foster, May 2005.
39 Taken from an interview by Louise Foster with an anonymous retailer, November 2004.
40 *Drapers*, 4 December 2004.
41 Taken from interview with Philip Green by Louise Foster, *Drapers*, November 2004.

CHAPTER 10: UNFINISHED BUSINESS

1 Interview with retail insider, May 2005.
2 *Sunday Telegraph*, 18 July 2004.
3 Judi Bevan, *The Rise and Fall of Marks & Spencer*, p. 37.
4 *Financial Times*, 4 October 2004.
5 Interview with retail insider, June 2005.
6 *Sunday Times*, 27 June 2004.
7 Ibid.
8 *Daily Mail*, 29 June 2004.
9 The OFT is obliged to look closely at any merger or acquisition involving a British company with a turnover of more than £70 million or where the combined group would command more than a quarter of the market.
10 *Daily Telegraph*, 29 May 2004.
11 Interview with Neill Denny, April 2005.
12 *Sunday Telegraph*, 24 December 2000.
13 Quoted in the *Financial Times*, 28 May 2004.
14 *Guardian*, 5 June 2004.
15 *The Times*, 1 June 2004.
16 *Guardian*, 11 June 2004.

CHAPTER 11: DIRTY TRICKS

1 *The Times*, 1 June 2004.
2 *Independent*, 11 June 2004.
3 Quoted in *Retail Week*, 11 June 2004.
4 *Sunday Times*, 27 June 2004.
5 Conversation with M&S, June 2005.
6 *Sunday Telegraph*, 27 June 2004.
7 *Daily Telegraph*, 2 July 2004.
8 *Daily Mail*, 30 June 2004.
9 *Sunday Times*, 27 June 2004.
10 Quoted in *Sunday Herald*, 4 July 2004.

CHAPTER 12: TANKS ON THE LAWN

1 *Financial Times*, 7 July 2004.
2 *Financial Times*, 8 July 2004.
3 Interview with City editor, May 2005.
4 *Sunday Times*, 11 July 2004.
5 *Independent on Sunday*, 4 July 2004.
6 *Daily Telegraph*, 10 July 2004.
7 *Sunday Times*, 11 July 2004.
8 Interview with Sir David Sieff, May 2005.
9 *Evening Standard*, 12 July 2004.
10 Ibid.

CHAPTER 13: THE DAY OF RECKONING

1   *Financial Times*, 5 October 2004.
2   There was also a technical argument about the actual scale of his support since some of Green's declared backers had so-called derivative contracts that did not have the same status as holders of ordinary shares.
3   *Daily Telegraph*, 16 July 2004.
4   *Daily Mail*, 19 July 2004.
5   *Observer*, 21 November 2004.
6   *Drapers*, 4 December 2004.
7   *Sunday Telegraph*, 18 July 2004.
8   *Guardian*, 15 July 2004.
9   *Independent on Sunday*, 18 July 2004.
10 *Observer*, 18 July 2004.
11 *Guardian*, 16 July 2004.
12 *Sunday Times*, 18 July 2004.
13 Interview with financial editor, June 2005.
14 *Retail Week*, 30 July 2004.
15 Interview with Neill Denny, April 2005.
16 *Retail Week*, 11 June 2004.
17 *Daily Mail*, 19 July 2004.

CHAPTER 14: BREATHING DOWN THEIR NECKS

1   *Campaign*, 23 July 2004.
2   *Financial Times*, 5 October 2004.
3   *Sunday Telegraph*, 25 July 2004.
4   Bhs Ltd Company Accounts, to March 2004, Companies House.
5   From interview with Philip Green by Louise Foster, *Drapers*, November 2004.
6   *Independent on Sunday*, 16 February 2003.
7   Taveta Investments Ltd, Annual Report for year ended August 2004, Companies House.
8   *Daily Mail*, 3 June 2005.
9   Interview with Richard Hyman, June 2005.
10 Ibid.
11 2005 Value Added Scoreboard, DTI, 31 March 2005.
12 *Guardian*, 22 October 2004.
13 From interview with Philip Green by Louise Foster, *Drapers*, November 2004.
14 Interview with Louise Foster, May 2005.
15 Interview with retail insider, May 2005.
16 *Retail Week*, 24 November 2004.
17 *Drapers*, 29 November 2003.
18 *Drapers*, 4 December 2004.

19 *Drapers*, 29 November 2003.
20 The categories include market share, profitability, brand awareness and consumer trust.
21 *Retail Week*, 25 February 2005.
22 *Sunday Times*, 27 February 2001.
23 *Verdict on Womenswear Retailers*, Verdict Research, 2004, p. 1.
24 *Drapers*, 4 December 2004.
25 *Verdict on Womenswear Retailers*, p. 16.
26 *Drapers*, 4 December 2004.
27 Interview with retail insider.
28 Interview with Robert Clark, April 2005.
29 *Drapers*, 4 December 2004.
30 Sales figures provided by Robert Clark.
31 *Independent*, 16 July 2004.
32 *Independent on Sunday*, 30 May 2004.
33 *Verdict on Womenswear Retailers*, p. 55.
34 Interview with retail expert.
35 Interview with Neill Denny, April 2005.
36 Interview with retail insider.
37 *Verdict on Womenswear Retailers*, p. 16.
38 Interview with retail analyst.
39 *Drapers*, 24 August 2004.
40 *Verdict on How Britain Shops for Clothing*, 2004, Verdict Research, 2004, p. 9.
41 Interview with Richard Hyman, June 2005.
42 *Verdict on Womenswear Retailers*, p. 28.

CHAPTER 15: LET THE STRESS BEGIN

1   Interview with Neill Denny, April 2005.
2   From interview of Stuart Rose by Louise Foster, *Drapers*, November 2004.
3   *Retail Week*, 19 November 2004.
4   Interview with retail expert .
5   Quoted in *Observer*, 27 June 2004.
6   *Sunday Times*, 8 May 2005.
7   M&S claim that the gap has narrowed since the study was conducted in February 2005.
8   *Retail Week*, 11 March 2005.
9   *Daily Telegraph*, 12 November 2004.
10 Interview with Richard Hyman, June 2005.
11 *The Times*, 15 December 2004.
12 Interview with Richard Hyman, June 2005.
13 Interview with retail journalist, April 2005.
14 *Daily Telegraph*, 10 March 2005.
15 *Sunday Telegraph*, 20 March 2005.

16   Interview with retail expert.
17   Interview with City retail expert, May 2005.
18   *Sunday Times*, 18 July 2004.
19   *Retail Week*, 24 September 2004.

CHAPTER 16: JUDGEMENT DAY

1   Rich List 2005, *Sunday Times*, April 2005.
2   Ibid.
3   *Mirror*, 22 March 2002
4   *Sunday Times*, 30 May 2004.
5   Interview with Gerald Weisfeld, February 2005.
6   *Observer*, 12 January 2003.
7   *Sunday Times*, 26 February 2002.
8   Taken from interview with Green by Louise Foster, *Drapers*, November 2004.
9   *Financial Times*, 26 June 2004.
10   Interview with Neill Denny, April 2005.
11   Interview with Sir David Sieff, March 2005.
12   *Independent on Sunday*, 19 December 1999.
13   Interview with Richard Hyman, June 2005.
14   *Real Business*, October 2004.
15   From interview with Green by Louise Foster, *Drapers*, November 2004.
16   *Financial Times*, 14 June 2004.
17   Interview with financial commentator.
18   Interview with Sir David Sieff, March 2005.
19   Interview with Robert Clark, April 2005.
20   *The Times*, 22 February 2003.
21   *Forbes*, 15 March 2004 and 10 March 2005.
22   *Financial Times*, 10 July 2004.
23   Interview with retail expert.
24   Interview with Sir David Sieff, March 2005.
25   *Retail Week*, 26 March 2003.
26   *Guardian*, 15 April 2003.
27   *Forbes*, 15 March 2004.
28   *Sunday Times*, 7 January 2001.
29   *Evening Standard*, 2 December 2004.
30   Interview with retail journalist.
31   Interview with Neill Denny, April 2005.

INDEX

Collins Stewart 81
Conduit Street 29, 31
Conran, Sir Terence 71, 115
Coopers & Lybrand 60
Corbett, Gerald 135
Costa, Ken 135
Cottage Homes charity 85
Cruise, Tom 198
Cummings, Peter 5, 77, 85, 86, 89, 142, 150,
    161, 212, 219, 220, 242, 246
Cupcraft Ltd 26
Cyprus 3–11, 43, 139, 143

Daily Mail 86, 163, 183, 184, 188, 220
Daily Telegraph 142, 144, 166, 188, 194
Darke, Neil 81
Davies, Erica 223
Davies, George 50, 156, 174, 199, 250
Davis, Sir Peter 152
de Montfort, Piers 105
de Savary, Peter, 61
Debenhams 111, 120, 127, 144, 148, 226,
    227, 229, 240
Denny, Neil 122, 126, 138, 152, 153, 166,
    213, 227, 231, 249, 261
Department of Trade and Industry 64, 82,
    106
Desmond & Sons 180
Desmond, Dermot 129–30,
Desmond, Richard 238, 240, 254, 259
Deutsche Bank 96–7, 142, 202, 211, 233
Dolcis 75, 79, 83
Donaldson Luftkin & Jenrette (DLJ) 96, 97,
    103, 107–9, 160, 188
Dorchester Hotel 113, 135
Dorothy Perkins 6, 92, 136, 138, 153, 216,
    217, 222, 224, 228, 229, 232, 238, 257
Drapers/Drapers Weekly ix, 25, 153, 154, 223,
    228, 230
Drury, Romney 131
Dyke, Greg 17

Earl, Robert 192, 246
Earth, Wind & Fire 9, 143
Ecclestone, Bernie 6, 97, 123, 181, 240
Eliades, Panos 62
Elizabeth II, Queen 158, 173, 254
Equitable Life Assurance 57
Etam 238
Evans 92, 136, 138, 142, 229
Evening Standard 31, 123, 200

Facia 81, 82–3
Faith, Adam 45
Fast-fashion 146
Ferguson, Alex 246, 259
'financial engineering' 149, 221, 253
Financial Services Authority 185, 187, 188,
    193
Financial Times 82, 106, 144, 152, 161, 190,
    203, 248, 252, 256
Finsbury 178, 184
Fletcher, Richard 135
Forbes 254, 259
Forsyth, Frederick 45
Foster, Louise ix, 154–5, 223
Franklin Resources 100–1

Freeman Hardy Willis 79, 81
Freemans 80, 84, 91
Frost, Sadie 223
FU's Jeans 36, 39

Galeries Lafayette 91
GE Consumer Finance 148
George at Asda 156, 227, 228, 229, 250
Goldman Sachs 160, 161, 174, 176, 184–8,
    202, 209, 215, 219, 246
Goldsmith, James 250
Grabiner, Anthony Lord QC 145, 181
Grabiner, Ian 55–6, 73, 74, 78, 145, 153, 248
Grant, Andrew 171
Grant, Hugh 150, 198
Gray, Elaine 6, 55–6, 69, 70, 71, 82, 120
Great Universal Stores (GUS) 18, 137, 171
Greaves, Jimmy 158
Green, Alma 5, 12–13, 18–19, 24, 26, 32, 40,
    44, 261
Green, Brandon 8, 65, 113, 210, 238, 245
Green, Chloe 8, 53, 65, 113, 139, 142, 210,
    245
Green, Elizabeth 13
Green, Philip
    50th birthday party 1–11; schooling
    13–19; apprenticeship in shoe trade
    19–20; early business career 22–4;
    handwriting analysed 24; failure of
    Joan Collins Jeans 25–6; other business
    failures 26; opens first shop 29; Bond
    Street Bandit 29–32; rescues Bonanza
    Jeans 33–5; acquires Jean Jeanie 37–8;
    at Lee Cooper 39–40; playboy years
    40–1; Tottenham Hotspur and Tony
    Berry 42; resigns from Lee Cooper
    Jeans 44–5; chief executive at Amber
    Day 47– 64; marriage to Tina 53;
    running Amber Day 54–60; *Private Eye*
    revelations 61, 63–4; acquires Parker &
    Franks (Xception) 65–7; attempts to
    resuscitate Owen Owen 68–71; move to
    asset stripping 71; sorts out Owen &
    Robinson and wins new friends in the
    City 72–3; assists Tom Hunter 73–7;
    admiration for Charles Clore 79; heart
    attack 80–1; rivalry with Stephen
    Hinchliffe 81; targets Sears shoe
    empire 84–6; moves to Monaco 86;
    meets Barclay brothers 87; raid on
    rump of Sears 90–2; targets M&S (1999)
    94–5; backing from the City 96–7;
    snubbed by M&S board 98; 'Project
    Mushroom' 102–3; and wife's share
    dealings 104–5; victim of M&S 'dirty
    tricks' 106–8; abandons bid 109;
    friendship with Aida Hersham 110; life
    in Monaco 113–14; takeover of Bhs
    114–26; pays out record dividend 127;
    row with *Guardian* over value of Bhs
    128–30; Retail Personality of the Year
    Award 132, 153; buys Arcadia 137–42;
    PG50 – The Movie 143; rise up the
    wealth league 3, 140, 149, 244; turns
    round Arcadia 144–9; British Retail
    Consortium 152; second M&S bid
    158–94; row with Lord Soames 204–5;